Curating Community

In *Curating Community: Museums, Constitutionalism, and the Taming of the Political*, Stacy Douglas challenges the centrality of sovereignty in our political and juridical imaginations. Creatively bringing together constitutional, political, and aesthetic theory, Douglas argues that museums and constitutions invite visitors to identify with a prescribed set of political constituencies based on national, ethnic, or anthropocentric premises. In both cases, these stable categories gloss over the radical messiness of the world and ask us to conflate representation with democracy. Yet the museum, when paired with the constitution, can also serve as a resource in the production of alternative imaginations of community. Consequently, Douglas's key contribution is the articulation of a theory of countermonumental constitutionalism, using the museum, that seeks to move beyond individual and collective forms of sovereignty that have dominated postcolonial and postapartheid theories of law and commemoration. She insists on the need to reconsider deep questions about how we conceptualize the limits of ourselves, as well as our political communities, in order to attend to everyday questions of justice in the courtroom, the museum, and beyond.

Curating Community is a book for academics, artists, curators, and constitutional designers interested in legacies of violence, transitional justice, and democracy.

Stacy Douglas is assistant professor of law and legal studies at Carleton University in Ottawa, Canada.

Law, Meaning, and Violence

The scope of Law, Meaning, and Violence is defined by the wide-ranging scholarly debates signaled by each of the words in the title. Those debates have taken place among and between lawyers, anthropologists, political theorists, sociologists, and historians, as well as literary and cultural critics. This series is intended to recognize the importance of such ongoing conversations about law, meaning, and violence as well as to encourage and further them.

Series Editors: Martha Minow, Harvard Law School
                    Austin Sarat, Amherst College

Curating Community

MUSEUMS, CONSTITUTIONALISM, AND THE TAMING OF THE POLITICAL

Stacy Douglas

University of Michigan Press
Ann Arbor

Published in the United States of America by

The University of Michigan Press

Printed and bound by CPI Group (UK) Ltd, Croydon, CR0 4YY

2020   2019   2018   2017   4   3   2   1

A CIP catalog record for this book is available from the British Library.

ISBN 978-0-472-07354-2 (hardcover: alk. paper)

ISBN 978-0-472-05354-4 (paper: alk. paper)

ISBN 978-0-472-12293-6 (e-book)

Cover image: "Devotion" (2013); cowhide, resin; installation view; by Nandipha Mntambo © Nandipha Mntambo courtesy Stevenson Cape Town and Johannesburg.

To my mom and dad.

Contents

Acknowledgments

This book is inspired by innumerable people. I must acknowledge my debt, first, to Davina Bhandar for her wise mentorship that ushered me into an exciting and rigorous intellectual environment at Kent Law School, where I met many of my colleagues, mentors, and great friends and from which this book grew. A list of just a few of these mentors includes Stewart Motha, whom I credit for many things, but especially for training me to think long, hard, and independently. Stewart's tenacious intellect combined with his great concern for justice will inspire me for the rest of my life. Also during this time my work was shaped by the ever generous and politically astute Donatella Alessandrini, as well as Davina Cooper, whose thoughtful and creative inquiries forced me to think more imaginatively about my work and the work of others. From 2008 to 2011, I was incredibly lucky to be surrounded by a group of inspiring feminist intellectuals at Kent too numerous to mention. The combined force of these scholars and activists made serving on the board of *Feminist Legal Studies* and *feminists@law* a deeply political experience that enriched me intellectually and professionally.

The arguments herein greatly benefited from countless conversations and debates with many comrades, but especially with Sarah Lamble, Sarah Keenan, Toni Johnson, Katie Cruz, and Suhraiya Jivraj, who were epic intellectual, emotional, and political advisors. Illan Wall and Carolina Olarte have been appropriately dissonant theoretical sounding boards from London Fields to Waco, Texas. Morgan Adamson and Paige Sweet provided their valuable eyes and passionate ears on more than one occasion. Chris Lloyd, Anastaziya Tataryn, Tara Mulqueen, and Daniel Matthews produced rich weekly discussions at Store Street in Fall 2011, the geographers and their allies in Minneapolis embraced me in my brief sojourn there, and Peter Fitzpatrick continues to provide me with enduring evocative engagement.

Thanks also to Sharlene Bamboat, Kheya Bag, Blair Ogden, Manuel Cruz, Alison Hugill, David Shulman, Yvette Russell, and Sami Khatib, for listening, editing, and conspiring with me on these ideas.

In Ottawa I continue to be enfolded into a rich intellectual community made up of many, but of whom I owe particular thanks to Emilie Cameron, Jen Ridgley, Rebecca Schein, Ummni Khan, Brian Smith, Fiona Jeffries, Pablo Mendez, Danielle DiNovelli-Lang, Sonya Gray, Alexis Shotwell, Justin Paulson, and Jennifer Henderson, as well as my students and colleagues in the Department of Law and Legal Studies. It is here that I also received top-notch research assistance from Tiffany MacLellan, Meghan Johnston, and Sophie Ho. I am also indebted for generous invitations to present my work-in-progress from Ruth Buchanan at the Osgoode School of Law, Scott Veitch and Dan Matthews at the University of Hong Kong, Emilios Christodoulidis at the University of Glasgow, Nathalie Casemajor at the Université du Québec en Outaouais, and Valerie Kerruish at the Altonaer Stiftung für philosophische Grundlagenforschung. My great appreciation goes to the Association for the Study of Law, Culture and the Humanities for their formal recognition of my work—an invaluable confidence boost—in 2014.

This book would not be enriched with primary research were it not for the support of educational staff members at the British Museum, the participants of the British Museum's 2009 Adult Learners' Week, and staff members at the District Six Museum and Constitution Hill in South Africa. These individuals graciously allowed me to come into their institutions to ask strange and broad questions about law, memory, and political community. My gratitude also to Nandipha Mntambo and the Stevenson Gallery in Cape Town for allowing me to use her wonderfully inspiring work on the cover of this book, as well as to Danielle Coty, Marcia LaBrenz, and the rest of the Editorial and Design team at the University of Michigan Press for their fantastic guidance. I am proud to work with a Press associated with one of the first public universities to declare that they would not release students' immigration status, in open defiance of President Donald Trump's Executive Order of 27 January 2017.

This research was generously funded by Kent Law School, *Antipode Journal of Critical Geography*, the Postgraduate and Early Career Network of Scholars (P.E.C.A.N.S.), the Association for the Study of Law, Culture and the Humanities, the Rosa Luxemburg Foundation (Berlin), and Carleton University's Faculty of Public Affairs. Earlier incarnations of some of the content has appeared elsewhere: A version of chapter 2 from this book appeared as "Museums as Constitutions: A Commentary on Constitutions and Constitution-Making," in *Law, Culture, and the Humanities* 11, no. 3 (Oct. 2015): 349–62 (DOI: 10.1177/1743872113499226). An amended form of chapter 3 was originally published as "The Time That Binds: Constitutionalism, Museums, and the Production of Political Community," in the *Australian Feminist Law Journal* 38 (2013): 75–92, and a much changed edition of chapter 4 appeared in *Law and Critique* in 2011 titled "Between Mo(nu)ments: Memorialising Past, Present and Future at the District Six Museum and Constitution Hill," vol. 22, issue 2, 177–87. Pieces of the argument herein were also used in a book chapter titled "Constitutions Are Not Enough: The Museum as Law's Counter-Archive," in *Law, Memory, Violence: Uncovering the Counter-Archive*, edited by Stewart Motha and Honni van Rijswijk (London: Routledge, 2016), 140–55. I am thankful for the permissions to reprint elements of my work here.

Infinite gratitude goes to my family for their unwavering encouragement and for putting up with my persistent need to slip away and do work. I would be lost without their love. And, lastly, I thank David Hugill for being a brilliant intellectual combatant, an endlessly understanding friend, and a constant spark of energy that makes every day exciting.

This is just a small list of my many exposures to the world. It is my firm belief in the truth of these contingencies, including my unstated reliance on the nonhuman world, that drives this project. Thus I also acknowledge the incessant sharing of being-in-common, the trembling contours of our selves, of others, and of the world, and I hope that we might soon reconsider our notions of the individual, of community, and, ultimately, of the political.

Introduction: Curating Community

I experienced firsthand the powerful narratives of museums as a child
growing up in a small city in Canada. Our school trips were often organized
outings to local museums, where we learned, through interactive exercises,
the history of our city and of Canada more broadly. On one particular ex-
cursion we were asked to pretend we were poor Irish immigrant children,
crammed into bunks on a ship, awaiting our arrival in the new country.
The staff instructed us to climb into the beds so we could relive the immigrant experience of our presumed ancestors. In many ways, this exercise
was unremarkable, a mundane interaction with the sort of naturalized histories that are so pervasive in the curricula of settler colonial societies like
the one I grew up in. But the experience has lingered in my mind for years,
raising questions about the intersection of memory, history, community,
and colonialism. Looking back, I wonder how it and other historical learning experiences shaped my youthful understanding of who I was and where
I belonged. By presenting Canada as a land populated by rugged immi-
grants and their descendants, these experiences taught me stories about
settler survival and perseverance. But they did not tell me anything about
the strategic violence that is so central to the history of white settlement
from which I descend.

Twenty years later, I found myself pondering these same questions at
the British Museum, an institution perceived to be the world's archive par
excellence. Founded by an act of Parliament in 1753 and officially opened

to the public in 1759, the British Museum's original collection was made up of two large donations, one by Sir Hans Sloane and one by King George II.[2] With more than six million visitors annually, the museum immodestly claims to possess "the greatest collection representative of human cultural achievement, ancient and modern, in the world."[3] Officials defend the museum's ownership and maintenance of these objects in the name of Enlightenment-inspired principles of cross-cultural understanding and tolerance. But they tell us very little about the strategic violence that is so central to the historical processes that made London the "natural" assembly point for such a collection.

Standing in this world-renowned institution, it occurred to me that museum experiences are not only about reinforcing ideas of nation and stoking the passions of nationalisms. Nor are they simply about celebrating sanitized presents and obfuscating violent pasts. They are also orienting events that teach us who we are and where we belong.

Margaret Atwood's poem about an imagined night in the Royal Ontario Museum encapsulates a central truth about the museum. The museum indicates that YOU ARE HERE. It tells a story about "you," as well as "your" relative location in the museum. This location is both physical and historical. At the same time that the museum offers carefully crafted physical routes through its collections, it also offers carefully crafted historical narratives about the relationship between objects and museum visitors that are intimately bound up with notions of community, time, history, and progress. The museum is predicated on a project of representing individuals and communities, rendering them in place in relation to a collection, nation, and history. YOU ARE HERE conveys a clear and definable subject—"YOU"—who is situated in a definite place—"HERE." It is precisely this project of "putting in place" that animates my interest in the museum. The museum told me a story about my country and myself, about who belonged where, and who belonged nowhere. In short, it told me a story about political community.

Yet the museum is not the only place where we are told stories about community. For example, questions of political community have also long been the focus of constitutional design and scholarship. Indeed, the constitution, like the museum, holds a powerful position as the authorizer of who belongs where and who belongs nowhere. It also articulates the dictum— though this time with legal authorization—YOU ARE HERE. In Canada, for example, debates over constitutional representation (or lack thereof) have been the key focus for indigenous peoples, the Québécois, and other equity-seeking groups. These debates and others like them stir intense feelings in all parties regarding their entitlement to history, sovereignty, and community. And the constitution is often imagined to be the primary site through which these concepts—as well as their sentimental attachments—are to be navigated. As the supposed producer and authorizer of political community, the constitution is frequently assumed to be the central device through which complex questions of politics and sociality should be negotiated.

But this is a demand that the constitution cannot accommodate. While constitutional negotiation may be able to provide some representational gains for groups seeking redress, the constitutional arrangement simply cannot attend to radical demands for, and possibilities of, comprehensively rethinking politics and sociality. Constitutions, like many museums, tell stories that reduce "community" to a representational politics. In so doing, they often promote a shallow sense of cohesion, boundedness, and shared experience while concealing the ways in which other forms of mutuality, contingency, and interdependence shape our lives.

This is as true for old colonial states and their affiliated constitutional monarchies as it is for countries undergoing radical legal and political transformation. In the South African context a unique convergence of the authorizing power of constitutions and museums is on display at Constitution Hill, a self-described multipurpose heritage site in central Johannesburg, officially opened in 2004. The site houses South Africa's new Constitutional Court and is built on the foundations of the city's Old Fort Prison Complex.[4] It also hosts a series of museums and exhibitions that showcase the rich history of the site. Site officials claim that "nowhere can the story of South Africa's turbulent past and its extraordinary transition to democracy be told as it is at Constitution Hill."[5] They differentiate between a vaguely construed "past" (i.e., apartheid) and a contemporary period of deliverance. The museum staff insists that the museum fosters democracy by educating people about their newly found constitutional rights. By venerating the 1996 Constitution and its ushering in of liberal constitutional democracy, apartheid is imagined as a distant and bygone phenomenon, eradicated by the arrival of a new political order. In short, the site tells a story of successful and complete transformation.

The sure-footedness of Constitution Hill's conception of democracy—

and its intimate relationship with an exaltation of the powers of the new liberal democratic constitutional order—is echoed in mainstream interpretations of politics in contemporary South Africa. Such thinking centralizes the role of constitutionalism and glosses over contestations about the legacies of apartheid by heralding the arrival of a redemptive political order. It links democratization to the promises of the Constitutional Court, interpreting the new legal institutions as the stable foundation of a progressive telos that will continue to carry South Africans away from their "dark past" and toward an increasingly democratic future. It assumes, in other words, that the legal architecture of liberal democracy is capable of meaningfully addressing the legacies of colonialism and apartheid. In short, the thinking that animates the political project of Constitution Hill equates the promises of the new Constitution with democracy itself.

While Constitution Hill and the British Museum are situated in two very different political and geographic locations, they are both institutions concerned with the representation of the world. The interactive adult educational programs that both museums administer, for example, are intended to help visitors negotiate history. To do so, they employ strategies that invite visitors to experience themselves in relation to the collected objects, thereby rendering visitors *in place* and *in time*. In this and other ways, the museums reproduce and consolidate normative conceptions of the individual, the community, of historical time, and of democracy. As such, they participate in the maintenance and perpetuation of the very categories that most of us use to understand the world around us. Museums, like constitutions, function as authorizers of the world, its history, its reality, and its possibilities.

But museum scholar Donald Preziosi reminds us that the museum is not a singularly repressive institution. Rather, it is "a family of institutions housing multiple anamorphic orientations."[6] The latter are processes that give coherence to things that are otherwise distorted or messy. In this sense, they represent objects and stories so that history can "be seen as unfolding, on its own, almost magically, before one's eyes."[7] In the case of Constitution Hill, for example, apartheid is imagined to belong to a bygone era, and the great potential of constitutional democracy is presumed to be leading South Africa into the future with evolutionary propulsion. This tidy telos suggests that there are no remnants of apartheid within the new legal order. The evolutionary force of this anamorphic orientation helps lend an authoritative gloss to the narrative of redemptive liberal democracy. The museum's conception of the political thus relinquishes considerations of how this supposedly "new era" continues to be riddled with the contradictions of apartheid and colonization. What is happening in these examples is a subjection of more fundamental questions of the political to the limited frameworks of state-based liberal democracy. The museum staff frame the parameters of their political projects through the lens of governmental directives and constitutional fetishization.[8] This reduction of the possibility of the political to the confines of the existing categories of law and politics is characteristic of the tension between "politics" and "the political" articulated by thinkers like Claude LeFort, Carl Schmitt, Hannah Arendt, and Jean-Luc Nancy.[9] It is also one of the central political and intellectual concerns of this book.

REPRESENTATION, SOVEREIGNTY, AND THE POLITICAL

To distinguish between politics and the political is to articulate a difference between the everyday concerns of institutional political activity (*politics*), on the one hand, and considerations of ethics, thinking, writing, and acting that happen at a distance from such pre-existing, institutionally inclined parameters, on the other (*the political*). This difference is especially crucial for considering horizons of possibility that extend beyond the aims and objectives of representative democracy. Without an autonomous and expansive concept of the political, imaginations of what is viable remain hopelessly tied to prevailing institutional norms and processes. Both Schmitt and Arendt lament the colonization of an autonomous concept of the political by the utilitarian logic of the contemporary liberal nation-state.[10] They argue for an excavation of a concept of the political that refuses to be diluted by the existing categories of sovereignty and representation, though with vastly different outcomes.[11] Connectedly, Arendt and Nancy claim that these categories are unable to account for the plurality of the world.[12] The act of representation creates an image of an individual and a community as a sovereign whole, but this image tells a lie; it denies the truth of our nonsovereign existence. Such renditions, even when appealed to under duress and in the name of a "strategic essentialism," cannot help but perpetuate a myth of the possibility of sovereign individualism and sovereign communities.[13] Below I elaborate just what is at stake in such a move, but for now let me emphasize that my hostility to a program of representation is not only about satisfying an abstract concern with circumscription. My resistance to representation is not merely a groundless foray into the oceanic depths of postmodernism.

Rather, it stems from a deeply political concern with inherited colonial imaginaries of justice. This project is important not only for societies where colonial contradictions endure, but also for other societies attempting to negotiate deep-seated historical divisions.

The limitations of a representation-centered approach are, in many ways, on display in the South African context. Over the past twenty years much has been written about the great potential and vast failures of the transformative constitutional project, a program that hinges on formal representation. The 1996 Constitution of the Republic of South Africa continues to be heralded by some for its institutionalization of justiciable socioeconomic or "third-generation" rights.[14] These grand promises were thought to mark the beginning of a decisive shift away from the racialized inequities that plagued South Africa for the preceding decades under apartheid. As I elaborate upon in chapter 4, though, twenty years later many of these racialized inequalities continue to persist.[15] While these failures cannot solely be attributed to the constitutional project, many South African authors and activists claim that the 1996 Constitution did little more than proclaim a commitment to democracy and antiracialism while maintaining the structural divisions that organized society under apartheid.[16] For these critics, the Constitution has not fulfilled its self-proclaimed aim to "heal the divisions of the past and [. . .] free the potential of each person."[17] This is not surprising, of course. Constitutions alone cannot free people and heal divisions. Such grandiose statements function as symbolic claims, meant to inspire a commitment to and an ethos of a social contract.

But constitutions are not only symbolic; they are also documents that police. Indeed, constitutions are authorized and enforced by a state that enacts them. They tell us who and what can be legally recognized and who and what is protected by their parameters: sovereign individuals living in a sovereign state. Symbolically and materially, they request our investment in them, on their terms, and ask us to partake in a mutual monumental promise to their project of representation. It is this mighty claim of the constitution and its place as the pinnacle of our collective political imagination that I take aim at in this book.

It is not only the constitution that sets its political aims as synonymous with institutional inclusion, however. The British Museum, like the local museum in Canada and the South African constitutional project, attempts to navigate legacies of empire by proffering better inclusion in its representational framework. In their interactive learning programs, members of the staff at the British Museum attempt to tell a history of the world through objects collected over centuries of colonialism and imperialism.[18] In addition to explicating this history, the staff promote a program of democracy based on state-endorsed conceptions of inclusion and assimilation. In chapter 2 I explain how the staff aim to bring nonwhite and immigrant individuals to the museum to counter its largely white and middle-class audience, as well as to promote a national agenda concerned with educational improvement.[19] These strategies of inclusion compel assimilation to the colonial apparatus by demarcating a sphere of the political that is overdetermined by sovereignty. Indeed, what these projects have in common is a belief in the power and potential of the instructional statement: YOU ARE HERE. Maintaining this project of necessary delimitation as the pinnacle of our democratic aims and objectives is an impoverished conception of the possibilities of the political. In response, this book articulates an alternative approach that takes the *interruption* of this liberal legal subject and its attendant political community as its task. Such a project is necessary not only to avoid the suffocation of the political by politics, but also to interrupt the centrality of sovereignty in our political and juridical imaginations.

CUSTODIAL PRACTICES

The term "curate" comes from the Latin *cura*, meaning "to care," and *curare*, meaning "to take care of."[20] The New Oxford American Dictionary defines "curator" as "a keeper or *custodian* of a museum or other collection."[21] Historically, the term "curator" was also used to refer to a pastor who held guardianship over a minor.[22] These etymological connections elicit ideas of "tending" to community. Of course, curating is a practice that is already popularly linked with museums. In general, though, it is associated with the practice of attending to the museums' *collections*. This book has a different focus: how the idea of *community* is curated at the site of the museum. Rather than look to museum objects, this project looks at the interactive educational practices deployed in adult learning programs at museums. As I explain in chapter 2, these programs are increasingly part of the modern museum experience and are presumed to help promote democratic engagement, diversity, and accessibility, elements that have long been noted as absent. However, while "caring" for and "tending" to community are often presumed to be actions with inherent moral worth, such a presumption problematically assumes that the production of community is a good thing. In contrast, this book explores the way in which the concept of "community" is used to stifle and suffocate the diversity of the world.

I argue that the interactive adult educational programming offered at museums often sets the production of community as its task. Didier Maleuvre argues that museums invite visitors to identify with a prescribed set of political constituencies.[23] For him, this arrangement channels the plurality of life into narrow representational frameworks. Similarly, Preziosi argues that museums render people *in place*.[24] He claims that, far from shaking the very foundations of being or challenging individuals into questioning their existence, the museum forestalls chaos by offering a view of the world as secure and ordered.[25] As I mention above, this security is communicated through anamorphic orientations, practices of classification that smooth and cohere the messiness of the world.[26] Chronological time, as I explore in chapter 3, functions as one such example of an anamorphic orientation by lending a coherent legitimacy to the idea of a human community steadily evolving over time. These orientations function as *custodial* tools in the production of an idea of community; they assist in its curation.

Moreover, while the term "curating" is most commonly associated with museums and art galleries, it is also relevant to constitutionalism. Indeed, constitutions produce an idea of community—"the people"—that they represent. According to Martin Loughlin and Neil Walker, "modern constitutional texts aspire not only to establish the forms of governmental authority (legally constituted power) but also to reconstitute the people in a particular way."[27] Like the custodial practices of the museum, these conceptions of community rely on stable categories that gloss over the messiness of the world; they offer a manageable conception of community that is amenable to constitutional arrangements. Jean and John Comaroff claim that the constitution acts:

> as an instrument of governance [that] allows the state to represent itself *as the custodian* of civility against disorder—and, therefore, as mandated to conjure moral community by exercising a monopoly over the construction of a commonwealth out of inimical diversities of interest.[28]

In contrast, constitutional scholars such as Jürgen Habermas contend that the constitution does not concretize community but changes with it. He claims that "a constitution can be thought of as an historical project that each generation of citizens continues to pursue."[29] But while it is certainly true that the constitution is open to amendment and change, its principal function remains the delimitation of community. By definition, the constitution bounds a body politic.

This book is concerned with the central role that the constitution plays in producing political community through a representational framework that valorizes sovereignty. It is thus interested in the way in which state-based categories of politics institute what Aletta Norval calls a "horizon of intelligibility—a framework delineating what is possible, what can be said and done, what positions may be legitimately taken, [and] what actions may be engaged in."[30] But my critical aim is not *only* state-based politics. After all, both the museum and constitutionalism share in the creation of this horizon of intelligibility; they share in the production of imaginations of sovereignty. By this I do not only mean the form of juridical sovereignty popularly linked with geopolitical authority, but also and especially the sovereignty that is imagined when we think of ourselves and the populations in which we claim status and belonging, whether state-based or not, as *bounded* or *boundable*. Considering this commonality between the two institutions is crucial if we are serious about acknowledging the truth of our existence with each other and the world around us as relational. It is not enough to only look to the constitution as the authenticator of the supremacy of the liberal individual and its corresponding community; we must also contemplate other sites that share a proclivity to launch imaginations of sovereignty.

AGAINST SOVEREIGNTY

This book reconsiders the political in order to challenge the purported necessity of representing community. I pursue this argument through the work of Jean-Luc Nancy, who argues for a "retreatment" of the political that challenges the utilitarian demand to speak to the everyday concerns of politics.[31] In his terms, projects that gloss over this consideration of the political become dangerous because they rely on normative categories, such as "the human" and "democracy," to legitimize their aims. He argues that we need to ask tough questions about who and what these categories serve.

Nancy takes specific aim at "community." He claims that the very idea of community—in its common conception as a delimited and bounded group of humans—is impossible because it is based on a paradox. When we draw a border around a community (or any other absolute for that matter), we are creating a boundary that is necessarily exposed to an outside. For Nancy, this means that nothing can ever be absolutely bounded and delimited; it is always in relation to its outside.[32] Nancy calls this relation "exposure" and claims that we are all always already exposed, not just to humans but also to the world.[33] He calls this infinite exposure being-in-common. Any postulation of a closed and atomized community or a closed and atomized individual is a denial of this relationality. Nancy claims that the task of justice is to render this infinite exposure of the world—being-in-common—legible.[34] One of the central ways of doing this is to interrupt narratives of community or the individual that continue to postulate it as secured and isolated. Community, like the individual, is without essence; it is nothing but infinite sharing brought about by the exposure of existence, and it is this infinite sharing that must be rendered legible. Images of political communities and individuals, whether in constitutions or museum exhibitions, offer up mythological stories, authorized by an insidious and false equation of representation with truth.

To some, this will sound like new-age, apolitical, ahistorical balderdash. But before such readers trigger their personal pomo alert systems, I invite them to explain how anything short of a radical rethinking of what constitutes "community" will offer us the tools that are necessary to negotiate just futures in a world ravaged by ceaseless violence, historic levels of displacement, and, increasingly, climate chaos. In my view, such a rethinking requires a thoroughgoing critique of the centrality of the sovereign individual at the heart of Western liberalism. This figure is perpetuated in modern political theory as the unencumbered man that enters into the social contract for protection of property in themselves and their territory. But for all the talk of protection that such arrangement achieves, it is precisely the political centrality of this imagined figure that continues to pose barriers to genuine forms of equity, not least because it is this thinking that perpetuates a durable mythology of individual and collective autonomy. Rather than recognize the ontological embeddedness of ourselves in the world—not only our biological debt to being birthed by another, but also our everyday existence that is facilitated by air, water, and food—we choose to pretend that it is the single modern individual and his private social affairs that should orient our legal and political lives. In so doing, we deny our relations with the world, telling lies about who and what is important, who and what needs protection, and who and what is affected by our actions. In what follows, I am definitively *not* proposing that all the ontological realities of biological life can or should be captured by law. Nor am I calling for an expansion of legal protections to include more natural features of the earth. What I am suggesting is that modern Western liberal law allows us to believe that justice is done when individual rights are protected, even at the expense of the world in which we live.

Anticolonial writers have long made this point. One of my earliest personal encounters with this critique was from Marie Battiste and James (Sa'ke'j) Youngblood Henderson in their book *Protecting Indigenous Knowledge and Heritage: A Global Challenge* (2000).[35] In this text, Battiste and Henderson discuss a scenario where the particularity of Western law's epistemology is thrown into sharp focus. The authors show that, in negotiations with indigenous stakeholders, Canadian government lawyers draw lines as borders to divide up territory, cutting communities off from vital connections to water systems and animal migratory routes.[36] Battiste and Henderson reveal the fundamental impossibility of communication between the two negotiating parties as the federal lawyers are unable to see outside of their philosophical tradition. This simple example crystallizes the discord between worldviews and what is at stake in such untranslatability. To engage with a liberal legal system is to participate in the recasting of cultural presumptions that flow from that tradition, such as the veneration of human lives above all others, the centrality of the liberal individual subject, and the dominion of human-drawn borders. Many other critiques of the legacy of sovereignty and the subject at its center in Western legal and political thinking have since emerged from anticolonial writers in North America such as Taiaiake Alfred, Glen Coulthard, John Borrows, Audra Simpson, and Andrea Smith.[37]

This book takes inspiration from these critiques, as well as from those launched by authors writing in the African anticolonial tradition, such as Mogobe Ramose, Tshepo Madlingozi, and Andile Mngximata. Ramose in particular develops a sustained critique of the heritage of the liberal individual, especially as it takes its form in the grammar of Western law. For Ramose, the legal subject imports a set of doctrines that frustrate our ability to think differently about being together in the world: "Western legal thought accords primacy to the legal subject as a concept: an abstract entity. . . . Language is indispensable to the indelible inscription of the legal subject into the vocabulary of law."[38] Ramose charges the standardization of law and its undergirding principles with conducting a diffuse form of "epistemicide" against African philosophy. As the liberal subject is deployed and redeployed in the grammar of liberal law, it facilitates a creeping hegemony of what is imagined to be possible and what a legal notion of justice is. He argues, in response, that there are other forms of law that have a different idea of the subject, a subject in flux, that is more realistically in tune with the realities of "the flow of life."[39] This can happen in *ubuntu* law, a law undergirded by a different epistemological structure, one that comes from the African philosophical tradition.

While I do not endorse Ramose's legal philosophy *tout court*, he offers important insights about the mythological sovereign individual as a persistent barrier to decolonial thinking. I draw inspiration from his work as I challenge the centrality of the constitution, with all its culturally inflected presuppositions, especially in postapartheid theories of law and jurisprudence that come from South Africa. While we may not be ready to do away with Western liberal legalism and its precepts just yet, there is a necessity to consider what is at stake as scholars and others continue to hold on with an ever-tightening grip, and in the face of contributions like Ramose's, to the legal traditions that are familiar to some, rather than those that proffer justice for many. Cultural assumptions about liberal legal justice as superior have long fueled dismissive reactions to anticolonial critique, and it is my aim to forefront what is at stake in and offer some alternatives to this repudiation.

Perhaps obviously then, I do not argue that the mere inclusion of constitutional principles inflected with indigenous overtones is a useful strategy for a decolonial project. The problem, as I emphasize throughout, is that the fundamental logic of the liberal legal system turns on a sovereign individual subject that is contained within a sovereign legal community. Incorporating indigenous concepts like *ubuntu* cannot disrupt the foundational presuppositions of the liberal paradigm. I explain this in greater detail, using two case studies, in chapter 5. This is also why extra-legal sites are important and why, for the purposes of this research, I turn to the museum as a site in the contemporary moment that can offer more thoughtful reflection on the inheritance of liberal epistemological tenets than the constitution can.

Moreover, it is not *only* the liberal individual subject that is a barrier to anticolonial thinking. Rather, the target herein is the figure of sovereignty as absolute, whether individual or collective, and this takes form in many places, not just the constitution. As I explain in greater detail in chapter 1, the paradox of the absolute confounds any attempt to draw a border around someone or some thing, including community. Therefore, the figure of individual or collective sovereignty, when imagined as complete, denies the ontological relations that make up the world. Sovereign declarations tell a lie about the possibility of the impossible absolute.

But this assertion may rub some readers the wrong way. After all, in the contemporary moment don't indigenous communities *need* to reclaim sovereignty from colonial states? Doesn't sovereignty need to be deployed, even if strategically, as a pragmatic tool of defense against territorial, governmental, economic, and cultural incursions? Yes. One hundred times, yes. But this strategy must also be clear-minded about what it is: a foray into a legal system that hinges on the mythological figure of the absolute. I use "foray" here in the most literal sense, as an incursion into hostile territory, because sovereignty as absolute is part and parcel of the terms, logics, and grammar that maintain the centrality of the liberal individual subject and its attendant state-centric borders. It seems that its deployment is only useful in a world where these precepts continue to have hold on our imaginations, in a sense, only in enemy terrain; while it may be a necessary tool for confronting liberal legal systems in a recognizable language, it can only offer solutions on the terms of that same system. This means a redeployment of the mythological figures of the individual and community that rest at its center, which continue to act as barriers to a philosophy of being-in-common, which in turn stifles the potential for decolonization and environmental justice.

Therefore, my aim is not constitutions per se, but rather the narratives of sovereignty that they import. Other devices can also import these stories and do. Indeed, this is what museums and constitutions have in common. They both have the potential to tell a myth about community, whether that be on state-based, ethnic, or anthropocentric lines. The propensity to tell these stories is also found in political movements and populist uprisings; it is certainly not confined to the constitution. Yet I argue that the constitution is structurally bound to at least some semblance of this myth; this is its legal function, it's raison d'etre. A constitution's essence of being is to help us draw a line around a community to say, even if for only utilitarian purposing, "this is who is in and this is who is out." Of course, these boundaries can be changed, refused, and misinterpreted but, in the end, the constitution stands as the state-sanctioned storyteller that enforces the imagined borders of community. In short, the constitution is the legal authorizer of the myth of sovereignty. Although such myths circulate elsewhere, including museums, they do not have to. Museums and other sites have the potential (although rarely realized) to interrupt such narratives and reveal the truth of community, not as bounded or boundable but as always already an ontological experience of sharing unrestricted to states, ideologies, or humans. It is this potential that I explore herein.

COUNTERMONUMENTAL CONSTITUTIONALISM

This challenge to the thinking of the sovereign individual and its attendant community poses a dilemma for constitutionalism. For how can the constitution, the framework for the articulation of political community par excellence, avoid the inevitable delimitation of political community? In short, it cannot. In this book I contend that the museum is more able to attend to this need for radical reflexivity because it has the potential to interrupt steady, strong, sovereign conceptions of political community. I therefore bring the museum and the constitution together to pursue a theory of countermonumental constitutionalism that serves as a resource in the production of nonsovereign imaginations of community.

South African constitutional and political theorists Johannes Snyman, Henk Botha, and Wessel le Roux are credited with introducing and popularizing the concept of a "countermonumental constitutionalism."[40] These thinkers argue that the constitution cannot be the sole site for constructing and interpreting national narratives of law and justice. They respectively turn to human obligation, an Arendtian conception of politics, and art as other modes of effecting national responsibility for democracy and resisting what le Roux calls constitutional spectatorship.[41] My concern owes a debt to these robust contributions, which have creatively and provocatively brought together the fields of constitutionalism and memory studies to consider how to create obligations beyond those delineated by the existing legal landscape.

Countermonumental constitutionalism in this book is made up of two components. First, a countermonumental constitutionalism does not exalt the constitution as the central tool in the production of political community. The museum plays a crucial role in this respect because it demonstrates that the constitution is not the only place from which imaginations of political community are launched. Remembering that political community is a product of practices at multiple sites works against the inclination to fetishize the constitutional arrangement as its central orienting tool. The second component of a countermonumental constitutionalism is the necessary interruption of community. The museum is key in this regard because, unlike the constitution, it has the capacity to facilitate this interruption. The constitution cannot simultaneously account for the plurality of the world and maintain its role as legal delimitation tool. To put this demand on the constitution is to ask it to undo itself, to demand that it perform what Emilios Christodoulidis terms "constitutional irresolution."[42] This demand *can* be placed on the museum, however. Indeed, while the museum, like the constitution, tends to set the production of community as its task, it can also engage in countermonumental memorializing practices that disrupt this persistent aim. The cultivation of these practices and their insistent interrogation of the logic of communion can offer a crucial supplement to the limits of constitutionalism. Museums thus offer the possibility of holding open the political rather than letting it be subsumed by politics.

I apply this theory of a countermonumental constitutionalism to recently articulated postapartheid theories of law. These theories, proffered by Johan van der Walt and by Drucilla Cornell and Nyoko Muvangua, articulate a postapartheid jurisprudence based on amendments to the adjudication process. In their respective arguments, these scholars attempt to locate the possibility of a more just South Africa through legal judgments that go beyond the protection of liberal democratic rights. But while these theories make significant efforts to hold the political open, they ultimately cannot for two major reasons. First, they maintain the centrality of the constitution in their theories. By focusing solely on the possibilities of adjudication to reconstruct a more just South Africa, they recenter the constitutional arrangement as the primary tool for such practices. Second, while they are critical of the limits of this constitution, their theories do not engage in the undoing of its central communing logic. This move forgoes a retreatment of the political. Indeed, rather than undoing the logic of community, they participate in its further production by adding—albeit critical—supplements to it. In contrast, a countermonumental constitutionalism can provide a helpful alternative. Such an approach introduces the site of the museum as a place that can also build imaginations of political community. But rather than build coherent and smooth sovereign imaginations, the museum can be tasked with pulling apart these imaginations in an attempt to undo the logic of communion.

The District Six Museum in South Africa offers a key example of how such countermonumental practices can be exercised. This museum is actively engaged in the undoing of conceptions of community. The staff at this museum see the task of troubling the concept of community as crucial for the undoing of logics and categories of thinking that have been inherited by colonialism and apartheid. While the museum is committed to revisiting history in the hopes of building an anticapitalist and anti-apartheid South Africa, it is also wary of the dangers of too easily falling into simple conceptions of history and community. This is particularly important for the staff as the landscapes of trauma and violence are layered with multiple and competing claims to land and history. Therefore, they simultaneously launch programs that interrogate notions of community, home, and race while also attempting to build an anti-apartheid city. I elaborate on these critical memorializing practices in detail in chapters 3 and 4.

In sum, pairing the museum with the constitution affords two vital opportunities. First, it decenters the constitution as the central tool in the production of political community. Second, the museum offers an external resource that can provide reflexive reconsiderations of community that the constitution cannot. In its reflexive role, however, the museum is not intended to augment or add to the constitution. Rather, the museum's practices of interruption are meant to challenge the very idea of community that undergirds the constitution; the museum is meant to undo sovereign imaginations rather than contribute to them.

I want to emphasize that my argument for the deflation of the role of the constitution is not a naïve retreat from a conception of the public. I am not calling for a radical dispersion of public life into privatized identity politics. Rather, my concern is passionately invested in the public sphere, who and what we think it includes and how it is maintained. Constitutions offer a supposedly universal method of communicating what the essential parts of our public is made up of, what basic tenets we can all agree to. But what do we do with those humans, nonhumans, and philosophies that are always already sidelined from this public due to a historically and culturally particular European predilection for sovereignty? My argument is that we need to maintain a role for the constitution, for these articulations of *publicness*, but that because it is a legal document that necessary delineates, necessarily cuts, it cannot also be the device that interrupts imaginations of sovereignty. The constitution cannot simultaneously delimit and offer reflexivity upon that closure; it is not structurally designed for this purpose.

Surely, some will retort that all representation delineates, that all institutionalization is necessarily reductionist. It is my view, however, that not all institutions are equally reductive. Where the constitution must, the museum can do otherwise. The museum is not structurally bound to offer the same neat story of sovereignty. Moreover, the museum—both those that are officially state-funded but also those that are not—is another institution that offers a site for imagining who and what makes up the public. Countless annual school trips from elementary to college age (often integrated with state-legislated curriculum), as well as tourist visits promoted by municipal, state, and federal governments, mean that the museum is a vibrant venue for thinking about popular conceptions of community but also a locus for effectively interrupting those conceptions. While other sites might also serve as productive places from which sovereign imaginations of community can be disturbed, I retain a focus on the museum precisely because of its place as a common and quasi-official authorizer of truth. This project thus takes seriously the question of being-in-common in the ontological realm, but only as it has ramifications for the ontic. My claim is that the constitution and the museum can work together—albeit with inversed emphases in their current treatment in legal and political arenas—in moving slowly closer to a world that has a more robust conception of the public as infinite sharing.

Astute observers will note that although I invoke Nancy's theory of being-in-common, which eschews the role of constitutions and contracts in an effort to rethink the political at a distance from politics, in the end I maintain a role for the institutional protections and (potential for) universal communicability offered by constitutions. In this vein, my argument seems more akin to an Arendtian one: critique sovereignty, yes, but hold on to some semblance of order, or, in her words, promises in a sea of insecurity.[43] I must emphasize, however, that my maintenance of the albeit shrunken role of constitutions comes less from a deep-seated fear, like Arendt (which paradoxically recasts the document as the guardian of security), and more from a pragmatic desire to speak to the contemporary moment. Constitutions are here now and not going anywhere quickly. The challenge then, I argue, is to simultaneously use them, acknowledge the hold they have on our collective imaginations as the pinnacle devices with which we organize society, *and* to disrupt that grip. This is not a flippant dismissal of these lauded documents but rather a passionate concern with the ways in which constitutional precepts actively condition horizons of legal and political intelligibility. If we want to imagine differently, I argue, we must confront our attachment to these documents and their imported language, subject, jurisdiction, and remedies.

CURATING THE ARGUMENT

This book argues that we must decenter the constitution as a key device in the process of transformation, but that it remains a necessary tool in the management of human conflict. This is a difficult argument to hold together; the first three chapters develop a critique of the constitution, while the latter two endorse its continued role in the contemporary moment. I demonstrate in those early chapters the extent and significance of the limits of representation in the project of transformation. Only once this is firmly established do I return to the constitution's necessary, if deflated, role for postconflict and postcolonial societies.

Chapter 1 introduces the tension between politics and the political by turning to political theorists and philosophers who have commented on the distinction over the course of the past century. Significantly, this tension has animated much of the theory concerned with themes of freedom, sovereignty, and community. These thinkers, such as Schmitt and Arendt, are also concerned with a thinking of constitutionalism, its role, its potential, and its limitations. Indeed, the tension between politics and the political animates much of constitutional thought, as scholars attempt to pair expansive notions of freedom with the limits imposed on this freedom by law.

Contemporary constitutional thinkers Martin Loughlin, Neil Walker, and Emilios Christodoulidis also attempt to address this tension. Each specifically acknowledges the limits of the constitution and then attempts to address this limitation through the constitutional arrangement itself or by turning to the politics of civil society. Both of these moves, however, remain focused on the production of community with the liberal individual subject at its center, when what is needed is a constitutionalism that can write the interruption of community.

Chapter 2 explores how the theme of community persists through the rise of the modern museum, as well as in calls for its reform. This enduring theme is made possible through ways of seeing—anamorphic orientations—that cohere the messiness of the world, produce smooth relations between objects and visitors, and help the museum tell a tidy anthropocentric story. Like the constitutionalism articulated by scholars in chapter 1, these orientations function to close down the world rather than open it up. In particular, this chapter takes aim at "new museum" approaches that take their conceptions of democracy for granted, presuming that increased interaction between objects and visitors can attend to legacies of disenfranchisement, colonial theft, and marginalized histories. Retreating the political means reapproaching these assumptions in order to more fully attend to their limits and to contemplate more expansive conceptions of the new, democratic museum.

Chapter 3 explores an example of an anamorphic orientation at work at both the museum and in constitutionalism: that of time as chronological progress, which is used at both sites to tame the political. In the case of constitutionalism, the notion of enduring time lends legitimacy to the authority of the state. In the case of the museum, chronological time is used to produce categories of community and the individual. In both cases, self-assured conceptions of past, present, and future are used to legitimize a narrow concept of the political. Yet these anamorphic orientations cannot entirely smooth and cohere the world. Indeed, my research at the British Museum also yields examples of unexpected confusion, miscommunication, and frustration between staff members and participants that interrupt the anamorphic proclivities of the museum. But although these sporadic events offer momentary contestations to the authority of chronological time, they do not go far enough in articulating the interruption of community. In order to do justice to being-in-common, we must engage in writing the "essencelessness of relation."[44] Rather than leave this up to unpredictable possibilities, the museum and the constitution must *actively* take up this task.

Chapter 4 demonstrates that articulating the interruption of community can take place through countermonumental memorializing practices at the museum. Although the museum, like the constitution, attempts to smooth the world through frameworks of sovereignty, there are also ways for it to resist this tendency. Countermonumental practices, such as those observed through the interactive adult educational programming at the District Six Museum, intentionally disrupt the cohering of community. And these practices have real ramifications for constitutionalism.

Christodoulidis, a key critic of constitutional fetishism, looks to the potential of civil society to challenge the limits of the constitutional framework. He argues that the powers of civil society, organized into a collective subject, offer the possibility of resistance. But while Christodoulidis engages in a critique of *constitutional* monumentalism, he ultimately endorses a monumental *politics*, one that hinges on the absolute immanence of the multitude that he derives from the work of Antonio Negri.[45] I critique this turn to the potential of constituent power and its self-assured position as the antithesis of constituted power. Rather than function in contradistinction to constitutionalism, a theory of politics motivated by a collective subject falls prey to the same dilemma of producing community. Therefore, although Christodoulidis and Negri begin by critiquing the stifling proclivities of constituted power, their exaltation of constituent power ultimately collapses into a program of politics. It is the site of the museum and its countermonumental memorializing practices—and not the constituent power of the multitude—that can offer an external reflexive resource that can challenge and shape the limits of the constitutional arrangement.

Chapter 5 draws on existing South African constitutional theory to fully articulate a theory of countermonumental constitutionalism. Here I explicitly build on the work already done by South African constitutional theorists that introduced the term in the 1990s. My approach works with the continued existence of the constitutional arrangement but adds a crucial reflexive resource to it: the site of the museum. Following Nancy's exigency, a countermonumental constitutionalism writes the infinite sharing of the world by interrupting secure and static articulations of community. I draw out this theory in relation to two recently postulated theories of jurisprudence. These theories, proffered by van der Walt and by Cornell and Muvangua, attempt to take seriously the contemporary constitutional arrangement in South Africa.[46] They both acknowledge the necessity of legal and political decision making. In response, they strive to make innovative additions to the existing adjudicational structure in the hopes of inspiring more just constitutional decisions in the future. Although both theories are valiant attempts at negotiating the stifling proclivities of the constitution, they do not go far enough in attending to legacies of colonialism and apartheid. This is because both center the constitutional arrangement as the key tool with which to inaugurate a postapartheid jurisprudence and therefore miss the opportunity to interrupt the logic of community. A countermonumental constitutionalism that embraces the role of the museum builds on these theories to better attend to their projects of creating a postapartheid jurisprudence.

Museums are like constitutions in that they both share a proclivity to produce community. Both rely on the idea that community can be produced and that their respective institution—the museum or the constitution—is a central conduit for the staging of this production. While this project of representation may be important and indeed necessary (issues returned to in chapters 4 and 5), this proclivity to produce community confuses representation with democracy. In other words, the museum and the constitution conflate their projects of representation with the vast realities of existence, including nonsovereign conceptions of the individual and communities. There is an urgent need to reconsider the boundaries of political community and its attendant conceptions of democracy if we are to pay heed to the reality of our relational existence and to anticolonial epistemologies. Constitutions and museums, if they embrace countermonumental memorializing practices, can attend to this need, reminding us of this reality. Rather than exalt either the museum or the constitution as the central device with which to navigate complex questions of community, this book argues that it is the critical use of both that proffers positive possibilities.

The pairing of constitutions and museums provides a theory of postcolonial transformation that resists the persistent imaginations of sovereign individuals and sovereign communities. Indeed, their pairing has the potential to offer a reflexive resource to the structural limitations of the constitution. In so doing, museums and constitutions can be brought together to produce a countermonumental constitutionalism that disrupts the centrality of the constitution as the key site for the production of political community and takes the interruption of stable and secure notions of community as its task. This alternative approach offers a new way to address the limits of conventional constitutionalism while attending to the complex demands of memory and community in the face of colonialism, apartheid, and other structural forms of inequity.

CHAPTER ONE

Constituting the Political

[B]efore even the tie of the Law, there is the network of the world.
—JEAN-LUC NANCY[1]

Carl Schmitt and Hannah Arendt, though divergent in their approaches and responses, focus on redressing what they see as the depoliticization and neutralization of the political in contemporary liberal democracy.[2] For them, the power and potential of human society have been hollowed out by the hegemony of state-based politics. In response, they resuscitate respective notions of the political to attend to the crisis. Jean-Luc Nancy's concern with the colonization of the political by politics is closely aligned with these critiques. Rather than see its subjugation to the already existing categories of everyday politics, Nancy sees the political as a necessary process of *opening up* conceptions of community.[3] This notion stems directly from his theory of being-in-common—an ontology that builds on Martin Heidegger's concept of *Mitsein*—that expresses the fundamental commonality of the world.[4] The truth of being-in-common highlights the poverty of exalting formal constitutional arrangements while missing out on the way in which community is always already beyond such delimitations.

Similarly, Martin Loughlin, Neil Walker, and Emilios Christodoulidis are three thinkers that engage in sustained debates about the role of constitutionalism in the production of political community.[5] They hold in common a healthy skepticism about lionizing the constitution as the key device in their theories of transformation. Indeed, they all also note the distinction between politics and the political. While all three differ on the precise role of constitutionalism, however, each keeps it central to his theoretical work; although all are interested in confronting the constitution's limits, they return to it as a key strategy for the production and safeguarding of political community. Where Loughlin is primarily concerned with elucidating a theory of public law that reveals the profound role of "right ordering," or *droit politique*, Walker is interested in thinking about the functioning of extrastate constitutionalism.[6] In contrast to both Loughlin and Walker, Christodoulidis focuses on conceiving of a reflexive constitutional arrangement that incorporates disorganization and "dissensus" without assimilating it, usually in support of a broadly anticapitalist, leftist politics.[7] With Loughlin, Walker, and Christodoulidis, the political is a system of limiting government or instituting popular sovereignty through a collective will. Like the anamorphic orientations of the museum, what is missed in this predilection is a rethinking of the political at a distance from these concerns.

The centrality of law in constitutional theorists' work is hardly surprising. Indeed, what are constitutional theorists to do if not theorize about the role of the constitution? Fundamental questions about community—specifically, the way in which an ontological understanding of community always already exceeds the confines of representation—are missed in the quick turn to constitutionalism as a founding basis. While a reconsideration of the political may cast doubts and concerns about this founding of political community, it does not necessarily result in its total rejection. My challenge to the grounds of constitutional theory is thus not a withdrawal from making normative judgments. I explicate this in more detail in chapters 4 and 5, but for now let me say that troubling the solidity of the ground upon which constitutional theory rests is a productive unsettling that provokes important questions about the constitution's assumed centrality as the foundation of political community.

THE CONCEPT OF THE POLITICAL

Writing in the first half of the twentieth century, former Nazi and German jurist Carl Schmitt takes aim at the contemporary concept of the political.[8] He is especially critical of its purported reflection in liberal democratic parliamentarianism.[9] Schmitt critiques this modern conception of politics for its neutralization and depoliticization of the political:

> Today nothing is more modern than the onslaught against the political. American financiers, industrial technicians, Marxist socialists, and anarchic-

syndicalist revolutionaries unite in demanding that the biased rule of politics over unbiased economic management be done away with. There must no longer be political problems, only organizational-technical and economic-sociological tasks. The kind of economic-technical thinking that prevails today is no longer capable of perceiving a political idea. The modern state seems to have actually become what Max Weber envisioned: a huge industrial plant.[10]

For Schmitt, liberalism substitutes the political with a project of universal inclusion.[11] For him, such an impulse dilutes and neutralizes the political, resulting in the state's becoming nothing more than "a revocable service for individuals and their free associations."[12] Only his concept of the political can transcend this nonpolitical organization of the state.

Schmitt outlines his own concept of the political as the essential distinction between friend and enemy.[13] This essential distinction functions to organize human beings into antagonistic groups, aligned or at odds with each other over the side they find themselves on. The political is not found in the content of the battle itself but at the point at which the categories of "friend" and "enemy" are drawn out.[14] In this way, the concept of the political is an autonomous one, devoid of substantive content other than this essential distinction, and it even precedes the concept of the state.[15]

The friend/enemy distinction is not just any drawing of a line in the sand. It is specifically a public distinction, one that encourages a division among humans into two opposing forces, rather than a private hatred.[16] Moreover, the distinction retains at its core an irreducible reflexivity that resists subjugation to institutional form. This allows for the concept of the political to be drawn and redrawn in any given moment. Christodoulidis contends that for Schmitt, "the political remains a horizon that resists substitution, because in this 'reflexivity,' what 'needs' to be done, and what is gained and lost by the 'harnessing' of conflict, remains an irreducibly political question."[17]

Although Schmitt is often invoked by radical left democratic theorists for his critiques of liberalism, his attachment to sovereignty, statism, and obedience has appropriately fitted him with the title of the "Hobbes of the twentieth century."[18] Indeed, Schmitt's hostility to liberalism does not make him antistatist. He is merely critical of the evacuation of the political by the liberal democratic state that shrinks away from its fundamental reliance on the sovereign decision.[19] Ultimately, however, he puts his concept of the political to use for the continued justification of state-on-state rivalry, returning his radical claims to a foundation in the state form.[20] But where Schmitt's critique of the neutralization of the political results in an endorsement of a stronger state, Arendt's similar critique leads to the *rejection* of sovereignty. Indeed, Arendt is a fierce critic of Hobbes and claims that his theory of the state as a centralized power-wielding force only leads to "the blind conformism of bourgeois society" and the destruction of plurality.[21] For her, plurality can only flourish under conditions that protect an autonomous conception of the political.

Arendt critiques what she sees as the blurring of the distinction between the political and the social. Drawing on Ancient Greek history and philosophy, she argues that the political must be a sphere privileged unto itself.[22] As in the Greek society she studies, Arendt sees the political as distinct from the private matters of the household. Rather, the private realm and its provision of biological necessities provide the very possibility of the political.[23] For Arendt, the household is a place where violence, force, hierarchy, and discrimination are tolerated; indeed, they are its inherent elements. The political domain, on the other hand, is the place where all citizens are considered equal and expected to participate in public deliberations with one another, deciding on everything "through words and persuasion."[24] This concept of the political is undergirded by Arendt's deep commitment to human plurality, a theory that rejects the primacy of individual *man* and emphasizes the *action of men*:

> Action, the only activity that goes on directly between men without the intermediary of things or matter, corresponds to the human condition of plurality, to the fact that men, not Man, live on the earth and inhabit the world. While all aspects of the human condition are somehow related to politics, this plurality is specifically *the* condition—not only the *conditio sine qua non*, but the *conditio per quam*—of all political life.[25]

Arendt's romantic conceptions of the Ancient Greek polis and theory of plurality lead her to condemn what she sees as a contemporary conflation of the political with the social. For her, this conflation begins with the advent of the modern nation-state.[26]

Arendt argues that with the rise of the nation-state, politics has become increasingly concerned with the organization of populations, rather than a protection of or interest in the political.[27] This shift in the understanding of politics, she argues, comes from an expansion of thinking about political community as the form of a family or household. What was once a strategy of securing the basic necessities of life so that citizens could become members of the polis has, in the modern period, become a hegemonic agenda of nationwide "housekeeping."[28] Under this program of politics, the political disappears and is reduced to mundane visions of equality that venerate conformism and inadvertently stifle plurality.[29] But this is not merely the result of a particularly paternalistic state formation.

According to Arendt, eighteenth-century political thought collapsed the notion of freedom into that of the human will. This silent substitution then formed the basis for the advent of a definition of freedom far from that found in her exalted polis. Rather, this shift founded freedom in sovereignty:

> Because of the shift from action to will-power, from freedom as a state of being manifest in action to the *liberum arbitrium*, the idea of freedom ceased to be virtuosity in the sense we mentioned before and became sovereignty, the ideal of a free will, independent from others and eventually prevailing against them.[30]

Arendt claims that the increasingly prevalent concept of individual sovereignty in modern political thought, and its attendant endorsement of the ability of humans to found political community through communal self-volition, is at the heart of the erasure of the political.[31] For her, this consistent attempt to capture political community through a representation of sovereign wills—whether in the form of a state, party, or revolutionary uprising—is always contradictory to human plurality.[32] These projects subjugate the role of "action" to stifling prescriptions of autonomy in both their individual and collective forms.[33] In doing so, the political is internalized and "the citizen" replaces "the individual."[34] The exemplary instances of such limited thinking, Arendt argues, can be seen in the revolutionary struggles against feudal tyranny in Europe. She claims that these projects for popular sovereignty all too often took the form of a perverted form of the political, which secured citizens against tyrannical abuses but proffered no positive theory for political community.[35] She famously states that "if men wish to be free, it is precisely sovereignty they must renounce."[36]

In contrast to the revolutionary traditions of Europe, especially that of the French, Arendt extols the revolutionary project in the United States. In marking a distinction between the two, Arendt traces the differences between what she sees as two distinct types of social contracts: "One was concluded between individual persons and supposedly gave birth to society; the other was concluded between a people and its ruler and supposedly resulted in legitimate government."[37] Whereas the former is premised on mutual consent between individuals to build a political community based on promises to each other, the latter represents the mere consent to be governed.[38]

The role of the promise is crucial for Arendt. Promises act as "islands of security without which not even continuity, let alone durability of any kind, would be possible in the relationships between men."[39] They provide some stability in the political realm without making absolute claims to self-mastery or autonomy.[40] Importantly for Arendt, promises bring together associations of people based on specific political interests, rather than "an identical will which magically inspires" a body of people.[41] Thus the promise maintains the importance of action at the heart of the political. It is the role of the promise, combined with an emphasis on collective deliberation, she claims, that animated the American Revolution and ensured its resistance to institutional sedimentation.[42] This promise, however, cannot be delivered without institutional support.

For Arendt, people need infrastructure within which the political can take place.[43] This requires a public space to meet as well as an institutional political framework to function as a site of authority.[44] To be clear, however, authority is not derived from a sovereign monarch, leader, or set of established rules. Rather, Arendt's conception of authority is one that gains its power *through contestation*. For her, "the amendments to the Constitution augment and increase the original foundations of the American republic; needless to say, the very authority of the American Constitution resides in its inherent capacity to be amended and augmented."[45] She argues that the Americans inadvertently copied the Romans in this respect by opting to situate their site of authority in the politics of humans, rather than a body of law that sat above them.[46] Arendt's concept of the political is thus a careful weaving of the potential of human promises, institutional infrastructure, public space, and human action.[47] For her, it is a delicate assembly of these variables that protects an autonomous conception of the political and, subsequently, human plurality.

Arendt's sophisticated approach to political community is a commendable attempt to avoid the dangers of collapsing the political into politics. Arendt draws on her fundamental theory of action to carve out a concept of the political that promotes public debate among humans. She is left with a carefully articulated notion of politics that resists the allure to found political community in constitutionalism or popular sovereignty. Her emphasis on a properly public sphere and its concomitant human deliberators, however, continues to set the production of a *world of the political* as her task.

Arendt ultimately grounds her expansive conception of human plurality in her theory of politics. Rather than allow her antifoundational observations on the tyranny of sovereignty and the limits of constitutionalism to debilitate the very possibility of political community, she uses them to insert a safety valve that allows for the positive articulation of politics. The safety valve comes in the form of the promise, "an island of security" in a sea of chaos.[48] Roberto Esposito critiques this latent theme of security or "conservation." Citing Jean-François Lyotard, he intimates that Arendt's theory is "'a thinking concerned with health' [. . .] a thought inflected more towards protecting than calling radically into question the mythologeme of *humanitas.*"[49] Although Arendt is unquestionably concerned with human plurality, she ultimately suppresses its limitlessness in favor of developing a politics based on human promises. In so doing, she draws a border around the "properly" political—a sphere designed to bring humans together to form political community—that mimics the problems I explore at museums. In contrast, Jean-Luc Nancy's relational ontology offers a way of thinking about the world as always in a process of sharing. It illuminates the dangers of *creating* a political world and encourages a retreatment of the political beyond the consideration of humans and promises.[50]

Like Schmitt and Arendt, Nancy is concerned with the colonization of the political by politics.[51] Yet where Schmitt pursues sovereignty and Arendt follows the potential of the promise, Nancy rejects such grounding.[52] He points out that such delimitations are always a betrayal of being-in-common and, as such, are a *production* of community.[53] Rather than closing down and institutionalizing political community, Nancy wants to open it, or rather draw attention to the ways in which it is always already *open.*

Inspired by Georges Bataille's denial of the possibility of absolute knowledge, Nancy draws out the contradiction of the "absolute."[54] According to Nancy, "the absolute must be the absolute of its own absoluteness, or not be at all. In other words: to be absolutely alone, it is not enough that I be so; I must be alone being alone—and this of course is contradictory."[55] What Nancy elucidates here is that on the one hand, in order to be absolute, the absolute must be exactly that; it must not be in relation to anything else. On the other hand, as it encloses itself, it necessarily makes a border that is exposed to something other than itself. In order to counter this exposure to another thing, in order for the absolute to be absolute, it must enclose itself with another closure, thereby defeating the possibility of its absoluteness. Consequently, the absolute is a contradiction.[56] This inescapable relationality means that there can be no individual or other totality that is immanent to itself (whether it be "community," "the state," or "the people"). The separate enclosure is impossible as a result of a lack of any definitive boundary between inside and outside; there is only the relation of exposure.[57] It is this inherent relationality that forms the ground for Nancy's conception of being-in-common.

Being-in-common is empty of any foundations based on a subject or a knowable, immanent community. It takes place—it is "what happens to us"—as it exposes the impossibility of absolute immanence.[58] Further, being-in-common means that beings cannot be thought of as either "internal" or "external" to themselves but, rather, always and necessarily *both*.[59] Nancy's ontology is therefore in stark contrast to contemporary metaphysics that attempt to think through notions of community based on a conception of the subject as self-contained, a problem that he claims persists in Heidegger's notion of being-with (*Mitsein*). For Nancy, Heidegger maintains a conception of the subject that is not sufficiently implicated in its ontological relationship with other beings; in Heidegger's conception of being-with, there is too much "being" and not enough "with."[60]

Community, therefore, cannot be thought of as an assemblage of individuals or as a product created by acting subjects; it is *nothing*, it cannot be made. It is a sharing between beings, the sharing of the inside and outside.[61] It is not, however, a willed sharing, as in a sharing instigated by acting subjects. It is the necessary sharing of existence, of being-in-common.[62] Moreover, this sharing is always incomplete, for a completed sharing would mean what was being shared had disappeared. Completed sharing would mean the annihilation of the space beyond the self that sets being in relation, and a denial of this space returns us to the mythical presupposition of representation. Community is not a completed work but rather is an *inoperative* and incomplete sharing that we are abandoned to.[63] Community cannot be bound by contracts or by the myth of absolute immanence.[64]

Nancy perceives narratives that posit the possibility of absolute immanence as "mythical."[65] In these stories, the "will of community" is legitimized as an active agent in the construction of a (false) possibility of communion.[66] This myth is mobilized as a truth about the potentiality of wills and, hence, of the community to know itself in its "totality."[67] These stories of absolute immanence lay at the heart of both right- and left-wing political projects:

> What one calls "totalitarianism" is the complete presentation of a sense in truth: myth, that is, but myth as reality, without the différance of its narrative. It is the immediate being-there or immanence of myth. In the fascist version, truth is the life of the community, in the Nazi version, truth is the conflagration of the people, and in the communist version, truth is humanity creating itself as humanity [. . .] On this account, politics must be destiny, must have history as its career, sovereignty as its emblem, and sacrifice as its access.[68]

Nancy's concept of the political involves a consciousness for the ways in which community is always already involved in the experience of sharing. Such a consciousness is incompatible with the myth of foundations or absolute immanence; it interrupts this myth by denying the positing of its completion. Against the inclination of mythic thought to make a foundation from a fiction, this consciousness interrupts myth and its project of narrating community as operative.[69] This consciousness resists the reduction of the political to an origin and encourages a thinking of community that exposes our ontological sharing. Nancy's thought poses a radical challenge to any attempt to found or secure community, whether it is through representation at the museum, through constitutionalism, or in Arendt's carefully articulated notion of politics.

Skeptics assert that this radical ontological claim has little to say to constitutionalism and that Nancy's theory marks a withdrawal from normative judgments.[70] Nancy's reply to such accusations is a biting reversal of the question. His ontology of being-in-common challenges self-assured theories of ethics and politics; his theory demands that such certainty be perpetually retreated. Nancy does not celebrate nihilism, nor does he advocate the abandoning of foundations as another solidity; he warns against the dangers of romanticizing the "fragment," claiming that it confers "all the autonomy, finish, and aura of the 'work of art.'"[71] Instead, his world is made up of

> the incessant tying up of singularities with each other, over each other, and through each other, without any end other than the enchainment of

(k)nots, without any structure other than their interconnection or interdependence, and without any possibility of calling any single (k)not or the
totality of (k)nots self-sufficient (for there would be "totality" only in the
enchainment itself).[72]

The problem is how to think political community in a way that embraces
this ontological sharing.

Nancy's thought poses a challenge to the institutionalizing proclivities
of both museums and constitutionalism. Where museological practices and
constitutional thinking seek to render legible a conception of the world,
Nancy seeks to undo this legibility. The world created by the representative
structures of museums and constitutions cannot do justice to this conception of the political.

CONSTITUTIONALISM AND THE EVACUATION OF THE POLITICAL

Some might argue that attempting to make constitutionalism answer to the
dilemmas raised by the distinction between the political and politics is ri-
diculous. Certainly constitutions are definitionally concerned with the everyday machinery of politics and as such cannot be faulted for a preoccupa-
tion with the agenda of the state and its management of populations. But
the distinction between politics and the political is also one made in the
contemporary constitutional theory of Loughlin, Walker, and Christodoulidis. Each of these thinkers values a consideration of the political at a distance
from politics in their efforts to draw out reflexive theories of constitutional
law. Ultimately, however, they all return to the power and potential of the
constitution in the production of political community. In the first case,
Loughlin's theory extols the powers of popular sovereignty and its ability to
shape the constitutional arrangement. In the second instance, Walker concedes the problem of constitutional fetishism yet maintains the centrality of
constitutionalism (albeit in extra-state form). Finally, Christodoulidis leaves
us with the potential of praxis of an underdetermined subject that returns us
to the conundrum of absolute immanence. In the section that follows, I outline these theories and how they depart from their radical trajectories to reproduce a concept of the political set on the production of community. My
point here is not to dismiss the normative concerns of these brilliant legal

thinkers but rather, taking inspiration from Judith Butler, "to interrogate what the theoretical move that establishes foundations *authorizes*, and what precisely it excludes or forecloses."[73]

Loughlin's concern is that legal scholars have forgotten that constitutionalism is founded by the political. He is keen to emphasize that prior to the establishment of a legal system comes a political moment that founds the institution of government. Following Schmitt, Loughlin asserts that the political precedes the legal; it is the political that supplies the foundation for law.

Loughlin's theory of the political is made up of three orders. Beginning with Schmitt's formulation of the distinction between friend and enemy, Loughlin contends that human conflict forms the foundation of the political.[74] This distinction comes before the creation of the state and before the creation of law. The second register of politics, however, goes beyond this preliminary stage to embrace the potentialities of state-based programs of governing. Here, in the second order of the political, politics takes place as a system that operates between the government and the governed in order to achieve a common goal of security.[75] In this instance too, Loughlin strives to demonstrate that law and government emerge from the political. It is struggles over determining the function of law—how it might protect, enable, or liberate a community—that dictate the form of governing. The third order of politics comes in the form of constitutional law. Loughlin claims that this third register functions to smooth out and balance the systems of state government via a fair, nonpartisan framework.[76] For him, constitutional law is the result of a collective political bargain. It establishes the rules that the people have agreed will guide and orient the relationship between government and governed. He does not claim that the constitution entirely grasps the politics of a people. Rather, the first and second registers of his outline of the political retain the ever-present possibility of disturbing, and thus shifting, the constitutional framework. For Loughlin, the fundamental importance of the political in public law lies in the foundational political practices of a people that create and sustain a system of authority (in the form of government).[77] This concept of the political, however, evokes two fundamental problems: namely, the limited boundaries of institutional politics and the paradox of an immanent power.

In the first instance, Loughlin's concept of the political is that it rests on the authorizing function of a constituent power that lays the imagined foundations of the political arrangement. This concept of "the people," however, has long been recognized as a paradox best formulated by asking: What force or authority do these "people" have *before* the creation of a constitutional arrangement? As Jacques Derrida puts it,

> [T]his people does not exist. They do not exist as an entity, it does not exist, before this declaration, not as such. If it gives birth to itself, as free and independent subject, as possible signer, this can hold only in the act of the signature. The signature invents the signer.[78]

It is fair to ask: In the name of what political project is this paradox being ignored? What political community is being fostered in its name?

Loughlin acknowledges this paradox—indeed, he identifies it as a problem at the heart of constituent power—but this admission does not pose a problem for his theory. Rather, he finds a way to integrate the dilemma by simultaneously acknowledging and sidestepping it. He proposes that a theory of "reflexive constitutionalism" can avoid the paradoxical foundations of the constitution by "treating the founding not simply as an historical event but as a reflexive undertaking through which 'the people' come after the fact [. . .] to embrace the norms enunciated in constitutional documents."[79] But it is unclear how this formulation accounts for the paradox of the origin. Rather than confront the profound dilemma the paradox reveals, Loughlin glosses over it. Here again, as in the case of Arendt, the radical possibilities of this instability of community are muted and stifled by the importation of a foundation that is imagined to secure it.

In more recent work Loughlin continues to elaborate the importance of a constituent power as the basis for the political. He refers to the fundamental power that orients and legitimizes the state form as *"droit politique."* Taken from Jean-Jacques Rousseau's *Du contrat social ou Principes du droit politique (The Social Contract), droit politique* is the concept of "right to rule" or "right ordering" that undergirds the entire state infrastructure.[80] In Loughlin's words *droit politique* "entails the creation of a world of our own devising."[81] But this call for the creation of a world of our own devising ignores the fact that the world is already *here*. Yes, right ordering attends to the everyday demand of politics—the need for the rule of law and a representational structure—but this cannot serve as the horizon of our political imaginations. Loughlin ignores the way in which community is always already beyond rights-based delimitations in the interest of attending to the demands of the existing categories of politics.

Although this may not be a surprising move for a constitutional scholar, it is Loughlin's own aim to set out a distinct theory of the political. Yet he collapses fundamental questions about community and plurality into the everyday practices of governing. His exaltation of political right is only relevant insofar as it legitimizes and orders the foundations of the state. The centrality of the state is a consistent theme in Loughlin's theory:

> [T]he state is the entity created by the foundational deed; the state is a collective representation of a people (a "we"). This basic philosophical idea of the state (otherwise, "The Nation") provides the founding assumption on which an elaboration of the precepts of political right becomes conceivable. This structure of political right generates a series of truths about the political world.[82]

Here Loughlin's explanation of the foundational role of the state in buoying the possibility of *droit politique* institutionalizes his first order of the political. Although the rules may be legitimately altered as a result of their underlying foundations, the rules (in the form of constitutional law) will mediate the resulting experience. Loughlin's account of the political is thus deeply connected to an institutional-based politics.[83] It is not only Loughlin's emphasis on the importance of the state form, however, but also his exaltation of constituent power that collapses his notion of the political into politics. Here again in his more recent theory he narrates into the spotlight the enduring figure of a "modern" "secular" constitutionalism legitimized by the self-authorizing power of an immanent autonomous people:

> [O]nly with the creation of the modern world [. . .] do we see the formation of distinct spheres of human activity—the economic, the scientific, the technical, the intellectual, and the political. And only with this differentiation can these regimes leave religion behind and develop their own autonomous modes of operation. [. . .] But the argument is not that the modern world is an irreligious world; religion lives on as a powerful influence in modern societies. The point is that it lives on as culture, and no longer as the basic structuring force of collective organisation.[84]

According to Loughlin, modern political authorization no longer comes from "above" but from "ourselves"; in this modern era, transcendence is rejected and immanence becomes its defining feature.[85] Here, *droit politique* and its self-satisfied anthropocentrism envelops and supersedes any prioritization of an autonomous concept of the political.[86]

Loughlin would likely refute this characterization of his work. Indeed, in several places he asserts that his project is distinctly *not* conflating the mundane concerns of governance with the political.[87] He claims he is emphasizing that public law is concerned with the task of drawing out, deliberating, and contesting its own parameters. Rather than simply see the constitutional arrangement as a set of limitations on individual and group power, he claims it should be the site from which power is launched, or in his words "generated."[88] And yet it is difficult to understand how he marries the critique of his collapse of the political into politics when he returns to an ultimate conception of freedom as "a status that is realized only within the state."[89] Moreover, Loughlin claims that his task is "not that of political philosophy [or] elaborating the structure of some ideal constitution [but] to understand the precepts through which constitutional ordering makes sense or [. . .] to understand the ways in which existing constitutional arrangements can be said to work."[90] Loughlin's self-proclaimed descriptive account of the political, however, cannot be separated from its role in reinforcing a normative idea about its content. It reinforces the myth that the political is merely about the mediation of government and governed and not about broader questions of community and plurality. An interruption of this logic refuses to accept the necessity of founding political community through representation. It takes as its task the undoing of the utilitarian impulse that undergirds this supposed necessity by demonstrating that community always already exceeds representations, whether offered by museums or constitutions.

Neil Walker challenges Loughlin's focus on the centrality of state-based constitutionalism. Rather than cultivate the idea of constitutionalism as something found exclusively within the domain of the nation-state, Walker writes explicitly about it "beyond the state."[91] He critiques the hegemony that state-based constitutionalism (what he calls "constitutional monism") has gained in the "Westphalian age" and its presumption that individual nation-states are the center of constitutional authority.[92] According to Walker, the supremacy of state-based constitutionalism is largely a result of self-referentiality. He claims that the authority of state constitutions "pulled themselves up by their own positivist bootstraps, drawing upon resilient sources of symbolic power and institutional strength."[93] In contrast, he claims that constitutions are no longer contained products of one particular country but rather are made up of agreements and treaties formed with transnational institutions like the World Trade Organization (WTO) and the European Union (EU).[94] To him, we may think of constitutionalism as being made up of "framing mechanisms" and that we can see those mechanisms in play both at state-based and poststate configurations.[95] For Walker, constitutional monism misses out on the ways in which political community is beyond the state.

Walker offers an intriguing challenge to a traditional thinking of constitutionalism, but his critique of the limitations of constitutional monism does not translate into its repudiation. Rather, he sees constitutionalism—as it functions within both domestic and international domains—as an essential part of political community.[96] Consequently, where Walker's approach to constitutionalism begins with a critique of the hegemony of constitutional monism, it ends not by challenging the continued power of constitutional discourse and its imagined centrality in the authorization and operation of political community, but with an endorsement of its function *beyond the state*. In other words, Walker does not seek to dismantle, disturb, or question the place of constitutionalism in the production of political community but instead wants to draw attention to the ways it is already operational in locations beyond the state and *affirm* its role there. This predilection maintains his theory as one primarily concerned with politics at the expense of the political.

Significantly, Walker attempts to address critiques of the exaltation of law in the formation of political community in his own work.[97] For example, he eloquently summarizes the critique of "constitutional fetishism." He explains that this fetishism gives

> undue concentration upon—even enchantment with—constitutionalism and constitutional structures [that] overstates the explanatory and transformative potential of constitutional discourse and frustrates, obstructs or at least diverts attention from other mechanisms through which power and influence are effectively wielded and political community is formed and which should instead provide the central, or at least a more significant, focus of our regulatory efforts and public imagination.[98]

Walker clearly elucidates the fundamental limitations of constitutionalism to take into consideration political challenges from outside its purview.[99] But although he agrees with this critique of the siren song of constitutionalism, in the end, he has little to offer in response. Ultimately, he

contends that such critiques are incompatible with our current epistemological situation:

> [T]here is no conceivable way within our present epistemic framework of
> thinking about large-scale institutional change without considering the role
> that law might have to play in that process of change. [. . .] So we reach the
> paradoxical conclusion that the very constitutional law which threatens to
> suffocate the political imagination nevertheless seems indispensable to our
> efforts to support and inspire that imagination.[100]

Walker's pessimism of the imagination is striking here, especially coming
from the same thinker who articulates the critique of the hegemony of constitutional monism as stemming from state constitutions' self-referentiality.
And yet he deploys the same circular logic. Like that of the constitutional
monists, his is a self-fulfilling prophecy; by claiming that political change
cannot be imagined without considering the role of constitutional law, he
validates his own claim about its centrality.

Moreover, given his clear elucidation of the critiques of constitutional fetishism, it is surprising to see him resort to a kind of ideological fatalism that
claims it cannot think without the law. Indeed, rather than take this own critique on board, Walker is more willing to gloss over it by asserting that such
critiques ultimately act as a "tribute [. . .] to the extraordinarily pervasive and
resilient power of constitutional discourse."[101] In the end, he admits that his
response has little to say to the charges of constitutional fetishism.[102]

But Walker, like Loughlin, holds on to the possibility for "reflexivity"
built into constitutionalism. He claims that "boundaries should be defined
such as to require healthy skepticism and interrogation of any claims which
seek to define constitutionalism [. .] within a final uncontestable framework."[103] But there is a contradictory logic here. Walker simultaneously argues for hostility to the boundaries of constitutionalism as well as for a do-
mestication of this hostility *as part of the process of defining constitutionalism.*
He does not find this contradiction to be a problem. Rather, he evades the
dilemma by asserting a claim reminiscent of the Pascalian wager.[104] He
claims that "there is no ground upon which we can say with absolute conviction that the values associated with constitutionalism and democracy hang
together, just as there is not ground upon which we can say with absolute
conviction that they do not."[105] Thus, although he concedes this fundamental abyss at the heart of the normative claims of constitutionalism, he prefers

to err on the side of the law. Ultimately, Walker's theory maintains a narrative about the necessary centrality of constitutionalism in the production of political community.

As with Loughlin above, Walker legitimizes a concept of the political that assumes the necessity of *making* political community. Although he acknowledges the dangers of overstating the power of constitutionalism, he ultimately sides with his own pessimism of the imagination, arguing that although it might "suffocate" our political vision, we nevertheless need it to "support and inspire that imagination."[106] Moreover, Walker justifies his endorsement of constitutionalism by claiming that although there is no way to say for certain that constitutionalism is central to democracy, there is also no way to know that it is not. This wager, however, does not consider the way in which constitutionalism itself—in its central goal of *producing* community through the representative structures of law—may be at odds with democracy. Consequently, Walker offers an impoverished imagination of the political that is suffocated by its conflation with the existing categories of politics.

Christodoulidis marks a departure from both Walker and Loughlin by arguing that theories of law and constitutionalism that claim exclusive authority over the creation and maintenance of political community are impoverished. These claims deny the very real role of—and need for—politics as a part of constitutionalism: "law cannot, as the republicans would have it, contain the politics of civil society and exhaust what these politics are about. The law cannot contain and voice our strivings for the communities we want to have and our aspirations for the people we want to be."[107] In contrast, he introduces the concept of "reflexive politics" into his constitutional thought, a politics that "keeps the question of its revisability [*sic*] always open and where the political constellation of meanings is always disruptable [*sic*]."[108] Unlike Walker and Loughlin, however, Christodoulidis argues that this reflexivity cannot be accommodated under the banner of constitutionalism.

Nevertheless, Christodoulidis continues to see a vital role for the constitution. Although he is critical of its exaltation as the central organizing force of political community, he continues to see it as "an important and indeed valuable place—in the politics of civil society in guaranteeing limitations on State power."[109] Christodoulidis's project is to keep the realms of law and politics distinct so that law is not used as the ultimate tool with which to think and organize political community. Rather, he sees law and politics as two distinct arenas, a distinction he makes using Niklas Luhmann's systems theory.

Christodoulidis claims that republicans ignore the functioning of separate systems to the great impoverishment of politics. This is most markedly obvious as republican constitutional scholars attempt to make constitutionalism reflexive and inclusive. According to him, this demand on constitutionalism is an impossible one because it attempts to make an inherently institutional concept (constitutionalism) open to radical transformation.[110] The problem is that institutional theories of law necessarily import boundaries about what can be contested.[111] Christodoulidis intimates that this is where systems theorists get it right: they explicitly show how institutional boundaries delimit what is "relevant" to the constitutional conversation rather than try to cover up the "mundane violence" of exclusion.[112] He claims that "legal argumentation as a practical discourse is always-already disciplined by the contextual conditions, [and] therefore no longer reflexive about them [. . .] there can be no structure-defying structures; the institution cannot see its blind spot and shake it off."[113] Therefore, the only way to get at, or rather get away from, these institutional footholds in law is not from within it but from elsewhere. Consequently, Christodoulidis develops a theory of politics that emanates from a constituent power.[114] Importantly, however, his endorsement of this constituent power differs considerably from Loughlin's. Christodoulidis stabilizes his notion of a constituent power via an underdetermined communal subject that is formed through praxis, that is, a subject that is always in a process of always becoming.

Christodoulidis describes this underdetermined collective subject by drawing on the Italian Operaismo and Autonomist movements, which sought to define the working class in ways that resisted its synonymization with "work." In order to both assert a collective identity *and* resist the hegemonic identification of workers with work (which maintained their link to capital), the Autonomists used a conception of self-valorization.[115] Self-valorization allowed for the articulation of a collective subject that remained underdetermined: "one in which both the subject and its praxis are underdetermined, expressing themselves in resistance but not exhausted in that form."[116] It is a subject that is only definable as an "unstructurable" potentiality and, as such, not reducible to a "political or juridical image."[117] It is a subject (under)determined by its praxis. Christodoulidis claims that

> praxis provides an opportunity for "presence" to register, because the subject and "its" action become mutually defining in a moment where the coinci-

dence is actual. This suspension of representation allows us to delay the characterisation of the subject until its undertaking of praxis, both subject and action emerging as representable in a moment of "real" self-referentiality.[118]

This simultaneously resistant and underdetermined subject can both communicate a struggle but also hold that struggle's meaning open, protecting it from sedimentation in institutional form. Christodoulidis explains the necessity of this dual function: "all politics need boundaries to be drawn because all representation needs boundaries, but these are boundaries to be transcended, positive markers to be questioned otherwise, indices of the *politicisable.*"[119] What is politicizable is imagined as the contestation over the role and limits of the institutional arrangement. Consequently, the political task at hand is maintaining the possibility for reflexivity, dissent, and disagreement over these boundaries.

While Christodoulidis emphasizes the need to draw attention to the limits of these boundaries, he does so by way of maintaining the role of constitutionalism in the production of community.[120] For him, the constitution is necessary for the protection of people against state power and for the articulation of politics.[121] He attempts to redress this concession by adding a reflexive caveat: he recognizes the power of politics practiced by civil society. Certainly this caveat challenges the inclination to look to the constitution for radical reflexivity (a demand it cannot meet), but Christodoulidis's turn to the politics of the multitude imports other limitations.

Christodoulidis's theory suggests that something can only be "politicisable" if it is made so by a constituent power. To be sure, Christodoulidis's theoretical unpacking of the problems of "representation" is thoughtful and cautious; he makes an "acrobatic effort" to articulate a politics of representation while undercutting its very possibility.[122] But, ultimately, he cannot rid his theory of an idea of a multitude that is knowable by its presence. While he acknowledges the danger of asserting a conception of an immanent community, he nonetheless produces one that is recognizable by its praxis. This community is not nothing; it is some*thing*. Christodoulidis's concept of the political is intimately tied to a foundation in a community of human actors that use their will to initiate and carry out their desired program. The equation of the political with the sovereign will of a community of human actors forgoes a consideration of the plurality of the world. It substitutes a thinking of the vast horizons of the potentiality of the world with the categories of existing politics. The political cannot be instituted by a program guided by the will of the people; rather, the political is an interruption of the very idea of "the people."

Christodoulidis's nuanced and thoughtful approach to the dilemma of constitutionalism demonstrates that it is not merely the enclosing proclivities of constitutionalism that collapse the political into politics. Even as he distances himself from what he refers to as the "republican containment thesis," his theory of reflexive politics falls into some of the same problems.[123] While he attempts to stray from a tradition of constitutional thinking that subjugates politics to law, his ultimate endorsement of the praxis of an underdetermined constituent power falls into a similar paradigm. Although intended as a challenge, Christodoulidis's theory of reflexive politics substitutes the communing logic of the constitution with the communing logic of the multitude.

WRITING THE INTERRUPTION OF COMMUNITY

Community cannot be thought of through rights, social contracts, or romantic notions of the people. Against the forces that seek to close the world by rendering it into a system of representation, resistance comes from world forming that seeks to interrupt these enclosures, what Allison Ross calls the "disruption of all closures of signification."[124] World forming is not the logic of the contract but the "incessant tying of singularities"; a praxis of the (k)not.[125] This, for Nancy, is "the law of the world."[126]

To be clear, world forming is not a project of creating a world that is *apart* from this world.[127] Nancy is clear; the world is here: "there [y] is the whole of the world. There is that there is."[128] Nor is this a project of creating *a* world; it is the forming of many worlds within one world.[129] Therefore, any conception of the world as a representation, and any representation of the world, is a betrayal of the world. This is because the representation of the world requires a subject to be outside of the world and this is an impossibility.[130] Justice is in this opening up, this sharing out, this exposure of existences.[131] But it is not a goal that can be attained, nor a program, or work. Justice is in the constant movement of this sharing, irreducible to an end, model, or product.[132] The exposure of this incessant sharing is the conception of the political that Nancy argues must be made sovereign in a new way.[133]

Significantly, world forming cannot be left up to a "rethinking." There is a political exigency to *articulate* community: "'articulation' means, in some way, 'writing,' which is to say, the inscription of a meaning whose transcendence or presence is indefinitely and constitutively deferred [. . .] the inscription of our infinite resistance."[134] The truth of being-in-common cannot be left to "the scintillations of a pure dispersion of singularities."[135] Rather, the articulation of being-in-common must be made in order to interrupt the productions of community that are used to legitimize conflicts over identity and land. This writing, however, must also interrupt itself; it must trace out the "essencelessness of relation" and ceaselessly expose us as in common.[136] Even as the foundations of the subject and of community are absent, the sharing of the world is not. And it is this sharing of the world that must be articulated, interrupting the myths of community that deny this being-in-common.

In order to do justice to the truth of being-in-common, museum practices and constitutionalism must articulate the sharing and exposure of the world. Such an endeavor entails a retreatment of the political that refuses to set the production of community as its task. This means that both museum practices and constitutionalism must refuse sovereignty, but not by taking refuge in this denial. Such refuge would only establish a new self-assured conception of the political with a new mythological veneer and coherence. Rather, a retreatment of the political at the museum and in constitutionalism means an incessant articulation of the infinite sharing of community. It means the constant writing of the exposure of existence, an exposure that interrupts the logic of communion.

CHAPTER TWO

Sovereign Orientations

However they are framed, museum objects—whether works of fine art, scientific specimens, mechanical inventions, ethnographic artifacts, fetishes, relics, or what have you—function as diagnostic devices and modular measures for making sense of all possible worlds and their subjects.

–DONALD PREZIOSI AND CLAIRE FARAGO[1]

Museums have become an important site of political contestation and controversy in the latter half of the twentieth century.[2] This is partly because the collections of many large national public museums grow directly out of histories of slavery, colonialism, and imperialism and have thus been accused of cultural appropriation, historical theft, and the propagation of civilizational hierarchies.[3] As a result, museums are at the center of debates over representation and repatriation that are contested on political, ethical, financial, and psychical grounds.

In response, contemporary curators, academics, and theorists have taken up the task of writing and working toward a "new" kind of museum.[4] This newly envisioned place, though differing vastly in proposed techniques, is overwhelmingly imagined as a more inclusive, "democratic" institution, aimed at righting the wrongs of historical museum practices. Future museological projects are proposed as interactive installations aimed at developing critical museum visitors, and others as theoretical gestures intended to reconceptualize relations between the museum and its visitors.[5] It is commonly asserted within this literature that museum practitioners should adopt these practical and theoretical reforms in order for museums to move away from their contentious foundations. In so doing, these reformist claims establish a moral responsibility to rehabilitate the museum in the service of a better future, and this future is commonly envisioned as ascertained through a corresponding drive toward "democracy."[6] The rehabilitated museum is then imagined to serve its appropriate function of representing and educating the public, or, as Didier Maleuvre contends, "reconciling the polis."[7]

The supposed necessity of representing community, however, fails to attend to the way in which community is always already a sharing of exposures that cannot be captured by an institutional framework. As contemporary museological literature equates democracy with the representation of political community, it abandons a retreating of the political that "ceaselessly expose[s] us as in common."[8] Moreover, these museums, as well as the attendant theoretical literature about them, invoke conceptions of underrepresented or excluded communities as if there is a truth about them to convey. This privation of community makes a *project* or *work* out of community. The aim of reforming the museum is therefore not merely a well-intended project of restoring what is missing (although its promoters may think of it that way); rather, these projects serve as active authorizers of the concepts and categories used to demarcate and delimit community. This production of community is fostered by the use of "anamorphic orientations"—practices of the museum that smooth and cohere the messiness of the world.[9]

The other snag in the new museum's claim to democratic supremacy emerges via a historical analysis of the emergence of the museum from monarchical collections in Western Europe. The supposed secularization of museum collections during the same social and political upheavals that brought about the advent of the modern state means that the museum's history has been intimately tied to discourses of citizenship and democracy. Despite its origins in antifeudal movements, however, the modern public museum maintained many of the traps of the hierarchical systems that the revolutionaries were purportedly trying to expel. This transposal is most obvious in the fact that new public museums became a site from which state agendas of governance and nation building were launched. The public museum was a site for instantiating a newly emerging public, positioned as the owners and keepers of national collections but also subject to its disciplinary demands. These modern themes of collective ownership and universal representation set the parameters for the museum to become a site of controversy and contestation over democratic ideals, representation, and reform in the nineteenth and especially the twentieth century.

Interestingly, constitutional discourse in Western Europe shares a similar trajectory. Indeed, the modern state is asserted to have emerged out of this same rejection of the monarchical tradition; the popular will of the people is now presumed to have taken its rightful place at the autonomous helm of the secular, liberal-democratic state. In both stories, the oppressive force of unelected rulers is imagined to be a distinct thing of the past. The new political landscape, ushered in by the revolutionary movements of the seventeenth and eighteenth centuries in Western Europe, claims to mark a distinct break from this earlier undemocratic tradition; liberal democracy is imagined to represent the pinnacle of political possibilities because of its authorization of man's power of self-determination. But this new landscape offers a suffocated notion of the political for both museums and constitutions, one that asks us to set our horizons on the power of sovereignty.

The formation of the modern public museum is intimately bound up with the social, political, and historical emergence of liberalism. Carol Duncan outrightly characterizes museums as sites of secular ceremonies.[10] She posits that the practices of museum-going form a complex of "civilizing rituals" that offer "values and beliefs—about social, sexual, and political identity—in the form of vivid and direct experience."[11] But these rituals are not just about state building. A critique of both the museum and the constitution as merely institutions dedicated to civic rituals, while true, does not go far enough. This characterization fails to identify the "destinal figure" of community and the production of the individual at their respective centers.[12] This tenacious attachment to the autonomous liberal subject and its normalized imaginations of sovereignty must be interrupted if we are to conceive of being together in the world differently.

Below I explore the work of "new museum" scholars that attempts to utilize interactive adult educational programming to reconfigure a project of political community in the name of democracy. In doing so, however, these attempts continue to centralize existing categories of community and consistently equate democracy with inclusion and better representation at the museum. In my view, such limited calls for reform cannot do justice to the ontological primacy of being-in-common nor can they proffer responses to legacies of colonialism. Attending to these complex legacies of exclusion and marginalization requires an unthinking of the hegemony of this atomized subject and its representation, which continues to hinge on imaginations of autonomy and sovereignty inherited from Western systems of law and politics that were institutionalized in museums and constitutions in the seventeenth and eighteenth centuries.

MUSEUMS AND THE ORGANIZATION OF THE WORLD

The institution of the museum has its roots in the history of Renaissance naturalists whose collecting habits greatly influenced the aristocratic and monarchical cultures around them.[13] Collectors kept studio rooms filled with a variety of found treasures that they hoped would unearth the world's secrets. Two of the most famed naturalists of the time, Conrad Gesner (Swiss) and Ulisse Aldrovandi (Italian), wrote encyclopedias and articles that conveyed a plethora of categories describing the objects they had collected.[14] Significantly, the naturalists' systems of classification differed considerably from those that animate the contemporary museum. Aldrovandi's description of a peacock using thirty categories of contemplation illustrates the difference.[15] This myriad of categories points to a larger scientific phenomenon of the time: the association of objects to the larger order of the cosmos.[16] This understanding of the natural world, however, gave way after the publication of work by Joannes Jonston, who used Aldrovandi's sketches but replaced the text with much more consolidated descriptions of the objects. This move inaugurated a new era in natural history that led to the "decontextualization of the world."[17]

At the same time, Renaissance princes were developing collections of their own. But rather than arrange their collections for the purposes of study and reflection, the princes' collections were organized as small-scale reconstructions of reality. Where the naturalists were skeptical of the ability to realistically represent reality, the princes' studio collections—held in *studiolos*—were organized as symbols of their great power and influence over the world; the modern museum experience grew out of this tradition.[18] These chambers, also referred to as "cabinets of curiosities," contained treasures kept behind closed doors.[19] The objects themselves were organized to represent the order of the cosmos and arranged in the *studiolo* so as to permit the prince a central spot from which only he could inspect each object.[20] This spatial positioning gave the prince exclusive right to mediate between the contents of his collection and the order of the cosmos that it represented. The layout of the *studiolo* was organized to reinforce the idea that sacred objects were to be possessed—and their significance translated—by the sovereign. Not only did these displays of the collections aggrandize the prince's personality and power by impressing his stature on his exclusive audiences, they emphasized his role in mediating access to the very knowledge of the world.[21]

Near the end of the sixteenth century these collections were largely transferred from the private viewing spaces of the sovereign to more popular spaces, a shift that was the product of several mutually reinforcing influences. One such influence was an increasing need to legitimize the role of the prince and the monarchical dynasty as a result of the destabilizing effects of the Protestant Reformation in Western Europe at the time.[22] Indeed, the advent of the Reformation was threatening to the Catholic monarchies' collective and authoritative control over knowledge.[23] In order to maintain some legitimacy in a rapidly changing landscape, the Catholic monarchies may have seen social value in tinkering with tradition and opening up the collections.[24] But these spaces, far from being for public consumption, were open exclusively to elite members of society, largely white male aristocrats, invited into the palace to take in the sights of the precious treasures.[25] Rather than mark a radical challenge to centralized power, however, the increased accessibility was a direct extension of the epistemological current that instantiated the primacy of the sovereign's role in the organization of the *studiolo*.[26] Therefore, the increased accessibility of collections through more public domains was not simply a retreat of the sovereign's influence. Rather, this more "public" showing of the princely collections continued to hold the supremacy of the sovereign as central to the viewing and understanding of the world.

The advent of the contemporary public museum descended from the revolutionary traditions of Western Europe. Its place as a public institution came largely as a result of antifeudal demands that transformed political and cultural society, especially the private ownership of royal collections.[27] As monarchic supremacy declined, museums came to be primarily public institutions funded and operated by the state. The collections were to be of service to the citizenry, displaying objects and artifacts for the masses. For example, opening in 1759, the British Museum was free to enter for "all studious and curious Persons."[28] Alongside the British Museum, the Louvre is another of the first large museums to be opened, funded, and operated by the state.[29] As in the case of the opening up of the prince's private collections, however, this further push toward more accessible collections did not necessarily disrupt the role of the sovereign. Rather, the new democratic institution envisioned by the revolutionaries simply substituted the centrality of the monarch with the centrality of the state; there was no radical transformation in the physical or symbolic organization of the objects.[30] The museum program implemented by the revolutionaries perpetuated the paradigm whereby an individual's relationship to the collection was an extension of his or her relationship to the state mediated through the sovereign.[31]

Strikingly, the persistence of this sovereign paradigm has also been identified in the advent of the modern state. For example, launching a critique against the French revolutionaries' practical and theoretical program, Hannah Arendt asks poignantly, "[W]hat else did even Sieyès do but simply put the sovereignty of the nation into the place which had been vacated by a sovereign king?"[32] Indeed, the revolutions of the seventeenth and eighteenth centuries did little to disrupt hierarchical legacies. As Bennett observes, the museum's objective was "to make a new conception of the state visible to the inspection of the citizen by redeploying expropriated royal treasures in a democratic public setting and thereby investing them with new meanings in embodying a public representativeness."[33] This new museum featured exhibitions aimed at displaying the transparency of the new democratic order, thereby validating the state and its rule. The shift functioned to interpellate the visitor, no longer as subject to the Lord, but as "citizen and therefore a shareholder in the state."[34] Under the new democratic organization, man was empowered to be the narrator of his own history, seeing for *himself* the objects of *his* state.[35]

The civic trend at the museum was part of a larger social, political purging of the monarchy and its associated Christian religious institutions. The public character of the state emerged from the struggle against absolutism during the transition from feudalism to capitalism, and with it arose the conception of the individual as a naturally self-sufficient, self-interested unit, leading to the burgeoning of the bourgeois public sphere and the masses' participation in it.[36] The substitution of the religious monarch with that of "the people" at the helm of the liberal state resonates closely with Schmitt's famous observation that "all significant concepts of the modern theory of the state are secularized theological concepts."[37] Schmitt intimates that although the modern liberal state is often conceived of as antithetical to the traditions of religious monarchs that preceded it, the arrangements of power persist and the paradigm of transcendence endures.[38] But although the new era of democratic transparency is intended to make the people the authors of their own political communities, the result is their paradoxical positioning as both gods of the new state and subjects of its disciplinary power.

Michel Foucault famously maps the transformation of political rationalities in Western culture through three consecutive epistemes—the Renaissance, Classical, and Modern—each with its attendant worldviews.[39] Where the systems of knowledge drawn on by Renaissance scientists emphasized the importance of items' myriad connections to the world (see the discussion of Aldrovandi above), the Classical episteme focused on drawing out unseen connections between objects and rendering them legible through representation. This shift paved the way for the introduction of modern scientific taxonomy. In *The Order of Things*, Foucault notes that until the middle of the seventeenth century,

> history was the inextricable and completely unitary fabric of all that was visible of things and of the signs that had been discovered or lodged in them: to write the history of a plant or an animal was as much a matter of describing its elements or organs as of describing the resemblances that could be found in it, the virtues that it was thought to possess, the legends and stories with which it had been involved, its place in heraldry, the medicaments that were concocted from its substance, the foods it provided, what the ancients recorded of it, and what travellers might have said of it. The history of a living being was that being itself, within the whole semantic network that connected it to the world.[40]

This form of historicism, however, gave way under the influence of the botanist Carolus Linnaeus to a method that was less interested in compiling information on the object and more focused on systematically synthesizing it.[41] This is the Classical episteme, dominated by knowledges that sought to taxonomize information. The method was predicated on a newly emerging epistemological thrust that sought to uncover hidden relations in and between beings, a method notably different from sixteenth- and early seventeenth-century conceptions of historical technique.[42] This shift led to the development of a classification system that allowed the "structure" of the objects to be "seen."[43] In other words, the semiotics of categorization became the primary form with which to convey meaning about the object. In so doing, the object of study became knowable as and through these categories. Whereas the previous method of classification compiled any and all information on the subject, Foucault argues that Linnaeus's procedure filtered this information into a visible structure.[44] This structure could then be communicated easily between multiple people as a shared understanding of the subject at hand. What may have been a complex of networks of meaning made up of legends, applications, use values, or ancient meanings for Renaissance naturalists was thus tamed into a smooth, coherent, and, importantly, *visible* description of the object at hand. Finally, the difference between the Classical and the Modern episteme is best characterized as one that shifts the importance from *taxonomic representations* of the object (i.e., natural history) to a concern with the object's properties of *biological life*. Foucault claims that the emergence of biological science in the Modern period brought along with it the notion of evolutionary thought and genealogical connection, a move that also meant a retreat of the emphasis on visible representations in the sciences.[45]

Significantly, this new attention to life processes and evolutionary thought also had repercussions in modes of governance. Foucault argues that the shift from the Classical to the Modern period brought along an attendant shift from sovereign, to disciplinary, and then biopolitical power, the latter a power concerned with the management of life and populations (rather than individual bodies) through techniques of normalization such as programs of monitoring and normalizing hygiene, as well as reproduction, birth, and mortality rates.[46] But these forms of power are not entirely distinct: "[T]his technology of power does not exclude the former, does not exclude disciplinary technology, but it does dovetail into it, integrate it, modify it to some extent, and above all, use it by sort of infiltrating it, embedding itself in existing disciplinary techniques."[47]

The emergence of evolutionary thought during the Modern episteme was a major influence on the organization of objects within the museum and, consequently, on the relationship between object, visitor, and knowledge. Specifically, the evolutionary narratives found their way into museum exhibition practices not only in the arrangement of objects animated by an evolutionary connection, but also in the framing of man as on a historical evolutionary path moving toward eventual flawlessness.[48] In the eighteenth century, relationships between visitors and the contents of the museum were no longer strictly officiated through religion or through the monarch as they had been before. In their new conceptions, museums exhibited objects in relation to a scientific rationality that conferred new symbolic meanings on the objects and, importantly, the relationship *between* objects.[49] In other words, the visitor was to be seen as standing at the end of the history that lay before them at the museum. This development of evolutionary thought subsequently paved the way for the program of education that would be the focus of the museum's agenda in the nineteenth and twentieth centuries.

The nineteenth-century public museum was a place where working people could be reformed and brought up to the civilizational standards of the middle class. This was purported to occur by having the working class attend the museum, where they would see their esteemed compatriots acting with good manners and, subsequently, would emulate the appropriate behavior.[50] In short, the middle class museum visitors were to set an example for the working class populations to follow.[51] These mid-nineteenth- and early twentieth-century plans for the museum were inscribed in its architecture, design, entrance policies, and dress codes as well as in its educational programming.[52] In fact, the United Kingdom's Education Act of 1902 explicitly established that time spent at the museum would count toward time spent in the classroom.[53] Moreover, these educational policies legitimized colonial and imperialist trends. This educational project aimed at the working class had a double function of managing behaviors and interpellating them into an imagined community of national subjects. Through the new evolutionary thrust of the museum, these subjects were imagined as a public organized by a unique time and place that distinguished them as a citizenry situated at the culmination of the evolutionary processes laid before them. According to Bennett, this order

> organized the implied public—the white citizenries of the imperialist powers—into a unity, representationally effacing divisions within the body politic in constructing a "we" conceived as the realization, and therefore just beneficiaries, of the processes of evolution and identified as a unity in opposition to the primitive otherness of conquered peoples.[54]

The evolutionary thrust of the educational programs at the museum continues today. Contemporarily, the museum extends a forceful narrative of universal education using the rhetoric of multiculturalism.[55]

The advent of the museum as a tool for popular education advances a conception of itself as part and parcel of a democratizing project while simultaneously acting as a chief producer of public manners and civility.[56] In other words, the museum makes a doubled-sided assertion. It claims to universally represent while, at the same time, it actively differentiates between populations both in how it grants (or does not) access to collections and through the representations it provides. This double bind creates a paradox at the heart of the modern public museum: as the museum claims to tell a universal story of history, it necessarily opens itself to an endless chain of critiques from those who can claim to be represented partially, poorly, or not at all. This was not the case with the collections and *studiolos* of princes and naturalists who made no such claim to universality. It is only with the advent of this purportedly transparent and comprehensively inclusive institution that it is opened up to "a constant discourse of reform as hitherto excluded constituencies seek inclusion."[57] In other words, the museum's claims to generality *produce* the onslaught of reformist strategies that animate museum studies today. Most importantly, these calls for reform and for better representation are structurally insatiable; the museum will never be able to satisfy them.[58]

The museum deploys representations of political constituencies that individual identities are then invited to comply with. In this way, "the museum constitutes a formidable model of civic membership, a ritual of social identification, in short, a technology of the subject."[59] In so doing, the museum aims to actualize a fantastical projection of a political community through the ritual encounters it provides between history and subjects.[60] And it is this elaborate system of privation that the representational framework of law and politics is also based on; it is at the heart of projects of nationalism, colonialism, and imperialism, as well as movements that oppose these forces by articulating themselves as oppositional communities. Museums that purport to be locally constituted and to have a voice "of the people" rely on discourses of authenticity that assimilate the individual into predetermined cultural or political communities.[61] It is not only through these demands for identification, however, that the museum participates in a closing of the world. It also occurs in the very foundational technologies of the museum.

Modern museology is predicated on an encyclopedic desire—and conviction that it is *possible*—to observe and know. To illustrate, Donald Preziosi compares the epistemological practices of the museum to a grammar textbook that he had as an elementary school student. The cover of the grammar book, he explains, was a picture of a room littered with prepositions in order to (literally) illustrate their spatial-temporal meanings. For example, in the picture Preziosi explains that the word "under" was written underneath a table. He claims that "I learned my prepositions by learning to "picture" the picture in which each word had its correct relative position."[62] Preziosi argues that the museum too encourages visitors to see the narrative interrelation between objects and subject matter. In so doing, visitors' imaginations are shaped by the modes of categorization prescribed by the museum. Preziosi deploys the term "funicity" to refer to this characteristic of the museum that he sees as foundational to modernity, "a conviction that the astute enough observer might be able to discern in an object the signs and traces of the origins and circumstances of production of that object or indeed of any artifact."[63] In short, technologies at work in the museum contribute to this sense of discernible coherence.

These technologies allow for the emergence of the knowable, locatable, and explainable notion of the individual in modernity. Museum visitors do not experience the potential loss of self; rather, through the unfolding of magical chronological time, they experience its putting-in-place, or legibility. Preziosi attributes this incessant fascination with order to the persistence of ancient Christian traditions in Enlightenment thought, practices "aimed at forestalling the holy or divine terror, [or] the *theios phobos* that Plato warned about."[64] Moreover, the opportunity to imagine a desirable, coherent self and attendant world offers visitors the chance to partake in a modern Western European exercise of recording and archiving. The anamorphic orientations at work ensure that difference and messiness can be domesticated and tamed, in service of "the dream of a totally transparent society."[65] This desire to make the world legible and knowable is central to the modern museum, and its anamorphic orientations are central to a project of taming the world.

REFORMING THE MUSEUM

The violence of these museological techniques is certainly not news to most. Indigenous individuals and communities, as well as postcolonial scholars and activists, have criticized the orientalizing effects of large public museums in Europe and the former colonies.[66] For example, exhibitions on traditional cultures have been charged with relegating societies to a vanishing past and denying contemporary complexities.[67] Many of the populations these exhibitions purport to represent are dynamic, living cultures made up of diverse and unique individuals.[68] Moreover, museum collections themselves are often crafted from objects obtained during times of war, colonial rule, and imperial occupation.[69] The subsequent exhibition of these items for the service of a particular national citizenry—especially in a national European or settler state context—has also been criticized for contributing to the maintenance of a hegemonic nationalistic ethnocentrism whereby one culture is empowered to represent the other.[70] This power dynamic is present in both attempts at representations of internal communities (for example, indigenous and "minority" groups within nations) and between nations (for example, repatriation debates concerning the Elgin Marbles between Britain and Greece).[71] In response, contemporary museum staff and scholars have launched various programs that aim to correct the legacies of these historical injustices. In what follows, I explore three major themes in the critical museological literature that aim to make the institution more democratic through the inclusion of historically excluded or oppressed individuals and communities: (i) the promotion of a more representative museum, (ii) thick democratic museological practices, and (iii) the proliferation of more interactive and "hands-on" museum exhibits. I argue that these proposals confuse their project of representation with democracy.

In her book *Making Representations: Museums in the Post-colonial Era,* Moira Simpson explores various histories of exhibitions from the United Kingdom to Canada and the subsequent calls for more adequate representation articulated by activist groups, individuals, and communities. She charts the legal, political, and social routes that people have taken to make demands on the museum to recognize institutionalized practices of orientalism, exclusion, and the perpetuation of colonial legacies through exhibitions. Her goal is to develop a museology that contributes to the cultural and economic development of indigenous communities.[72] In doing so, she appeals to her readers to take seriously representational and restitutive claims on the museum. It is her hope that, if made successfully, such claims will assist in the legitimation of indigenous rights and, subsequently, the increased political, social, and economic standing for those individuals and communities.[73] One significant element of Simpson's proposal for a more inclusive museology—alongside calls for repatriation of Aboriginal artifacts—is the support and encouragement of Aboriginal Keeping Places and Cultural Centres.[74]

Postcolonial critiques of the museum have resulted in the development of a rich body of literature and alternative curatorial and museological practices in the public museum of the twentieth and twenty-first century.[75] According to Marstine,

> theorists call for the transformation of the museum from a site of worship and awe to one of discourse and critical reflection that is committed to examining unsettling histories with sensitivity to all parties; they look to a mu-

seum that is transparent in its decision-making and willing to share power. New museum theory is about decolonizing, giving those represented control of their own cultural heritage. It's about real cross-cultural exchange.[76]

Accusations of museums' poor portrayal practices fundamentally rest, however, on the notion that adequate representation is achievable. This assertion runs up against at least four fundamental problems. First, depictions of individuals and communities through museological practices are necessarily limited and will, therefore, always be fundamentally unable to answer entirely to these claims. Any museological display that claims to represent a reality outside of its walls can always be accused of formulating an incomplete picture. Second, representation—whether it is in the museum or within the constitutional arrangement of the modern state—carries with it a set of attendant disciplinary techniques. Having a place as a citizen in the modern state also means being subject to its biopolitical management. This is a particularly critical concern for indigenous groups in the North American context who want to contest state-endorsed conceptions of community, history, and politics. The prospect of representation, while it offers the promise of a state-recognized legibility, means endorsing the colonial state's monopoly on the terms of the arrangement.[77] Third, the representational argument asserts that there is something true to be represented, whether it is a culture, community, or object.[78] This investment in representation carries with it an attendant attachment to an origin that is an impossibility. Denial of this impossibility allows us to tell mythological stories about sovereign selves and sovereign communities, which fail to attend to the truth of our existence. Lastly, as these projects import the myth of sovereignty, they recenter the modern Western concern with atomization, both individual and collective. It is this persistence of the absolute, of sovereignty, however, that acts as a barrier to anticolonial thinking.

Museum scholar Amy Lonetree would likely take issue with my position. She criticizes what she refers to as "abstract" and "postmodern" approaches at the museum on anticolonial grounds.[79] For her,

> abstraction isn't a correct choice for a museum hoping to educate a nation with a willed ignorance of its treatment of Indigenous peoples and the policies and practices that led to genocide in the Americas. Our survival, as many people have argued, is one of the greatest untold stories, and the specifics of this difficult and shameful history need to be told.[80]

While I am sympathetic to this argument (note the psychic fragment that I begin the book with), I am also hesitant to postulate the need for a true community or true story to be represented. This is both due to the problematic figure of the destinal community but also because of an uneasiness with the designation of "real" versus "abstract" storytelling. Who is given the power to decide what stories are told, in what way, and with what "real world" consequences? Mark Rifkin explores the powerful prospect of using indigenous poetry and fiction to write conceptions of sovereignty that resist the racial logics and colonial categories proffered by the United States settler state government. He refuses a distinction between what might be considered abstract writing and formal politics. Rifkin argues that to make this distinction between the figurative and the real is to deny the way the real is made up of "repeated institutionalized acts of figuration, which create and sustain the material conditions in which peoplehood can be signified and lived."[81]

Representations cannot but cohere and tame the world through their anamorphic orientations, and this closing down of the world is antithetical to democracy, not in service of it. This does not mean, however, that there is no place for museums. While, taking inspiration from Lonetree, we might not want to abandon representationally reparative projects in their entirety, I want to surface important concerns about what is at stake in investing in promises of restoring community in the name of democracy. Ultimately, a project of reform based entirely on more adequate representation—a framework that hinges on the centrality of the liberal democratic subject and its attendant sovereign community—offers a hollow conception of the political, especially as we attempt to address legacies of colonialism that are constituted by the deeply intertwined relationship between the material and epistemic.

Some practitioners and theorists of critical museology, acknowledging the pitfalls of seeking reform through more adequate representation, posit the concept of "thick democracy" as a basis for a new kind of museum. This concept is intended to extend *beyond* internally proposed reforms, which its proponents argue retain dominant social relations fostered at the museum. Thick democracy promotes the value of dialogue in the production and execution of a museum exhibit. In other words, rather than tinkering with the portrayal once it is formulated—as in often the case in representational claims—thick democracy ensures that represented individuals and communities are partners in the creation of the exhibit itself.

Viv Golding uses this concept in her project of exploring identity in young "socially deprived" youth from Brixton, a neighborhood in south London.[82] Golding extols the approach because it "is more concerned with the raising of new voices in a critical dialogue to promote the rule or power and 'strength of the people.'"[83] But in so doing, Golding draws on aims and objectives echoed in the UK government's *Skills for Life* program that also orients programming at the British Museum, which I discuss in the next chapter. Indeed, her concept of thick democracy resonates with the language of the state in its efforts to achieve "community cohesion" and "common citizenship."[84] Moreover, she praises the implementation of an alternative interactive learning strategy in the museum called Automatic Rap. She argues that it promotes the importance of "claiming the power to name and [to] actively take ownership of the individual place in a global world."[85] Citing the United Nations International Convention on the Rights of the Child (UNICRC), she goes on to say "these notions were related to the rights and responsibilities of individuals and the groups that are enshrined in law."[86]

　　Although Golding contends that her vision of thick democracy is "distinct" from popular notions of democracy in "Western systems of power," it maintains the centrality of liberal state-based institutions.[87] Even as she attempts to forward a program that challenges conventional conceptions of democracy, she perpetuates a state-centric vision whereby the government of the day is a legitimate arbiter of rights, purveyor of law, and director of community relations. This is evident not only in her invocation of the Labour Party's policy on community cohesion, but also as she venerates the importance of "rights and responsibilities of individuals [. . .] enshrined in law."[88] Arguably, Golding offers this discourse, stemming from the UNICRC, as a transnational alternative to the limited trappings of the nation-state. Indeed, in her attempt to open up the historically narrow conceptions of the citizen, she draws on a conception of the international institution that is popularly believed to be a sacred protector of extra-state human rights. Like her state-based concept of democracy, however, the justice sought through international conventions set by the United Nations continues to turn on a logic that centers the same conception of sovereign individuals and social contracts. While Golding seeks to challenge the limited politics of Western state-based democracy, her attendant exaltation of the United Nations convention fails to identify the consistent underlying logic in both.[89] Golding's concept of thick democracy does not seem to distance itself from the dangers of state-based reforms that she critiques. Golding's concept of thick democracy thus remains embedded within the given categories of politics that stifle the political and, with it, the possibilities for rethinking community and democracy.

James Clifford also attempts to draw out a more inclusive theory of museum exhibition development. Though his goals resonate with those of Golding's, Clifford does not explicitly use the concept of "thick democracy." Instead, drawing on the work of Mary Louise Pratt, Clifford proposes that reformists begin to think of the museum as a "contact zone."[90] He claims that a contact zone can function such that the "the collection would become part of an ongoing historical, political, moral relationship between the culture that produced the objects and the members of another culture who would come to view them."[91] Clifford offers this theoretical proposition especially as a way to acknowledge and work with the historical legacies of imperialism and colonialism that necessarily shape encounters at the museum. Indeed, Clifford claims that "a 'contact' perspective emphasizes how subjects are constituted in and by their relations to each other. . . . [It stresses] copresence, interaction, interlocking understandings and practices, often within radically asymmetrical relations of power."[92] Straying from the trend of atomistic individualism in museum reform strategies, he invokes a seemingly alternative discourse that privileges relationality and "copresence" among subjects. Clifford's concept of the museum as a contact zone aims to recognize and address unequal power relations within the museum and transcend hegemonic conceptions of the individual. But his conception of copresence retains at its foundation separate and distinct subjects who find their copresence through their interactions. His theory hinges on a concept of individuated subjects that happen upon their copresence through acts of volition, rather than as a result of the ontological sharing of their existence.

Another strategy of attempting to address the hierarchical and exclusionary practices of the museum is a move toward more interactive museum exhibits through concentrated physical and mental stimulation.[93] These exhibits popularly involve sensorial exercises that aim to further engage visitors with collections and their historical contexts.[94] Emulating other popular public spaces, many museums have adopted unique audio-visual and alternative educative techniques in order to challenge traditional hierarchical interactions between the visitor and the institution.[95] These strategies, however, are also bound up with what some practitioners see as an increasing need to maintain visitors' dwindling attention spans and stimulate annual visitor rates.[96] Competing motives of the museum staff, administration, and government directives are of course influenced by a complex configuration of social, political, and economic criteria.[97] Frequently, these interactive experiences at the museum explicitly encourage visitors to think and feel like others through time and across geographical space. This multisensory experience aims to dislocate the centrality of the visual experience of the museum in favor of an "engagement in which sight, hearing, and touch interact to produce a more embodied, active, and participatory relationship to the museum, and to other visitors."[98]

Authors Terry Russell and George Hein, however, are critical of the emphasis of "hands-on" approaches to the museum. They assert that a "minds-on" approach is more effective and more democratic as it promotes thoughtful engagement with the subject matter while also dissolving a binary that falsely links the mind to inactivity and the body with activity.[99] Within this approach, Hein proposes four types of pedagogy to promote democratic engagement with museum visitors. Beginning with the least amount of engagement, Hein outlines a "didactic, expository" model.[100] Under this model, visitors are asked to participate in an exercise, but the museum remains the authoritative source of knowledge. This might involve a quiz or set of questions in which the participant hazards a guess and then is told if the answers are right or wrong. In a second model, museums offer individuals "stimulus response."[101] This takes the form of the previous example but involves a reward for answering questions correctly. Hein's third model is a model of "discovery" whereby individuals are encouraged to explore on their own and to have an educational experience that does not necessarily tell them "right" or "wrong" answers.[102] Lastly, the format of "constructivism" is a directly dialogic installation that seeks to engage individual visitors through their common experiences as "humans."[103]

Some attribute the recent development of the interactive museum such as that outlined by Hein and Russell to the advent of neoliberalism.[104] These critics suggest that making individuals responsible for their own historical and educative experience may correspond all too coincidentally with the transnational encroachment of free market values of individualism and corporate control into previously held public service sectors.[105] But although the move toward a more interactive museum has resulted in "a series of transformations in [visitor's] socio-sensory environments,"[106] a critique of the neoliberal turn at the museum does not address the problem I am focused on here. While this may be an observable trend, this framework of critique does not get to the heart of the matter. Interactive programs remain focused on the development of a unique experience with community and culture. Rather than dispensing with the guiding force of these destinal figures, interactive programming reinvigorates it, promising a chance at ultimate communion through a more immersive experience. These reforms reinforce a conception of democracy that is predicated on better representation, rather than destabilizing the concept of community at its core. As my genealogy of the modern museum indicates, this investment in sovereignty is as likely to appear in postwar and revolutionary museums as it is in exhibits borne out of neoliberal societies. This is not a rejection of a historical analysis but a demand for a longer view that is able to perceive the influence of liberalism on our collective imaginations, which goes beyond the last forty years of Hayekian-inspired economic thinking.

INTERRUPTING ANAMORPHIC ORIENTATIONS

A rethinking of the political means a rejection of the equation between the foundation of community in institutional representations and the political. This is essential to the untying of the (k)nots of community and a thinking of the (k)not as still to be tied:

> It is in all respects not only reasonable, but also required by the vigor and rigor of thought, to avoid recourse to representations: the future is precisely what exceeds representation. And we have learned that we must grasp the world once more outside of representation.[107]

This is not a call for a new or different representation of the world, nor is it an abandonment of all sense, grounded in a new foundation of nihilism. A concept of the political that does justice to being-in-common is a writing of ontological sharing. It is against the destinal figure of community. It is against the anamorphic orientations that classify, order, and cohere relations between objects and museum visitors. It is against the ascription of essence to objects, visitors, and history that denies their existence as exposure. It is against the museum's attempts to smooth the world from its form as a "properly incongruous incongruity."[108] But what precisely are these orientations that smooth, and therefore close, the world?

Preziosi explains that, in modernity, not knowing what you are looking at in a museum is tantamount to not knowing *when* you are.[109] He uses this provocative statement to point to the centrality of temporality in the construction of the modern subject at the museum. He claims that the subject who gazes on the object occupies a place simultaneously inside and outside of history. They are at once the product of history, at the end of history, and, significantly, linked to the future. Foucault too cites the importance of time and temporality at the modern museum: "the project of organizing in this way a sort of perpetual and indefinite accumulation of time in an immobile place, this whole idea belongs to our modernity."[110] Indeed, one of the key anamorphic orientations at work in the museum is that of time as historical progress, deployed at the museum to establish relations between visitors and objects. The museum is "designed to engage and be operated by its users, who literally (re)enact history and chronology *choreographically*."[111] It is this conception of time as historical progress that is one of the key driving forces of the destinal figure of community at the museum and the subject of the next chapter.

CHAPTER THREE

The Time of Sovereignty

In the collections of the British Museum the world can write the new histories that it needs to understand its past and shape its future.

–BRITISH MUSEUM[1]

We place our vision of a new constitutional order for South Africa on the table not as conquerors, prescribing to the conquered. We speak as fellow citizens to heal the wounds of the past with the intent of constructing a new order based on justice for all.

–PRESIDENT NELSON MANDELA, INAUGURAL SPEECH[2]

Museums and constitutions are imagined as tools for righting historical wrongs and setting the course for a better future. Above, the British Museum asserts its centrality in the production of "new histories" that the world needs in order to "shape its future." And, articulating the principles of what was soon to be the 1996 South African Constitution, former president Nelson Mandela claims that the new juridical order will both attend to the "wounds of the past" and construct a new future that will result in "justice for all." Both statements draw on a conception of time that moves from the past to a redemptive future. It is a naturalized notion of continuous time that provides the backdrop for these prophesied transformations. As such, conceptions of time become central in orienting the relationship between an imagined past and an imagined future by telling a narrative from which political projects, communities, and subjects are imagined, rendering the messiness of political community into an ordered whole. In this way, time functions as an anamorphic orientation at work in the museum.

    Chronological time is also a pivotal device in the production of the conception of state-authorized sovereignty. The notion of continuous time emerges, at least in part, from the transformation of a theological organization of the world to the rise of the modern state. During this period, interpretations of time shifted from fixed and finite to enduring and infinite. The emergence of continuous time bestowed the institutions of the modern state with the quality of permanence, bolstering the state's claim to sovereign authority. These institutions have continued to gather their legitimacy from this conferral of continuous time while denying their theological inheritance. The coterminous rise of time as infinite and the development of the modern state have resulted in a deep attachment to the notion of enduring time for contemporary conceptions of political community.

Carl Schmitt asserts that these theological underpinnings of the modern liberal state must be revealed.[3] In his terms, the façade of parliamentary democracy only dilutes the truth of the sovereign moment of the decision. He critiques the mythical sense of permanence that is conferred on the modern state and its conflation with sovereignty.[4] For Schmitt, the illusion of enduring institutionalized power only masks what is actually a temporary, fleeting moment of sovereignty found in the decision.[5]

Walter Benjamin also takes issue with the authoritative concept of time as continuous and chronological.[6] He recognizes the way in which the authority of contemporary sovereignty rests on a particular notion of temporality. But where Schmitt responds to the paradox of the supposedly secular modern state by galvanizing the sovereign remnant at its core, Benjamin wants to deactivate, or depose [*Entsetzung*] it.[7] This requires conceiving of an alternate temporality that defies both the time of politics (parliamentary democracy) as well as Schmitt's time of sovereignty (that of the decision). Benjamin finds his alternative in the notion of messianic time, a temporality that demonstrates how interruptions and cessations in the naturalized flow of chronological time can depose sovereign authority.[8] His troubling of time as evolutionary progress exposes the perils of accepting the myth of the necessity of liberal temporal periodization.

In this chapter, I elucidate how the notion of continuous time is used to orient and authorize the categories of politics, community, and the subject at the museum. This gentle shaping of the horizons of intelligibility informs what kinds of politics, communities, and subjects are authorized as thinkable. For example, senior staff members at the British Museum equate their conception of democracy with the inclusion and cohesion of diverse communities and the attendant achievement of a redemptive future. Another political aim articulated by these staff members is one that, resonating closely with George Hein's form of "constructivist" pedagogy mentioned in chapter 2, unites humans across vast historical expanses by making participants realize that "we're all human."[9] They are, in other words, occupied with the production of a community of humans who recognize their similarities across generations. Through such narratives, the contemporary museum visitor is imagined as situated at the end and as the culmination of a progressive teleology.

This notion of time as progress is not only articulated by the staff, but also by students participating in museum programs. Students, like the staff at the museum, use a concept of chronological time to articulate their ideas of how to improve the world, a notion of linear time that assists in the production of "what counts." This trend persists in interactive adult educational programs not only at the British Museum but also at Constitution Hill and the District Six Museum. Although the latter occasionally troubles clear delineations between past and present—for example, by drawing attention to the ways the legacies of apartheid animate the contemporary social, political, and economic landscape in South Africa—it too draws on chronological time to authorize its political objectives.

These anamorphic orientations are also contested, however. Indeed, the authority of the museum's aims is disrupted through frustration, misunderstanding, and confusion. In these moments, the messy and distorted elements of the world overwhelm the museum's systems of classification. Thus, although time as an anamorphic orientation helps lend an authoritative gloss to the political projects at the museum, it is not totalizing. Rather, while linear, continuous time functions to cohere political community at the museum, it is also interrupted and made *inoperative* by the interminable messiness of the world. While these sporadic interruptions may be the kind of messianic events that Benjamin is inclined toward, such disruptions do not only have to be left to entirely unpredictable occasions. The significance of these events can also be embraced by the everyday practices of the museum. In other words, the museum does not only have to function as a manager of the world and its populations, it can also participate in its disruption and provide an interruption to the logic of communion. At the end of this chapter I intimate that while museums *can* interrupt this logic, they *must*, not only in a haphazard way through confusion and misunderstanding, but through a continuous writing of the essenceless of community.

TIME AS AN ANAMORPHIC ORIENTATION

The notion of time as "unlimited progress" took hold near the end of the thirteenth century.[10] This interpretation differed greatly from the previously held conception of time as finite, an understanding that was perpetuated and guarded by the authority of the church throughout the Middle Ages. Before the thirteenth century, time was largely thought of as something that was created by God and that could be taken away at any given moment. Thus, the imminent arrival of the end of the world, as propagated by the Christian teachings and given authoritative weight by the Holy Roman Empire, maintained a conception of worldly time as fixed. While the afterlife might provide immortality for individuals in heaven, the perpetually looming end of the world meant the end of worldly time.[11] Near the end of the thirteenth century, however, this began to change and the notion of time became increasingly considered as potentially limitless.[12] According to Ernst Kantorowicz:

> [T]he limited span of terrestrial Time [. . .] lost its ephemeral frailty and limitation, and its character also changed morally: Time no longer appeared predominantly as the symbol of caducity, of Death; Time [. . .] became a vivifying element, a symbol of endless duration.[13]

Of course, these secularizing changes took place gradually, but as they did the guardians of immortality were transferred from heaven to earth.[14]

Significantly, this transfer of continuity and endurance from the sacred to the profane provided the basis for the emergence of the modern secular state.[15] Whereas previously the Church was thought of as the primordial institution that would last until judgment day, the transfer of continuous time to man meant that the functions of the state were the new institutions of endurance. As James Martel summarizes:

> The idea of a Church that would last until the day of judgment was readily transferred to the courts, to the state's fiscal holdings and to the dignity and crown of the monarchy. All of these functions were said to "never die" (as opposed to the mortal individuals who fulfilled these roles at any given time). Eventually these so-called para-ecclesiastical institutions left the Church itself behind.[16]

Although the rise of the modern state did not immediately follow this change in conceptions of time, nor did the transition occur all at once, the shift paved the way for the contemporary conception of time as enduring and, importantly, the modern concept of sovereignty. This transfer of ever-lasting—or sempiternal—time to the state was one of the main progenitors of its authority, giving the state a "sacred veneer" and making it "an exalted institution in form and purpose."[17] In this way, the contemporary notion of sovereignty is deeply bound up with the conception of continuous time.

Schmitt criticizes champions of liberalism for denying and disguising the role of decisionism that lies at the heart of parliamentary democracy. Where liberal democratic constitutionalists, like Hans Kelsen, think they can predict all legal situations with a set of positive laws, Schmitt argues there will inevitably be situations that exceed the boundaries of constitutions, charters, and bills of rights and will require a decision made by an human actor. He declares that "in the exception the power of real life breaks through the crust of a mechanism that has become torpid by repetition," and he is frustrated that liberalism's main advocates deny this central truth.[18] Because these exceptional times must be navigated decisively in the interest of state security, Schmitt is critical of the trappings of institutional checks and balances that suffocate the moment of the decision.[19] For him, sovereignty does not rest in constitutions, but rather "sovereign is he who decides on the exception."[20] For Schmitt, the enduring time of the state that purportedly authorizes its legitimacy covers over the finite, fixed, and fleeting time of true sovereignty: that of the decision. He is not concerned with eradicating this truth, but with naming it and treating it for what it is.[21] Schmitt, however, ultimately channels his decisionism into institutional form; indeed, he is firmly statist. Therefore, while he claims that the piercing time of the exception can break through the torpid time of liberalism, he ultimately follows what he sees as the undeniable power of sovereignty.[22]

Benjamin takes up a similar critique of the time of the state, though with a dramatically different outcome.[23] Benjamin agrees with Schmitt that liberalism is a hollow conception of the political (though he takes particular aim at social democrats and other leftists),[24] but his response is nothing like Schmitt's endorsement of the sovereign decision. Benjamin's "On the Critique of Violence" is a redoubtable rejection of the logic of sovereignty and the utilitarian impulse behind it. For Benjamin, sovereignty is not inescapable; there is a way to resist it or depose of it. In order to do so, however, we must first recognize the proliferation of what he refers to as the means/ends relationship that animates all law. This relationship is a circular logic that uses "means" to justify "ends" or vice versa. He argues that in either case, the logic of means/ends is a justification for violence; it feeds a cyclical relationship of law-positing and law-preserving violence.[25]

To demonstrate, Benjamin draws on the distinction formulated by sociologist George Sorel between two different types of strikes.[26] The first is the general political strike, a mobilization aimed at reversing power relations so that the oppressed come out on top. In this scenario, the means/ends relationship remains firmly intact, even if power dynamics are inverted. Whether the dominant group is in the position of power or those roles are reversed, both groups seek to secure their place at the helm, thereby maintaining the structure of power that legitimizes violence. They have in mind a *telos*, a form, or a goal; they have intention. The political strike is thus overdetermined by the logic of the means/ends relationship whereby strike action is taken in order to achieve a preconceived end.[27] The second type of mobilization is the proletarian general strike, a form of action that directly opposes the logic of the means/ends relationship of the political strike. In the proletarian strike, workers stop the functioning of state apparatuses by refusing to work. They have no additional political agenda or preconceived goal. This is a strike for the strike's sake. Rather, in withdrawing their labor their actions thwart state power as well as the logic of intention and utility that undergirds it.[28] The proletarian strike is, as Werner Hamacher claims, a way of "being without intention"; it does not posit a new program or goal but rather interrupts the circular logic of the means/ends relationship.[29] Thus the proletarian strike without intention is law-*deposing* rather than law-founding or law-preserving.

Benjamin describes the difference between the violence of the means/ends logic and its passive antithesis as the difference between mythic and divine violence. The former, for him, is the product of the utilitarian-driven, power-asserting force of law. Constitutional law is a prime example as it legitimizes the power and authority of the victors in the very foundation of the social contract. This authorization grants the power-holders the ability to distribute rights to those it has vanquished through law-establishing violence.[30] Constitutional law glosses over the fundamental inequity at work by assuming that those who fall under this new law can be considered equal even when one group grants the rights and the other is bestowed with them: "[W]hat comes out here, in all its awful originality, is the same mythic ambiguity of laws that may not be 'overstepped' as Anatole France lampoons when he writes: they ban rich and poor alike from sleeping under the arches."[31] Mythic violence is at the center of all law; it is the process of giving mythical force—whether through contractual obligation, guilt, or other remaining imposition—to rules.

Time as progress is a tool that lends itself to the authorization of law-founding and law-preserving violence. Indeed, Benjamin takes aim at the authoritative weight of chronological time, calling it the "strongest narcotic of the nineteenth century."[32] Accordingly, he takes aim at forms of historiography that recount chronological events in this teleological narrative. Benjamin famously tells the story of the *Angelus Novus*, taken from the title of Paul Klee's painting, which portrays an angel, open-mouthed and moving away—backwards—from something he cannot stop staring at. Benjamin likens this scene to the depravity of the contemporary obsession and naturalization of progress. The angel is looking at the past but where we see history, the angel sees nothing but tragedy after tragedy, compiled into one giant catastrophe. And although the angel would like to stay to make things better, an unstoppable wind is blowing him backwards into the future. This storm is what we call progress.[33] In contrast to the unthinking conception of time as progress, Benjamin holds a political and philosophical commitment to conceiving of a temporality unconstrained by hegemonic historiography and finds one divergent conception of time through his notion of divine violence.

In contrast to the sovereign fetish of mythical violence, divine violence cannot be willed or brought forth by intentional human agency. It is not concerned with achieving sovereignty but with deposing it. Like the proletarian strike, it does not invent a new order or program but merely offers a fleeting moment of interruption:

> Where mythic violence is law-establishing, divine violence destroys law; where the first sets bounds, the second wreaks boundless destruction; where mythic violence apportions blame and calls for expiation simultaneously, divine violence expiates; where the former threatens, the latter strikes; where one is bloody, the other, albeit lethal, kills without blood.[34]

Although the characterization of divine violence as powerful and momentary sounds like Schmitt's time of the decision, Benjamin opposes such a will-dependent conception of the political. He rejects the fetish of man-made sovereignty that perpetuates violence in the name of utilitarianism.[35]

Divine violence does not institute a new order, for that would be a reasser-
tion of mythical violence. But what then does this mean for the practices of
constitution writing and museum exhibiting and their critics? What room is
there in Benjamin's theory for a retreatment of the political?

James Martel argues that we can find the possibility for human agency in
law-deposing moments in Benjamin's *The Origin of German Tragic Drama*.[36]
He explains that as German playwrights in the sixteenth and seventeenth
centuries attempted to exalt the authority of the monarch, because of their
ineptitude they inadvertently subverted it.[37] Rather than portraying the sovereign as strong and authoritative, which was their intention, their dialogues present him as uncertain and wavering.[38] They fail to recreate the
bombastic baroque form they meant to write and instead *inadvertently* expose the fallibility and foundationless authority of the sovereign.[39] Crucially, it is this *unintentional* exposure of the baselessness of the sovereign's
supposedly eternal authority that can serve as a catalyst for what Benjamin
calls a *real* state of emergency.[40] This state of emergency must also be paired
with a new conception of history, one that draws attention to the fallibility
of the hollow claim of sovereignty. One way to do this is through the method
of montage.[41] Rather than perpetuating themes of wholeness, unity, or representations of history the way they "really were," montage draws attention
to the fragmentary nature of the world and resists its sovereign presentations; it has the capacity to radically alter our conception of history.[42]

Benjamin's project of thinking of the "presence of the now [*Jetztzeit*]"
through the form of montage resonates best with surrealism.[43] It is in his essay on the avant-garde art movement, written in 1929, that Benjamin proposes a "way of seeing things that recognizes the everyday as impenetrable
and the impenetrable as everyday."[44] He claims that the surrealist André
Breton redeems the ephemeral by "causing the mighty forces of 'atmosphere'
that lie hidden in these things to explode."[45] For Benjamin, it is the surreal-
ists and their "secular illuminations" of the everyday (without dreams,
opium, or hashish) that contribute to the potential of thinking another mo-
dality of history.[46] The surrealist montage, in opposition to the additive
method of historicism, can arrest and "blast open the continuum of history."[47] His was not an unthinking celebration of chaos, though; Benjamin
was also cautious about the romanticism and undialectical nature of surrealism.[48] Benjamin's target was not only periodization per se but a critique of
bourgeois classifications that rendered invisible the historical contingency
of an object. Inspired by Marx's critique of commodity fetishism, Benjamin

saw a need to trouble the categories of thinking about the past and future inherited from liberal capitalism.[49]

Benjamin's project is not a lament for a lost past that must be restored and made right, but instead it is a resistance to the forces of narrative that hinder the potentialities of the past and the present. It is Benjamin's aim, like the project of atomic fission, to blast open these energies and release them from the restrictive enclosures that suffocate them.[50] Benjamin excavates these potentialities from literature, objects, and language in order to offer a way of thinking about the past, present, and future, while avoiding teleological propulsion to a redemptive future.[51] His insights offer a tool with which to critique the naturalization of chronological time that lends an aura of authority to the museums' educational programming; his thinking challenges the construction of neat conceptions of politics, community, and the subject.

THE BRITISH MUSEUM, LONDON

Since 2004 the British Museum, mirroring similar developments in the United States, Canada, and France, has been directly developing and implementing "hands-on," interactive educational programs for its visitors. Ranging from material aimed at children to high school teachers, the programs are considered to offer new ways of engaging with the museum's collections. Beginning in 2004, the museum began offering an annual program called Adult Learners' Week, an event for organized groups of adults from further education colleges, community centers, libraries, and *Skills for Life* classes (offered by community centers throughout London). Trip organizers choose between a set of prearranged tour themes for their visit that are aimed at developing participants' literacy and numeracy skills in line with the UK government's *Skills for Life* strategy adopted in 2001.[52] According to the museum staff, these strategies are particularly key for adults whose first language is not English, including long-time London inhabitants, economic migrant workers, and refugees and asylum seekers. Thus this project is largely oriented around adult literacy for individuals whose first language is not English. Of course, the presence of the guiding force of this government strategy means that, in some ways, it is unsurprising that the museum's notions of democracy are aligned to a state-sponsored conception of community cohesion. The notion of time as continuous, however, is intimately woven into both staff members' *and* participants' characterizations of their experiences at the museum.

The political project imagined by the staff at the British Museum is intimately tied to a teleological conception of time that has its end in a redemptive future. Although purportedly concerned with literacy skills, the program's goals also go beyond a concern for "English for Speakers of Other Language" (ESOL) students' language training. Rather, staff members embrace a larger project of working toward social cohesion by attempting to draw in various "excluded audiences" to the museum. As one staff member notes, one of the aims of the programming is to get participants to return to the museum with their friends and family:

> We do also value the need to diversify our audience and to create a diversity within our audiences. Because, as with a lot of museums, our representation of audiences is predominantly white European and yet we have a collection that represents two million years of humanity [Hopefully participants will] tell their friends, that they'll share with their friends. So there's a wider engagement aspect to it which also relates more to targeting excluded audiences—so black and ethnic minorities and refugees and asylum seekers, people with mental health, homeless people, of which, you know, sort of being in the center of a large metropolis, all these kinds of groups are on our doorstep.[53]

The temporal order of the political project is one that reflects on an unfortunate past (a museum audience that lacks "diversity") with a view of modifying the present in the hopes of redeeming the museum in the future. Contained within this goal is an unspoken assumption about the virtuosity of universal representation used to augment the communing logic at work.[54] The compulsion to achieve this redeemed future means that the inclusion of underrepresented audiences at the museum takes precedence over an examination of reasons why those populations are excluded or choose to exclude themselves in the first place.

The notion of time as continuous and redemptive also carries with it a transnational hope for a future universal humanism. For at least one staff member, the political project being carried out at the museum is one of making people understand that all humans are similar. For her, this pedagogical project is of the utmost ethical importance for resolving conflict and maintaining peace among human beings. The museum is essential, as it allows individuals to recognize consistencies among humanity across time: "[I]t makes people recognize their similarities . . . that we're all people, you know?"[55] Staff members emphasize this aspect in the programs by drawing links between museum objects and what they see as their contemporary incarnations. For example, in one session staff members ask participants to guess whether preselected Ancient Egyptian objects are for "rich" people or "poor" people. In another example, staff members highlight what is identified by the museum as a cosmetic pot used by Egyptians to apply makeup. Staff members help students guess what the object is by dramatizing the application of putting on eyeliner. In a final example, in programs dedicated to learning about astrolabes, staff members repeatedly liken the ancient objects to modern-day wristwatches. In interviews afterwards, staff members emphasize that they think the most important aspect of the learning programs is to make people recognize their similarities across historical time. They say their goal is to create a universal experience for students that emphasizes their similarity as "humans."

This emphasis on transhistoricizing concepts, objects, and experiences is consistently imagined to take place through a linear conception of time, traveling from an ancient and outmoded past to a modern present. This projected narrative is a prime example of an anamorphic orientation at the museum. Here the notion of continuous time is used to both connect humans across historical time and to situate the contemporary visitor at the end of its teleological force. Students can identify themselves as users of modern equipment such as eyeliner and watches that, although connecting them to the past, also distinguish them as modern. Moreover, the desire to make contemporary connections means that objects are consistently translated into existing identifiable categories. Rather than consider the objects as they might open up new and different ways of thinking of being in the world, they are reduced to what staff members identify as "simple" categories "because everyone knows them."

In subsequent interviews about their experiences at the museum, many students also take up the narrative of redemption through time. The vast majority of students proclaim the value of learning about the past in order to improve the future. One student claims that the objects in the museum are a "clue for new generation and we have to understand behind, past. We have to understand because we will lose now and we will improve now. If we don't know behind—if we don't know past—we can't improve now." Imagined improvements range from avoiding war to dealing with environmental catastrophe. In these cases, the past is a tool that can be put to service in imaginings of a better world for "us" and, significantly, for future generations. Another student claims that "everybody have to think about the future. To think how you can be in the future. Everybody need to think about the future."

The subject at the British Museum is also overwhelmingly determined by discourses of evolutionary time. Museum staff members as well as language tutors repeatedly discuss the importance of *developing* subjects, that is, teaching students particular skills and traits for what is purported to be a better *future* person. In the adult learning programs at the British Museum, it is not merely the cultivation of any form of selfhood but about the development of a *responsible* subject.

The metaphor of "stepping-stones" and "finding one's own voice" is deployed repeatedly when speaking with museum staff members about the programs. Staff members state that the programs are about "driving down and drilling down much more into personal responses and personal experiences and developing students' ideas." Another staff member claims that "it works best if people are made to feel that they can contribute something . . . you know, to allow people to feel that they have a voice." Although a seemingly benevolent gesture, this programming resonates with a broader agenda of making individuals responsible. The strong outcome-oriented tone of the programs came through interviews with staff members at the museum who repeatedly mention that the program's impetus is to have adult participants return to the museum with their families. In this way, individual participants' repeat visits are the tool with which to make the museum more diverse:

> [I]f people come for a class, under the guidance of a tutor they meet someone who's welcome, who's friendly, then on that very level, hopefully that's a stepping stone to make them feel confident to come back.

Moreover, teachers from the language centers also engage in this discourse. One language tutor in an interview claimed that returning with friends and family is a key goal of the program. The tutor contended that to

> return itself is the whole idea of being self-motivated. Because the courses we run [at the colleges] are ten hours and that isn't enough for their learning to go forward. They have to take responsibility to do stuff outside the classroom

themselves to make any real progress . . . that which we would like them to make. They have to take responsibility outside the classroom, manage their own time so it's sort of symbolic of that.

The tone of the programming of making participants responsible is hardly surprising given the basis for the adult learning course was initiated due to a New Labour directive called *Skills for Life*. My aim here, however, is not to engage in a critique of neoliberal pedagogical reforms at the museum but to draw out the way in which the development of the subject—whether neoliberal or not—is contingent on a temporality that is the basis for its emergence in the first place. In other words, the subject is only conceivable as it fits into the narrative of unfolding chronological time.

Students too speak about the museum as a site from which they can personally learn. One student states that "for me it's good to go to the museum to learn everything about the history, all the different countries, all the different nationalities. Around the picture you can discover the many different aspects, the different life of the countries." This student claims that the museum is a site for developing historical knowledge about the world. The museum is the place from which this authoritative information can be gleaned for personal knowledge. Another student states that the "museum is necessary for me because I can understand and I can search everything there. I can feel I am living that time. Because past is necessary to our now and future. That's important we have to carry past in the future and now." Consequently, the subject at the British Museum is one that experiences not just a putting-in-place, but also a putting-in-time, a self-legibility through the structure of evolutionary time.

Of course, it is impossible and in many ways unimportant to determine if this discourse is gleaned strictly from the learning programs at the museum. As explored above, the notion of continuous time is deeply mired in the fabric of our very conceptions of political community.[56] Therefore it is not my intention to draw causal connections between the interactive adult educational programs and students' experience of them; I wish only to point out that the conception of continuous time as progress is drawn upon to legitimize ideas of "what counts" as a political project. Here students, in a way similar to staff members, use the notion of time as progress as the backdrop upon which to base their ideas of how to improve the world. Certainly, the museum's political project does nothing to unsettle or trouble this experience; harking back to Preziosi, the anamorphic orientations of the museum offer a putting-in-place, or legibility, of the self. This normalized narrative of evolutionary time then stands as authorizer of the political projects built in its name.

CONSTITUTION HILL, JOHANNESBURG

The political project at Constitution Hill is envisioned as one that plays out in a chronological narrative of redemption from a "dark past." Notably, the word "apartheid" is never uttered by the staff; it is only ever referred to through the deployment of euphemisms such as "our dark past," "our dark days," and "a history" and contrasted with imaginations of a South Africa moving steadily forward with evolutionary propulsion.[57] Though it is consistently characterized as moving away from the past (the unnamed specter of apartheid), it is also a project of educating participants about the contemporary liberal democratic institution of South Africa, as well as one of making individuals responsible for achieving a great future. In all cases, continuous time forms the backdrop upon which the political projects are set.

The political project of democracy building is conceived in much less global and humanistic terms than at the British Museum. At Constitution Hill, there is no project of social cohesion that aims to bring marginalized groups into the hegemonic cultural center. Rather, staff members are clear and concise in their aims of using the past to make a more democratic future that will come through "learning about their constitutional rights as entrenched in our law books." Here, the evolutionary thrust of chronological time is intimately connected to a discourse of law and democracy. The past, the present, and the future are all knowable categories that can be wielded in service of the political project of democratization. One staff member states that

> the whole point of the site is the lack of democracy back in our past. And this whole site revolves around democratic rights and, and democracy itself . . . this is a very democratic site, in terms of what wasn't here and what now is based on our highest democratic institution here, which is the Constitutional Court. What do I mean by democracy? Democracy is equality for all, and equal say for all.

Schmitt and Benjamin contend that this conflation of evolutionary time with the authority of the modern state suffocates the political with the framework of liberal democracy. In the case of Constitution Hill, continuous time lends legitimacy to the fictitious equation of democracy with constitutional rights and assists in the determination of what is legitimate to think of as the political in the South African context.

The subject at Constitution Hill is one that heeds the call of "heritage" and responds by carrying it forward into the future. For the staff at the museum, history is dead and of no use because nothing can be learned from it. Heritage, on the other hand, can be put to work in the service of a brighter future:

> History is dead. History is something on a piece of paper that nobody learns from. They kind of read it then forget about it ten minutes later . . . but heritage is something very important. . . . That's what you choose to carry with you forward.

Subjects, as they are imagined here, are individuals that learn about the past (at the museum) and choose to take new knowledge with them into the future. The good and desirable subject is intrinsically predicated on an evolutionary temporality that moves from a dark past into a redeemed future. The pedagogic thrust at the museum is to encourage subjects to embrace this temporal logic. This project is essential for democratic futures, but although the past is to be learned from, it is not to be taken forward; only the *lessons* from the past are to move with the subject into the future. The terrible past should not be forgotten, but it should not hinder the forging of a new liberal-constitutional democracy. In this newly imagined place, and in stark contrast to the practices of the District Six Museum, colonial legacies are of little relevance in the present.

THE DISTRICT SIX MUSEUM, CAPE TOWN

The time of the political at the District Six Museum also operates on an imagined future of emancipation. The pedagogic thrust is to create a postapartheid city and postapartheid subjectivities. This conception of a political project, like the other museums, also hinges on a temporal logic of imagining a new world beyond the present. For example, staff members describe a recent interactive workshop that

> cuts across all subject areas. It involves literature, it involves oral history, it involves human rights elements, so how you'd reimagine cities along nonracist, anticapitalist, all those lines. You know, how do you create a city that is friendly for everybody—a city that doesn't forcibly remove people.

At the District Six Museum, the future departs from apartheid legacies that continue to linger from the past into the present; the museum posits two different conceptions of time. First, there is the possibility of a new future that, like both the British Museum and Constitution Hill, offers the promise of redemption from a troubled past. Importantly, however, staff members at the District Six Museum do not equate their vision of a redeemed future with universal inclusion. Rather, the communing logic is held with suspicion here, especially for its association with state-led projects that erase legacies of historical inequalities, especially along class lines. This differs markedly from the time of inclusion fostered at the British Museum. Second, and also in contrast to the other two museums, the District Six fosters a conception of the past as deeply embroiled with the present. Rather than asserting a notion of historical time as moving steadily along a teleological line of evolutionary progression, there is no clear distinction between the past and present. Indeed, for the staff, the present is ravaged with the legacies of racism through the continued operation of historical structures of power and privilege. Much of the interactive educational programming at the museum is dedicated to creating awareness about the inheritance of apartheid legacies, especially the persistence of material wealth among middle- and upper-class white populations and of corporate benefactors of apartheid. Staff members indicate that their role is to help articulate these differences so that the "hidden" power of historical privilege can be destroyed:

> We also try to bring to the surface the kind of, what we call the hidden curriculum that operates as hidden. It's where people engage with each other and the differences that are unstated become the most dangerous differences. . . . So what we try to do is surface that.

This alternative to continuous linear time resonates with Benjamin's notion of "now time" [*Jeztzeit*]. "Now time" stands in contrast to the "empty, homogenous time" of history that proceeds in the name of progress. Instead of deploying a notion of continuous redemptive time as the guiding force of their notion of the political, the staff at the District Six Museum wants to contest and reflect on this construction of it and its covering over of material inequalities in order to reveal the contemporary legacies of apartheid.

The museum is also committed to playing with time to confront uncomplicated conceptions of "community." One central element of the museum is the Floor Map, which is an enlarged depiction of the District Six neighborhood. Old and new residents from the neighborhood are asked to walk on the map and mark their home. But because of the multiple generations of people who have lived in the neighborhood and the multiple histories of forced removals (from colonial expansion to apartheid-era relocations), participants often find that someone else has already claimed their place on the map. The Floor Map intends to have visitors undergo this difficult experience as a way of forcing difficult questions about home, ownership, and justice. According to one staff member,

> this consciousness precipitates, or rather has the potential to precipitate crisis. In having to think him or herself in relation to others, the visitor is forced into thinking of his or her relationship with these others. It is here that the Museum is at its most dangerous as a pedagogical space because the visitor is in a sense now no longer protected by the frame of the grand narrative defined by the Museum.[58]

Participants are thus encouraged to reimagine community along lines that defy linear historicity. This results in a palimpsestic understanding of time and place that allows for multiple and shared claims to the land to be made at the same time. The Floor Map is also intended to shake secure understandings of "community." Rather than a putting-in-place, the museum uses alternative conceptions of temporality to construct a crisis in the notion of community for the visitor. The crisis challenges visitors to reconsider their notion of themselves, as well as their relation to others. Moreover, the museum's emphasis on disrupting clear and singular narratives is not limited to the Floor Map. As Sanger explains, the museum also fosters a critical approach in its youth programming:

> [W]hen we work with the memory of forced removals and apartheid generally, we rarely present youth with one linear narrative and instead encourage

them to "discover" the past from their present historical, social, cultural and geographical vantage points. Exploring forced removals then, might start with an investigative project where young people research the ways in which people today are being displaced. At many of these workshops, city center gentrification projects, economic migration, child trafficking and war are entry points into engaging with the multiple narratives about forced removals encountered in the museum space.[59]

In its embrace of this alternative approach, the District Six Museum pursues an opportunity to reconsider the political at the site of the museum. The aim of the museum's political project, however, is not without its means/ends logic. Indeed, staff members are confident in their programming goals and strategies; they see their uncovering of the hidden connections between individuals as synonymous with justice.

One of the most important objectives of the pedagogic programming is to impart a sensibility about historical injustices and material inequality onto participants. Staff members claim that "we try to then teach them to reflect on the very many different things that make human beings uncomfortable when they come into a situation with people they perceive as different." Staff members imply that individuals who participate in this program are transformed into more *truly* democratic subjects. They note that although people purport to be living in a democratic age, they continue to engage in undemocratic practices of racism, classism, sexism, and homophobia. For them, the true democratic future will be made up of individual subjects who know what it means to "live democracy":

> People have learned not to use racist concepts because there's legislation that protects people. But what we find is that for us, that's not democracy, learning to sanitize your language. What you really have to do is deeply embrace people who are different to you. And so our programs that deal with democracy, and that's really everything, is sometimes a deeply painful process for many, many people, but once people learn to work with it, they begin to really understand and live democracy.[60]

The subject at District Six is asked to take up a temporal task that is carried into the future in the name of ethics. In this way, the naturalized temporality is imbued with a moral force and the subject is burdened with the task of imparting its truth. The District Six programming thereby also deploys temporal periodization in the service of their political project. Although they offer a more materialist, Benjaminian-inspired navigation of history, ultimately they too deploy a self-assured conception of the political that must be pursued in the interest of creating a different kind of community.

THE TIME OF INTERRUPTION

Although time functions as an anamorphic orientation that tames the political at the museum, it does not do so completely. While museum staff members and visitors participate in the circulation of a naturalized idea of time as progress, it is not without interruption. Interactive programming at the museums is also marked with consistent themes of misunderstanding, frustration, and confusion.

At the British Museum students often misunderstand the museum staff's instructions. When staff members ask students to complete a task—whether it is making an astrolabe, constructing a collage about life and death, or decorating a ceramic plate—the activity is peppered with audible confusion about how to carry out the instructions. Students were asked to construct their own astrolabe but then did not understand how they functioned. When staff members took the students outside to use them, participants struggled to understand how to make them work. While students found the experience funny, the staff found it frustrating.

In another exercise students were asked to pick a word that was significant to them and to write it on a ceramic plate. Students were then supposed to decorate the plate. This activity was intended to encourage reflection on the use of text, symbols, and design in ancient Islamic architecture, but it seemed a confusing task for most. There were many questions about the aims and objectives of the exercise. The guide tried to explain by showing past examples of completed tiles (created by other tour guides, not students), but even after multiple explanations the confusion did not subside. The result was that each individual creation was quite different. Some students had written poems, while others had written one small word in the center of the plate with no decoration. In postworkshop interviews, staff members expressed irritation at the in-class miscommunications. They claimed that the activity "didn't work" because students didn't understand the intention of the exercise.

There was also confusion among students when they recognized the same freelance tour guides at multiple museological sites in London. Many staff members at the British Museum are precarious workers, holding multiple insecure contracts at multiple institutions, moving between museums, and often delivering different workshops to the same students (certainly more fodder for contemplating the influence of neoliberalism on the contemporary institution). As a result, students found it difficult to keep track of their museum experiences because they had undertaken numerous trips to multiple places with their school group and encountered the same guide. After their trip to the British Museum, students sometimes found it difficult to recall what they learned and why it was important. When asked about their memory of the programs at the British Museum, some students wondered if I was asking them about seafaring, something they had learned at the Maritime Museum in Greenwich. Or perhaps I was inquiring about the cute sofa beds they had seen on display at the Geffrye Museum almost three miles away in Hackney.

These examples of misunderstanding, frustration, and confusion represent an interruption in the persistent theme of the destinal community at the site of the museum. In other words, they mark a cessation in the authority of the museum and its monopoly on the authority of time. Like Benjamin's playwrights who inadvertently drew attention to the fallibility of the sovereign by exposing its hollow authority, these examples from the museum offer instances of the inoperativity of the museum's programming. The anamorphic orientation of time that coheres the world is interrupted, and the messiness of the museum is made visible in these moments. Consequently, although the notion of continuous time can suffocate a rethinking of the political, it does not preclude the possibility for these kinds of interruptions. Although anamorphic orientations tend to smooth and gloss over the messiness of the world at the museum, they cannot entirely cover it up.

These sporadic moments, however, are not the only way to interrupt the cohering proclivities of the museum. The museum can also—and I argue that it must—*actively engage* in practices that refuse to stifle and smooth the world. In the next chapter I highlight what alternative memorializing practices at the museum look like and how, rather than leaving interruption to sporadic miscommunication, they can write the interruption of community as part of a political project that refuses the logics of sovereignty.

CHAPTER FOUR

Monumental Politics

We therefore [. . .] adopt this Constitution as the supreme law of the
Republic so as to—Heal the divisions of the past and establish a society
based on democratic values, social justice and fundamental human
rights; Lay the foundations for a democratic society in which
government is based on the will of the people and every citizen is
equally protected by law; Improve the quality of life of all citizens and
free the potential of each person; and Build a united and democratic
South Africa able to take its place as a sovereign state in the family of
nations.

    –PREAMBLE, CONSTITUTION OF THE REPUBLIC OF SOUTH AFRICA 1996

When the interim Constitution was adopted in 1994, a new order had
been ushered in and South Africa would never be the same again. The
prolonged period of oppression and authoritarianism had passed. Its
place had been taken by a new constitutional order founded on values
including human dignity, the achievement of equality, the
advancement of human rights and freedoms, non-racialism and non-
sexism and the rule of law. [. . .] Nowhere are these struggles of the past
and the ideals espoused in our basic law better and more poignantly
expressed than in the siting of the Constitutional Court and the
development of Constitution Hill.

    –CHIEF JUSTICE PIUS LANGA (2006)

The preamble to the 1996 South African Constitution sets out monumental
ambitions for the new legal order. Not only does it aspire to heal the divisions of the past, lay the foundations for democracy, and build a united
South Africa, it also declares its mission to free the potential of each person.
Yet these aspirations are not confined to the Constitution itself. Even twelve
years after its introduction, the Constitution continues to animate public
discourse about the visions of a "new" South Africa.[1] Significantly, the prom-

ise of the 1996 document has also found its way into contemporary museums. The Constitution not only sets out monumental ambitions, it has itself become monumentalized.

The danger of centralizing the Constitution in the negotiation of political community in the South African context has been widely noted. Aside from its proclivities to smooth and cohere the world, the Constitution's role in the perpetuation of inequality even after the "end" of apartheid has been criticized. Scholars such as Andile Mngxitama and Tshepo Madlingozi, as well as new and old political and community organizations such as NOPE![2] and the Pan Africanist Congress of Azania (PAC), with its strong student wing,[3] decry its empty promises of justice. Mngxitama calls the post 1994 settlement the "rainbow miracle" that has its foundations on stolen land and wealth and, as a result, "cleanses itself of all radical pretensions and unapologetically embraces the liberal fiction of formal equality."[4] Madlingozi claims that since 1996

> the privatization and commodification of municipal services has meant that basic services such as health care and the provision of water and electricity have become inaccessible to the majority of South Africans. The combination of the discourse of human rights with neo-liberalism has meant that redistribution has fallen off the agenda of the ANC.[5]

On this point, it is important to note that while the Constitution is much lauded for its guarantee of justiciable second-generation socioeconomic rights, the nation's ability to deliver on this promise is directly tied to available national resources.

The sharp disjuncture between the promise and material costs of such promises has already come to light in the case of *Soobramoney v. Minister of Health, KwaZulu-Natal*.[6] In that case, a man, Thiagraj Soobramoney, needing emergency dialysis treatment claimed that under section 27(3) ("No one may be refused emergency medical treatment") and section 11 ("Everyone has the right to life"), the Addington Hospital was obliged to provide him with treatment. Citing section 27(2), the Constitutional Court ruled that these provisions were dependent on "the resources available for such purposes" and had to be interpreted in such context.[7] Consequently, Soobramoney was denied treatment, although he died from his illness before hearing the decision from the Constitutional Court.[8]

According to Mngxitama and Madlingozi, the constitutional promise cannot be fulfilled without a redistribution of the wealth accrued by the rich and middle-class white populations during colonization and apartheid. For Mngxitama, the continuity in capital control by white populations in South Africa means that the structural racism of the nation-state continues. He claims, drawing on the antiracist and anticapitalist writings of Steve Biko, that "the post 1994 political terrain is punctuated more by continuity than rupture [and] inaugurated a born again racism, which finds expression in the constitutional precepts, laws, practices, and life chances in society."[9] Indeed, since 1994 South Africa has faced growing urban poverty, the loss of almost one and a half million jobs between 2008 and 2010, and a systemic lack of access to housing, water, sanitation, and electricity for the urban poor.[10] The pacifying words of the new Constitution serve to entrench the status quo that has been adopted by what Mngxitama refers to as the "post 94 black political managers."[11] What South African scholars have termed "constitutional monumentalism" covers over these critiques, relegating apartheid to a bygone past that differs from the present time of constitutional democracy.[12] The monumental narrative equates law with justice and positions the new Constitution as the catalyst in the country's emancipation.

There are, of course, also arguments in support of the monumentalization of the Constitution. Karl Klare argues that "South Africa's legal culture and legal education are in need of a transformation or leavening that will bring them into closer harmony with the values and aspirations enacted in the Constitution."[13] Lourens du Plessis also takes seriously the opinion that the monumentalization of the 1996 document could be beneficial. He argues that some could see the outcome of *State v. Makwanyane and Another* (1995), in which the Constitutional Court declared capital punishment unconstitutional, "as relying on the Constitution [as] a monument to the values of democracy and constitutionalism."[14] Moreover, Drucilla Cornell and Karen van Marle argue that a dismissal of law as hopelessly stifling "the agonal energies of politics" misses the potentially important work that the Constitution can do.[15]

As foreshadowed in chapter 1, however, monumentalism is not only relegated to constitutions. As I mention there, the proclivity to produce community is not limited to the transcendental. Even those that reject the authority of the instantiation of society's legal stability in an external source such as the constitution can fall into the same trap. Those that argue for the unleashing of humanity's immanent power in the name of freedom often mobilize a destinal figure of community at the center of their political projects. One of the foremost believers in the power of immanence is the Italian philosopher and political theorist Antonio Negri.

Negri rejects constitutionalism in pursuit of the constituent power of the multitude. His approach is similar to that of Hannah Arendt's in that he too shares a hostility toward the transcendental legitimation of freedom. Negri, however, sees Arendt's turn to the power of the promise as a compromise of her radical theory. For Negri, any institutional instantiation of community (what he calls constituted power) suffocates the potential of the multitude (the constituent power). In sum, Negri believes in the immanent power of the people. Although he takes great pains to underdetermine this "people," his theory is deeply invested in the idea of a knowable community; while he does not erect a literal monument in the name of the people, he deploys monumental predilections through his political theory.

The discussion of transcendent and immanent accounts of freedom is crucial for this conversation, as I want to make clear that the problem at hand does not only lay with constitutions. Rather, the tenacious silhouette of sovereignty finds its way into museums and into radical oppositional politics such as those espoused by Negri and of which we hear faint echoes at the District Six Museum. Therefore, this chapter productively brings debates in political philosophy about postfoundational freedom into conversation with an existing corpus exploring the role and form of memorials and monuments in the South African context. These two seemingly disparate sets of literature are intimately linked, as they mutually explore the limits of representation at the same time as they recognize the urgent need to remember. The result is an argument about the importance of the *form* that remembrance takes. Different techniques are able to tell different stories.

What I show here is that the approaches initiated by the District Six, both in their interactive education programs and physical presentation (or nonpresentation) of memory, are better equipped to write the interruption of community than Constitution Hill. Rather than gloss over the deep dilemmas of articulating community, the staff at this museum focus on excavating it as an attempt to deal with the legacies of colonialism, apartheid, and neoliberal governance in contemporary South Africa. Museum staff members prioritize creating a crisis of community in order to confront the ways in which the legacies of these practices produce horizons of intelligibility. For them, this intense internal experience is intimately bound up with the political work that needs to be done in order to build an antiapartheid and anticapitalist South Africa. Because of this, the District Six offers some

insights into what a "structure-defying structure" might look like in a setting
that is distinct from constitutionalism yet similarly concerned with issues of
memory, justice, and political community.[16]

MONUMENTAL POLITICS

For Arendt, legitimating power in a transcendent source, in a place that is
external to the human world, is the pathway to totalitarianism. In the face of
the limitations of transcendentally located authority, Arendt proposes the
potential of performative acts such as the promise as a source upon which to
build political community. These acts allow for the power and potential of
human innovation to help build *some* source of stability for politics while
guarding against foundational overdeterminism.[17] Thus Arendt lauds the
performative speech-act of the promise for its gesture to the power of reci-
procity and mutuality made when people "get together and bind themselves
through promises, covenants, and mutual pledges."[18] This return to the
power of the promise, while underwritten with antifoundational aspirations, compromises the radical potential of her critique. Rather than completely open up institutional strictures she is so critical of, Arendt's theory
pauses here in the name of a desire for security.

Negri too is critical of the stifling limitations of institutionalized, transcendent Power (*potere*) on the immanent power (*potenza*) of the multitude,
or what he calls "constituted" versus "constituent" power.[19] Negri refers to
the transcendent form of power given to representational instruments, such
as constitutions or parliamentary democracy, as constituted Power. He
claims that "constitutionalism is transcendence, but above all constitutionalism is the police that transcendence establishes over the wholeness of bodies in order to impose on them order and hierarchy. Constitutionalism is an
apparatus that denies constituent power and democracy."[20] Constituent
power, on the other hand, describes the "'creative work of strength' that is
made up of a 'multitude of singularities.'"[21]

Consequently, Negri critiques Arendt for what he sees as her eventual
stabilization of political community in transcendent form.[22] For Negri, Arendt's concept of the promise places the source of authority in a sacred
covenant above the immanence of the multitude.[23] He claims that although Arendt begins by refusing contractualism, she "ends by praising it;
she begins by grounding her argument in the force of constituent power

and concludes by forgetting its radical quality."²⁴ Therefore, where Arendt turns to islands of security to found political community, Negri insists that this institutionalization is a renunciation of constituent power. He insists that constituent power and its absence of foundation is a positive concept of freedom:

> The expansiveness of strength and its productivity are grounded in the void of limitations, in the absence of positive determinations, in this fullness of absence. Constituent power is defined emerging from the vortex of the void, from the abyss of the absence of determinations, as a totally open need [. . .] Lack of preconstituted assumptions and fullness of strength: this is a truly positive concept of freedom.²⁵

For Negri, the absence of foundation is the defining feature of the multitude. It is this "vortex of the void" that gives it its radical democratic strength.

But Negri's conception of constituent power raises some questions. For instance, if constituent power truly is a foundationless "expansiveness of strength,"²⁶ then how is it possible that constituted Power can limit it? Is it not counter to Negri's own definition of constituent power to postulate that constituted Power has the capacity to stifle the power of the multitude? The confusion can be understood by considering Negri's project through two different, but intimately connected, arguments.

In the first instance, Negri explains the relationship between constituent and constituted power in historical terms. In this register, constituted Power has been used as a tool of domination by the state over the potential of constituent power. Constituted Power's monopoly on political authority (via representational parliamentary politics or formal constitutions) has contributed to a hegemonic conception of the terrain of political possibilities as entirely framed by formal systems of representation.²⁷ This historical and political understanding of constituted Power allows Negri to distinguish between the inherently suffocating properties of transcendental forms of authority on the one hand and the "creative strength" of constituent power on the other.²⁸

In the second instance, however, Negri wants to deny the distinction between the two forms of power. Drawing on an ontology he derives from Baruch Spinoza, Negri's metaphysics imply that a distinction between the transcendent and the immanent is impossible. For him, there is only always already constituent power: the biopolitical power of the multitude.²⁹ Therefore, establishing the foundations of the political in a transcendent source is not simply bad politics, it is out of the question. The Power (*potere*) that is ascribed to these transcendent sources is nothing more than an illusion. As Michael Hardt describes in his preface to Negri's *Savage Anomaly*,

> in the metaphysical domain the distinction between Power and power cannot exist; it merely serves a polemical function, affirming Spinoza's conception of power and negating the conventional notion of Power [. . .] there can be no distinction because there is only power. In metaphysics, Power is an illusion.[30]

Negri likens Spinoza's and his own project to that of the foundational Marxian critique of capitalist liberal democracy. He claims that much in the same way that under capitalism "economic value is made autonomous with respect to the market," the representation of the state as transcendent to society is also a mystification.[31]

Negri negotiates these two different yet interconnected registers of his argument. On the one hand, he argues that the historical and political landscape of the past few centuries of political thought has been dominated by a usurpation of democracy via the transcendent practices of representation. On the other hand, in an ontological register, Negri says that this distinction between transcendent and immanent power does not in fact exist. In both cases Negri appeals to the "ontological strength" of the multitude and its radical potential to destroy the "prisons of constituted power."[32]

Importantly, Negri argues that this constituent power defies representation. With reference to the work of Bataille and Nancy, Negri claims it is as "real as it is absent."[33] Constituent power is

> always open, both temporally and spatially. It flows as potently as freedom. It is at the same time resistance to oppression and construction of community; it is political discussion and tolerance; it is popular armament and the affirmation of principles through democratic invention.[34]

And yet Negri's simultaneous claim that constituent power is as "open as freedom" suggests the necessary question: With such infinite openness, how can it be defined as anything at all (i.e., "the multitude")? In other words, how can "nothing" be categorized as "something"? Indeed, for all of its purported absence, Negri does believe that constituent power is some*thing*; it is constant innovation that "opposes the concept of sovereignty."[35] Moreover, Negri explicitly claims that his task is to defy the traps of constituted Power by creating "an image of the subject that allows us to sustain adequately the concept of constitution as absolute procedure."[36] This confounding double movement between claiming a knowable category of the multitude (an image of the subject) and the simultaneous dispelling of it (absolute procedure) provokes crucial questions.

The dilemma harks back to a similar problematic found in Christodoulidis's concept of praxis explored in chapter 1.[37] Christodoulidis explicitly draws on Negri's theory of becoming to develop his concept of an underdetermined subject defined by its praxis. What both theorists cannot get away from, however, is that despite all their qualifications of the constituent subject (emphasizing its openness and fluidity), it remains something that is *there*. This constituent power of the multitude is definable by its absolutely immanent presence. For Negri and Christodoulidis, the multitude is defined by its creative strength. But Nancy's work exposes the dangers of postulating an absolutely immanent community:

> [I]t is precisely the immanence of man to man, or it is man, taken absolutely, considered as the immanent being par excellence, that constitutes the stumbling block to a thinking of community [. . . .] Consequently, economic ties, technological operations, and political fusion (into a *body* or under a *leader*) represent or rather present, expose, and realize this essence necessarily in themselves. Essence is set to work in them; through them, it becomes its own work.[38]

This absolutely immanent multitude, even as defined by its revolutionary becoming,[39] absolute procedure,[40] or praxis,[41] functions to *produce* an idea of community. This community, though claimed to be underdetermined, is still a community, bounded and secure and in denial of its inherent relationality to the world.

Peter Fitzpatrick also recognizes the tension between what Negri contends is the "absence" of a definable community and the simultaneous appearance of a self-constituted "multitude." Fitzpatrick claims that Hardt and Negri's concept of the multitude is at once

> illimitably including and expansive [. . . .] Yet this same multitude is a contained "subject" that assumes a coherence through its domination by a type

of vanguard labor. Furthermore, our authors can themselves encompass the multitude and articulate its primal "demands" as a small collection of "rights."[42]

Fitzpatrick draws attention to the suspicious return by Hardt and Negri to the language of rights near the end of *Empire*. Fitzpatrick points out that if the multitude was as illimitable as the authors set out, the authoritative position they take as its spokespeople would prove much more difficult.[43] Most important in this critique, however, is Fitzpatrick's observation of the return of an immanent community that has the ability to articulate these claims to rights. In a letter published in 2011 from Negri to a former Tunisian student, the latent republicanism of Negri's underdetermined constituent power comes to the fore as he articulates the possibilities of a postrevolutionary Tunisian political community. In the letter Negri endorses "strengthened legislatures" and "popular sovereignty" claiming that "the legislative and governing power needs to be put back on its feet [and] ought to be exercised directly by the young and by revolutionary groups."[44]

The vitality of the multitude and its agential powers defies the ontological primacy of the sharing of the world. Indeed, the embrace of the absolutely immanent merely replaces the role of the transcendent in thinking about political community; the absolutely immanent offers a new figure with which to orient the political. As Devisch claims, an unquestioning acceptance of the immanent "pretends all too quickly to have overcome the horizon [. . . .] Exactly this movement is what makes it to be caught again in the logic and to be the creation of a new 'Figure.'"[45] It is not, however, that there can be no such figure. The figure of being-in-common must be articulated, but, importantly, through a writing of community that interrupts its completion.

Christodoulidis notes that the constitution cannot be asked to accommodate radical reflexivity because it is structurally bound to build and bind community.[46] So he turns to the potential of civil society for pushing the boundaries of the constitutional arrangement. It is only this external pressure that can stretch the possibilities of the political; this potential cannot be found in the constitution itself. Christodoulidis's answer to this dilemma, though, continues to hinge on a logic of communion. Rather than take the undoing of community as his task, Christodoulidis hangs on to the possibility of absolute immanence through a theory of the multitude that he takes from Negri. While one of the key elements of a countermonumental constitutionalism is destabilizing the constitution as the key tool in the production of community, a second necessary component is the writing of the interruption of community.

The museum, like Christodoulidis's civil society, offers a reflexive resource outside of the constitutional arrangement that contributes to the decentering of the constitution as the key site from which imaginations of political community are launched. Unlike Christodoulidis's civil society, though, it also offers a site from which the communing logic of the constitutional arrangement can be interrupted. Although the museum can proffer narratives of community that deny the reality of our ontological being-in-common, like those explored in chapters 2 and 3, it does not ubiquitously do so. While the anamorphic orientations of the museum play a heavy hand in taming the political at the museum, there are also ways for the museum to employ disruptive memorializing practices. Because the museum has the potential to undermine the task of representation—where the constitution cannot—it is a necessary element in fulfilling the second component of a countermonumental constitutionalism.

MONUMENTALISM VS. COUNTERMONUMENTALISM
AT THE MUSEUM

Johannes Snyman makes a distinction between monuments and memorials.[47] Where memorials are antidotes to forgetting victims of past injustice, Snyman claims that monuments mark a decisive moment as a new beginning and embody the historical self-perception of the founders of the monument. According to Snyman,

> the subject of the monument in this sense is a collective "we," symbolising an uninterrupted continuity between the represented heroes [. . .] and a possible public who ought to identify with what is represented, thereby binding themselves to the tacit oath of allegiance to the collectivity the monument celebrates.[48]

In contrast to the celebration of a present collectivity, memorials speak to the importance of a collectivity over time. Memorials serve as reminders in an effort to ensure that the victims of past injustice are never forgotten.[49] Cornell and van Marle also remark upon this distinction:

[A]lthough monuments and memorials share a concern with memory, they differ significantly in the way they remember. Monuments celebrate and memorials commemorate. For example, after a war has been won, a monument will be created, celebrating the heroes and achievements of war. Memorials are created to commemorate the dead.[50]

Both monuments and memorials are erected as visual markers to an event or community. Whether exalting the present community or defining its connection across time, these practices function to manufacture a sense of collectivity. The relation between the two can be likened to the relationship between law-making and law-preserving violence explored in chapter 3. Although the two practices seem to differ in their approaches, they share in the production of a new law of debt and obligation. Whether it is a monument to defend the past or a memorial to defend the future, both conjure up a community of defenders. What is required instead is a memorializing practice that eschews this persistent theme of community. Such a practice may be found in Snyman's concept of a countermonument, which differs from both monument and memorial.[51]

For Snyman, a countermonumental gesture resists the colonization of memory not only by avoiding official narratives but also by rejecting the notion of representation itself. A countermonument "destroys itself as a spatio-temporal edifice."[52] According to le Roux, a countermonumental act, in the act of representation, represents that the unrepresentable exists.[53] Snyman describes Jochen Gerz and Esther Shalev-Gerz's *Monument Against Fascism* in Hamburg as an example of a countermonument. This piece, an obelisk signed by the residents of Hamburg as testament to their enduring opposition to fascism, was gradually sunk into the ground by the artists over a period of ten years. For Snyman, this piece exemplifies a resistance to monumentalism by actively erasing the monument itself. In the artists' words,

as more and more names cover this 12-metre tall lead column, it will gradually be lowered into the ground. One day it will have disappeared completely, and the site of the Hamburg *Monument Against Fascism* will be empty. In the end it is only we ourselves who can stand up against injustice.[54]

This last statement by the artists—that "in the end it is only we ourselves who can stand up against injustice"—provokes some questions about the possibility of this as a countermonument. While the structure itself may dis-appear, thereby erasing the possibility of it as a *literal* monument, the monumental *proclivities* to communion remain. Indeed, the artists' statement demonstrates that there is still a possible "we" who can stand up against "injustice." These monumental claims assert the knowledge of a presupposed "we" and a presupposed notion of "injustice" (which presumes an attendant notion of "justice"). While there is certainly an imperative to take up the memory of and vigilance owed to the victims of fascism, one of the primary tasks of countermonumentalism is also to undo secure notions of collectivity, immanentism, and justice, such as those articulated here. Self-assured notions of who is on the right side of history and who is not, as well as where and what justice is or is not, can easily be imagined as key authorizers of so-called "legitimate violence." Although the *Monument Against Fascism* may not serve as an ideal model of a countermonument, it does serve as an example of the complex tensions between monumental and countermonumental memorializing practices. The distinction is rendered clear in the exposition of the divergent memorialization practices offered by two museums in South Africa.

Constitution Hill attributes great importance to the constitutional moment as a way of remembering past injustices in order to build a brighter, more democratic future. Thus the memorializing techniques of the museum resonate closely with Snyman's conception of monumentalism. As I argue in chapter 3, the political project at Constitution Hill plays out in a chronological narrative of redemption from a "dark past" that is moving steadily toward a brighter future. This teleological narrative is used to tame an idea of the political into one that accords with a state-endorsed equation of democracy with the rule of law.[55] This monumentalization of the role of the constitution in the production and maintenance of political community is further projected onto the very art and architecture of Constitution Hill.

A key feature of the site is the Great African steps. These steps are strategically situated between "Number Four"—the notorious building where black and colored men, largely on pass offenses, were taken and imprisoned for indefinite amounts of time—on one side and the transparent glass of the new Constitutional Court on the other.[56] Visitors are told that a walk on the steps "is a walk between the past and the future, with the legacy of apartheid on one side and the values of freedom, equality and dignity on the other."[57] Staff members tell visitors that the Constitutional Court is a symbol of freedom, equality, and dignity and, most importantly, that it stands in stark contrast to the legacy of apartheid. In this narrative, the power and potential of

the new liberal democratic constitutional order are exalted through the design of the site itself.[58]

Inside the Constitutional Court building, the tour guide points out the
Ladder of Freedom, a large-scale artwork installed in the main foyer. The ladder's bottom rungs are wrapped in barbed wire and confined circumferen-
tially by metal caging. As one follows the rungs of the *Ladder of Freedom* upwards, the barbed wire gives way to a rung made of ivory (which we are told
reminds us, like elephants, to never forget) and at the top, one of a snake
(which we are told represents wisdom). The ladder tells the emancipatory
story of a nation struggling through apartheid and arriving at constitutional
democracy with evolutionary narrative propulsion.

Significantly however, the ladder does not lean upon any wall or supporting structure, nor does it, for example, end at a copy of the new Constitution. Instead it points upwards, implying an arrival at an unseen destina-
tion or an unfinished journey. Thus the ladder may be interpreted as offering
a more open or undetermined future for the nation. Certainly, without the
tour guide's proffered interpretation of the piece, one might conceive of its
constitutive elements differently. Ultimately, however, staff members at the
site do little to interrupt its narrative of national community and national
time.[59] Indeed, the ladder, as experienced through the official tour, frames
the historic time of the nation as beginning with apartheid. The museum
thereby plays a formative role in deciding what constitutes the history of
South Africa:

> [B]y choosing a particular version of history, by making choices of whom/
> what to include and whom/what to exclude, judges are therefore indeed
> making deeply political choices. And in doing so, they are assisting in the
> construction and maintenance of what it is legitimate to think of as South
> Africa's history.[60]

This piece with accompanying narration tells us that there is a singular and
monumental history to convey and it is one of a nation that has been redeemed through its journey from apartheid to a constitutional democracy.

Le Roux has also written about the design and architecture of Constitution Hill. He gives a fascinating background to the construction of the site,
including outlines of the initial competition for its design and statements
from workshops.[61] Le Roux argues that the entire site, far from completely
monumentalizing the new constitution, is rife with tensions between its

monumentalization and countermonumentalization. One example he offers is the inclusion of the stairwell that used to belong to the "awaiting trial block" of the former prison. This stairwell sits prominently in the foyer of the new Constitutional Court building. Le Roux claims that the old brick stairway, as it sits among the new materials that make up the rest of the building, "serves as a dramatic reminder of the way in which our courts and criminal justice system were implicated in the daily administration of, and struggle against, apartheid."[62] Another example is the art installations that animate the hallway of the court building. He claims that these installations disrupt the constitutional monumentalism that is propagated in other parts of the site. He claims that the result "is a powerful aesthetic expression of the tensions between the monumental and memorial or counter-monumental constitution, which is latent in the whole design of the Constitutional Court building."[63]

While le Roux's insights are important in drawing attention to the ways in which the site can be read as countermonumental, the thrust of the current programming make it difficult for such alternative readings. While moments of interruption can certainly be read into the site, the memorializing practices, as articulated through staff interviews, program overviews, and official tours, remain deeply invested in the monumentalizing of the new constitutional order and its guiding force for the orientation of political community.[64] Almost 1,500 kilometers away in Cape Town, however, there is a distinctly different practice of memorialization happening at the District Six Museum, one that defies the equation of democracy with the new constitutional order.

In contrast to the memorializing practices on offer at Constitution Hill, the interactive adult educational programs at the District Six Museum offer examples of countermonumental memory practices that *interrupt* rather than *produce* a stable conception of community. This occurs as the museum employs programming that operates in nonreductive, antiessentialist, and agonistic ways. Its approach resists the exaltation of liberal equality that erases difference and instead promotes contestation and disagreement. Specifically, the countermonumental approach is demonstrated by the museum's resistance to organizing through one foundational text or spokesperson, commitment to imagining fluid subjectivities, and surfacing of the largely unspoken role of materiality that shapes the postapartheid landscape of South Africa.

In the first instance, the museum resists having an identifiable spokesperson or foundational text. Instead, the museum speaks about itself through multiple books of collected essays, interviews, and oral histories and through the design of the site. Staff members at the District Six Museum foreground their skepticism about the possibility of ever representing (or desiring to represent) a true or coherent identity of the museum. They emphasize the idea of the museum as not a "community" museum but a museum "in-community" that operates on nonhierarchical principles and "takes serious account of an engaged public as both consumers and producers of its work."[65] This approach is also reflected in the design of the site. The museum is set inside a converted old church that sits inconspicuously on a busy street in central Cape Town. Its walls are decorated with paintings, photographs, and newspaper articles that, while well-preserved, are arranged in the form of montage. The District Six Museum refuses to forcefully declare its presence or delineate a clear institutional narrative.

Moreover, the District Six Museum is committed to interrogating presuppositions about identity and representation and does so through its educational programs. One such program explicitly asks participants, "what would it mean to live against the history of one's modes of self-description?"[66] Here museum staff members emphatically draw attention to the construction of subjectivity and, in so doing, make explicit the limits of representation. Their educational work resists the compulsion to assert a naturally existing community organized through so-called objective signifiers such as "nation" or "race."[67] This is demonstrated in two of the museum's recent campaigns, The Return: Re-imagining the City and the Hands Off Prestwich Campaign.

In the first case, the museum held a set of meetings and workshops under the title The Return: Re-imagining the City with a variety of different audiences that discussed the history of District Six. The workshop was followed by an exercise that explored the meanings of "return," "community," "race," "class," and "gender" and aimed to reconceptualize historicized understandings of these categories, as well as peoples' investment in them.[68] Participants were asked to role-play by taking on imagined identities of individuals who lived in District Six in order to foster complex understandings of loss and trauma. Re-enactments included conjuring up imaginations of both the forced removal and the future restitution process. Moreover, the staff explicitly linked the forced relocation of the District Six community (including the removal of indigenous groups during colonialism) to other occurrences of forced removals. In so doing, the museum refused to make the political project nationally focused or solely concerned with legal rights to property. According to Sanger,

> what is evident is that history and memory work is not neutral and not always a benign practice [. . . .] [W]e do not attempt to tell the great and definitive narrative of forced removals in South Africa. Instead, through our exhibition and storytelling we ask visitors to start a journey into the past from a very local and intimate space—that of the experience of one community in one part of Cape Town. This helps to make connections to the present and other similar experiences nationally and internationally.[69]

As a result, the restitution process, as well as "the return," is not assumed to take place solely within formal legal and national institutions. Moreover, the workshop does not sublimate a definable, knowable community but rather provokes questions about the notion of community. The promise of the future, as well as the potential for the role of law in the struggle for a postapartheid city, is contested at the District Six Museum.

A second example, the Hands Off Prestwich Campaign, revolves around a private contractor's accidental unearthing of approximately eight hundred human skeletons in Cape Town in 2003.[70] The South African Heritage Department wanted to use the remains for scientific research, but in accordance with heritage policy, it was required to open a sixty-day consultation period in order for possible descendants to come forward to claim biological kin status.[71] Although the museum wished for the remains to be left where they were out of respect, they refused to interact with the state in ways that reinforced racialized narratives of affiliation. According to Soudien, "they refused to make their kinship with the dead in a way which would conform to a language of "blood", and more pertinently, the expected language of race."[72] Therefore, the Hands Off Prestwich Campaign articulated a position against the state in solidarity with the dead on the basis that they both share—although in very different ways—the experience of dispossession. Rather than having a previously identified and static notion of community, the staff at the museum extended its notion of solidarity beyond state-endorsed as well as "scientifically" compulsory lines of being and belonging.

For the staff at the museum, classifications of race are steeped in the vocabulary of apartheid. Therefore, the staff constantly engage in processes of interrogating its meaning. Staff members draw on the work of Nazir Carrim in order to try to "break with the singular racialized identities that have con-

tinued to press down on [the youth of South Africa] and define them in narrow ways."[73] Sanger quotes directly from Carrim to explain:

> [O]ne could be a daughter in a family, a pupil in a school, a friend in the
> neighborhood, a human rights worker in the community and a South Afri-
> can or British for example. It is also important to note that these identities are
> in the same person all of the time and operate simultaneously. In addition,
> these identities also change. One could get married and become a wife in the
> family, one could move to another country, and so on. It is also important to
> note that these multiple identities are not always in harmony or balanced.
> They may be in tension with each other and, at moments, may even contra-
> dict each another.[74]

Staff members employ this approach both in their interactive educational
programming and in the practices of the museum more widely. For instance,
staff members and members of the community are deeply invested in disrupting the characterization of District Six as a "colored space." While the
city of Cape Town places demands on the museum to present itself as a representative of a "colored" community, the museum refuses to adopt what it
feels is an overly simplistic and homogenizing characterization.[75] Anwah
Nagia, the chairperson of the District Six Beneficiary Trust, claims that "this
politics is the very politics which was responsible for the dismemberment of
the District Six—a poisoned racialised way of understanding the world.
Whites here, Africans there, and "coloureds" over there."[76] This does not
mean, however, that the District Six Museum retreats from making critiques
of racism and race privilege. Rather, staff members at the museum also focus
on the way racism continues to animate the South African landscape. According to these staff members, this means that their imaginings of restitution are at a distance from state-based legislation that covers up the persistence of material inequalities.

The museum operated illegally under the apartheid regime and successfully ran its programs through community fundraising. Since 1994, it
has operated legally but is now faced with the task of resisting state bureau-
cratization as well as liberal notions of democracy that attempt to cure the
ills of racism through the legislated sanitization of racist language. Their
work with students aims to open up what they see as the more difficult
problems of achieving democracy in South Africa: historical privilege, economic disparity, and the painful confrontation of both. In encouraging a

historicized notion of power and privilege, the museum hopes to force open questions of institutional political power and dematerialized conceptions of racism:

> [P]olitical power is one thing but very often politicians are at the whim of those who control the corporate world and so that becomes something that is not dealt with. And the moment you try to deal with that, it's seen as racist. So, if you try to talk about the fact that the corporate world is still controlled by white South Africans who benefited from apartheid—that becomes an issue because you are being racist. But I think racism there becomes an argument where peoples' comfort zones get threatened.[77]

The emphasis on corporate beneficiaries of apartheid and its relation to contemporary political power in South Africa disrupts the powerful discourse of reconciliation that is so emphatic in postapartheid South Africa. Madlingozi documents and critiques the discourse of reconciliation for its erasure of the prevalence of material and social privilege. He argues that struggling for material claims of redistribution "are a thorn in the side of the new government" because they "expose the poverty of [the] elite compromise" of the postapartheid regime, which sees some individuals in positions of privilege while maintaining apartheid and colonial legacies of wealth and power.[78] While the museum wants to contest the legacy of racialized categories inherited from apartheid, they also maintain a crucial focus on how these categories are used in the creation of material inequality that continues to unfold along racialized lines.

Consequently, the memorializing practices of the District Six Museum resist the monumentalization of a definable political community such as that which emerges at Constitution Hill. Here the District Six museum offers a provocative interplay of challenges to fixity that promote more open and fluid imaginations of political community. In so doing, the District Six's countermonumental memorial practices do not recast the state or law as the necessary orienting devices of political community. Rather, the museum deploys memorializing practices that interrupt the very notion of community.

It could be argued that in some cases the museum comes close to celebrating the absolute immanence of community. For example, there is a strong emphasis on "exclusion" at the museum and the attendant need for "including multiple voices" and creating a "radically inclusive imagination of the city."[79] These claims raise the question: inclusion into what? But the

District Six Museum does not exalt this figure; it emphasizes its commitment to interrupting simplistic definitions of community. Rather than maintain a conception of an absolutely immanent multitude, the museum privileges the disruption of the articulation of community. According to staff members,

> memory in this reckoning is an engaged space in which agents invoke and perform multiple, ambiguous and contradictory subjectivities shot through with the push and pull of the ambient politics of the past, present and the future. These multiple inflections surrounding memory force it into a crisis at the moment of its enunciation, at the moment when it is having to be pulled together into a statement of what it is.[80]

Consequently, while the District Six Museum's memorializing practices emphasize the ongoing constitution of the subject (what one staff member calls "the making of consciousness" and what Christodoulidis refers to as *praxis*), they do not entirely fall into the trap of immanentism. These practices aim for crisis, contradictions, and difficult reckoning with the complexity of the self, the community, and the meaning of politics. These practices at the District Six Museum resist the founding of political community by both transcendent and immanent means. They avoid romanticizing radical indeterminacy by daring to *write* the interruption of community through their programming. Rather than shrinking from the responsibility of writing this interruption, reveling in a self-assured conviction in the power of fragmentary aesthetics, they reapproach the political, interrupting the myths of sovereignty, whether in the form of constitutions or radical oppositional politics, that tell us: YOU ARE HERE.

CHAPTER FIVE

Toward a Less Constitutional Constitutionalism

[At the District Six Museum] these multiple inflections surrounding
memory force it into a crisis at the moment of its enunciation, at the
moment when it is having to be pulled together into a statement of
what is.

    −CRAIN SOUDIEN[1]

Literature's revelation [. . .] does not reveal a completed reality, nor the
reality of a completion. It does not reveal, in a general way, *some
thing*—it reveals rather the unrevealable: namely, that it is itself, as a
work that reveals and gives access to a vision and to the communion of
a vision, essentially interrupted.

    −JEAN-LUC NANCY[2]

Against the "pulling together" (in the words of the District Six Museum staff)
or tying up of community (as in a social contract), countermonumentalism
is the undoing of communion. It takes as its task the cessation of a stable
conception of community and any attempt to institutionalize it by means of
representation. In this way, countermonumental constitutionalism differs
from the theories of Walker, Loughlin, and Christodoulidis, as well as those
of Schmitt, Arendt, and Negri. Where these theorists share a predilection for
instituting political community through a constitution, promise, or concept of absolute immanence, countermonumental constitutionalism challenges the centrality of the constitution as the key tool in the navigation and
negotiation of political community, and it writes the interruption of community, whether it is produced in the name of transcendence or immanence.
It is not enough to replace the centrality of the constitutional arrangement
with another set of strictures delimited by the boundaries of a constituent

power. Countermonumental constitutionalism takes the undoing of a knowable community as its task.

This does not mean, however, that there is no role for the constitution. Although the constitution offers a limited horizon of the political, it is a necessary device that performs a central role in the day-to-day functioning of nation-states the world over. Constitutions help human communities share a set of normative expectations and execute decisions necessary for social, political, and legal life. To insist that constitutions are entirely worthless fails to consider the reality of their entrenchment in the contemporary global legal landscape and their symbolic function as aspirational devices. Moreover, to assume that getting rid of the constitution does away with the problem of the suffocation of the political also misses the point of my extended focus on the similarities between constitutions and museums. Indeed, museums function in much the same way as constitutions when they deploy the common practice of smoothing and cohering narratives of the world. The problem then is not with constitutions per se but rather with the proclivity to produce community, to tell a lie about the possibility of sovereignty. The difference is that where constitutions are bound as legal documents to make a cut, a state-authorized and enforceable defining perimeter around who is "in" and who is "out," museums can do otherwise. Museums can play with myths of sovereignty, can interrupt them and show us a truer story about community, not as state-based or anthropologically bounded, but as devoid of the legacy of liberal autonomy that continues to animate our imaginations. Chapter 4 detailed examples of this from the District Six Museum. Therefore, in the end, constitutions retain an important role in countermonumental constitutionalism, but they cannot be the central nor singular tool in the production of political community. A countermonumental approach must include a location external to the constitution that can offer a reflexive resource that takes the interruption of community as its task. The museum is one such site.

The pressing need for a countermonumental constitutionalism is made clearer when contrasted with two recently published theories of postapartheid jurisprudence—one proffered by Johan van der Walt in *Law and Sacrifice: Towards a Post-Apartheid Theory of Law* and the other by Drucilla Cornell and Nyoko Muvangua in *uBuntu and the Law: African Ideals and Post-Apartheid Jurisprudence*. Both contributions offer insights into how reflexive judicial reasoning and constitutional principles might inspire a commitment to restorative justice in the South African context. In the first case, van der Walt argues that law needs to acknowledge the sacrifice of every legal decision. In so doing, he adeptly maneuvers the critiques of metaphysics launched by Heidegger and Nancy to demonstrate the poverty of law's denial of the plurality of the world. In the second, Cornell and Muvangua elaborate a theory of postapartheid jurisprudence based on the use of *ubuntu* as a constitutional principle. They claim that the African concept can import a challenge to the Western foundations of law that privilege individual rights and, consequently, shift the notion of democracy within judicial decision making beyond an atomistic framework. They claim that the use of *ubuntu*, by opening up who and what is included within the ambit of the constitution's aims, can pave the way for a more humane social, political, and economic landscape in contemporary South Africa.

A postapartheid jurisprudence, however, must go beyond mere adjudicational amendments. The grand promises of the new South African constitution have done little to address the interlocking issues of poverty and racism that mark the contemporary social and political landscape. The perpetuation of the constitutional framework as the central site from which to attend to legacies of apartheid and colonialism functions to marginalize and erase competing claims of the political that do not start from the same assumption. A reconsideration of the political for a postapartheid jurisprudence means rejecting the centrality of the existing constitutional arrangement as the key locus for transformation.

It is important to note that these authors carefully attempt to distance themselves from a simple exaltation of the potential of law to address legacies of apartheid. Crucially, van der Walt confronts the limits of law head-on. He claims that every government decision marks a retreat from plurality, yet he ultimately channels his argument into an authorization of the existing system, albeit with a judicial caveat. He explains that all we can do in the face of law's inevitable sacrificial proclivities is acknowledge the sacrifice. But such an acknowledgment does little to interrupt the fundamental communing logic of the existing order. Countermonumental constitutionalism builds on this theory; along with van der Walt, it acknowledges the need for and violence of the decision, but adds to it by decentering the role of the constitution (and its attendant sacrificial logic), using the site of the museum as a place for staging the interruption of sovereignty.

Some might argue that my theory of countermonumental constitutionalism merely substitutes the constitutional project with another, equally prescriptive program. Indeed, I am advocating for an institutionalization of the writing of interruption of community. For me, this is an ethical project in the service of attending to legacies of colonialism and apartheid but also for the acknowledgment of being-in-common, a truth that holds promise for all societies and individuals. The recognition that we are not simply autonomous individuals but beings deeply implicated in the lives of each other and the world could and must have profound effects on the ways we choose to remember, think, live, and govern. I say this with normative force; this is a calling for an undoing of the logic of communion. It is a "call-*ing*" as opposed to a "call" because it is not a static slogan or singular motto. It is an incessant task-*ing* of the need to write the interruption of community. This necessitates the rendering inoperative of an identifiable subject or community, as well as their orienting devices such as humanity, or immanence, under the banner of sovereignty. Countermonumental constitutionalism—an approach that strives to communicate "no sense other than the relation itself"—is up to this pressing task.[3] This writing of inoperativity is the task at hand.

ACKNOWLEDGING SACRIFICE

Van der Walt's *Law and Sacrifice: Towards a Post-Apartheid Theory of Law* offers a provocative proffering of an alternative jurisprudence for South Africa. Responding to the lasting legacies of racism and inequality that dominate the country's landscape, van der Walt draws attention to the ways in which the continued destruction of plurality is fostered by the unacknowledged sacrificial orientation of constitutional adjudication.[4] What he means is that decisions, when taken by government or the courts, create a narrative of justice that erases the multiple other possible outcomes of any contestation. In so doing, they erase what he calls "the plurality of the public."[5] Importantly, van der Walt's conception of plurality is not merely a collective of liberal, rights-bearing individuals coming together in a governmentally sanctioned public sphere. Rather, his conception of plurality is inspired by Heidegger's concept of *lēthe*—what he claims is "the infinite possibility and possibilities of existence from present actualizations of existence,"[6] or what might be more succinctly characterized as the "irreducible plurality of existence."[7] It is this irreducible plurality that he seeks to recuperate from the sacrificial disposition of the law, particularly as it is suffocated in the process of adjudication.

In contrast, van der Walt develops a theory of law that draws attention to the workings of this sacrificial logic, this retreat from plurality, in every judicial decision. In recognizing the sacrifice, van der Walt claims that the lost plurality is retrieved (though never entirely) because it keeps alternative claims to justice in play and emphasizes that the ground upon which such decisions are made are contingent, not absolute.[8] According to van der Walt, under this alternative jurisprudence "the dismissed aspiration remains in play alongside the one favored on a particular day. It can always come back to restate its claim."[9] Significantly, he does not attempt to claim that such recognition will necessarily "level the playing field" of the gross disparities among individuals and communities in South Africa.[10] In fact, van der Walt argues that such a task is impossible not least of all because there is an "absence of universally shared criteria as to what a level playing field is."[11] He does claim, however, that by keeping these dismissed claims legible the otherwise vertical relationship of law and constitutionalism can be "horizontalized" or, more accurately for van der Walt's theory, re-horizontalized.[12]

By horizontalization, van der Walt means the leveling out or equalizing of all social relationships, including those between the state and its subjects. It is a re-horizontalization because van der Walt sees this project as rehabilitating the roots of an original promise of revolutionary constitutionalism. This promise is the radical commitment to equality set out by the French at the turn of the eighteenth century. For him, the French Revolution's oath of allegiance against feudalism and its refusal of private privileges reflects the essence of an original recognition of the horizontality of mortals.[13] It is this original horizontality that van der Walt argues was forgotten under apartheid and that must inspire a postapartheid theory of law.[14]

Van der Walt claims that his idea of a horizontality of mortals comes from the work of Nancy. Specifically, he asserts that his theory of keeping multiple claims alongside each other emulates "the radical equality before the law that Nancy can be said to invoke when he writes about *l'horizontalité des morts*, the horizontality of mortals."[15] But this is a puzzling characterization of Nancy that seems at odds with the ontology of being-in-common. Where van der Walt seems assured in the compatibility of horizontality and law, Nancy rejects this association. Rather, the horizontality that van der Walt is trying to recover is always already beyond such attempted delimitations. Moreover, the horizontality is also beyond that of mere "mortals." For horizontalization to aptly characterize the philosophy of being-in-common, it would have to draw attention to the persistent experience of sharing. This is not a world of mortals but a network of the *world*.

Moreover, van der Walt's theory has little capacity to reconsider the structure of the constitutional arrangement that undergirds the adjudicatory moment. While judges may choose to record a decision that acknowledges the multiple other possible outcomes of any given case, this amendment cannot render legible the destruction of plurality that founds the institutional arrangement itself. This elision is made most obvious as van der Walt substitutes his ontological conception of *lēthe* with a "legal community." In so doing, he reduces his notion of plurality to an already delineated community marked by the bounds of law; the "legal community" becomes a given and, therefore, a grouping lacking substantive reflexive possibilities:

> [I]t is not enough to suggest that a broader understanding of the rule of law that allows for more than one "correct" answer to a legal question resolves the constitutional crisis that comes to haunt us whenever a judge has to decide a case [. . . .] It must also address the *destruction of the plurality of voices that constitute a legal community* whenever the judge selects one answer and presents it as the law that applies to the case.[16]

Here van der Walt underscores that the destruction of plurality happens as voices that constitute a legal community are silenced. What is missed in this conception of plurality, however, is the ways in which the destruction of plurality occurs in the very constitution of the "legal community." Although van der Walt writes this sacrifice into the structure of adjudication, his theory offers no such reflexivity on the arrangement itself.

To be sure, van der Walt emphatically claims that he is not attempting to *retrieve* plurality but only mark its ruin. Indeed, this point distinguishes his approach from those of theorists who make a paradoxical demand on the constitution to both delimit and hold such delineation open. But he nonetheless draws out a theory that maintains the centrality of the constitution in the negotiation of political community because he sees it and its role in making decisions as unavoidable. While constitutional decisions are necessary, however, they do not function as the beginning or end of the negotiation of political community. There are other sites that can offer ways of shifting the terms of the constitutional arrangement and contest its inherently limited framework. As the staff at the District Six Museum knows well, the very categories of thinking and limits of our imaginations are influenced by legacies of colonialism and apartheid. Therefore, the undoing of these categories and the troubling of easy conceptions of community must be the political task.

Van der Walt's focus on the role of adjudication means that the entire project is centered on the role, potentials, and limitations of the decision. This prioritization reduces the vast ambit of a postapartheid theory of law to what van der Walt characterizes as "juggling."[17] In his theory, the juggler is engaged in a process of constantly throwing and catching, always with a light touch and never holding on to any one thing for too long. But this juggling does indeed involve a decision. According to van der Walt, the decision should never extend "the reach of sacrifice beyond what has to be decided here and now."[18] He claims that this metaphor suggests "someone lost, not because he or she had no legitimate claim, but because the ambiguity of multiple desires and the miasmic doubling of claims to justice had to be reduced, for a moment, by sacrificing some in favor of others."[19] But this assertion raises the question: Who decides what has to be decided here and now, and why does this decision constitute the beginning and end of a postapartheid theory of law? Moreover, the recognition of the sacrificial logic becomes mobilized as part of the authorization of its continued legitimacy. Existence is certainly not legitimately sacrificed to liberal constitutional arrangements. Nancy claims that "if we must say that existence is sacrificed, it is sacrificed to no one, and is sacrificed to nothing."[20] Consequently, although van der Walt begins his theory with an emphasis on the irreducible plurality of existence, he eventually elides the radical implications of this ontological starting ground.

Van der Walt's postapartheid jurisprudence acknowledges the persistence of inequality in the existing order and, importantly, recognizes that the constitution is structurally unable to accommodate the plurality of the world. Without an external site with which to interrupt these stable iterations, however, his theory misses the chance to consider the exigency of attending to a reconsideration of community at a distance from these institutional strictures. In contrast, countermonumental constitutionalism acknowledges the destruction of plurality but also offers the museum as a site from which to challenge the limitations of the existing constitution. Such an approach better attends to van der Walt's desire to engage in radical ontological deconstruction *and* maintain a normative commitment to politics.[21] In short, a countermonumental constitutionalism bolsters a postapartheid theory of law that takes seriously the potential benefits of constitutional reform while also acknowledging its structural limitations and, as a result of these limitations, locates an alternative site (the museum) from which to launch interruptive presentations of community.

The persistence of community in van der Walt's theory is also apparent in his lionization of law's Western European foundations. He promotes what he calls the "Christian, Kantian or Millsian" foundations of Western law as he simultaneously raises suspicion regarding the use of *ubuntu* in South Africa. Juxtaposing *ubuntu* to what he classifies as a more robust European-inspired legal process, van der Walt claims that

> a rigorous jurisprudence must be dissatisfied with the feel-good flavor of a jurisprudence that has done little more than add a local, indigenous and communitarian touch to the Christian, Kantian or Millsian respect for the individual that informs Western jurisprudence.[22]

Van der Walt goes on to disparage *ubuntu* further by warning against its vague meaning and its potential for cooptation into conservative and patriarchal projects. He goes so far as to warn against what we may find if we pursue this supposedly mystical and unknowable jurisprudence. He claims that rather than a feel-good conception of law, we may "find that African cultures often or at least sometimes exacted a fine of a number of head of cattle as punishment for murder, on the one hand, and capital punishment for the theft of cattle, on the other."[23]

Stewart Motha points out that this observation casually elides the "staggering excesses of European imperial endeavours" that have taken their deadly tolls on populations around the globe.[24] In other words, in his characterization of *ubuntu* law as less rigorous than its European counterpart, van der Walt obscures the violent legacies of Christian, Kantian, and Millsian legal foundations by reinforcing their self-proclaimed seat at the height of the chain of juridical civilization. This exaltation of Western law and philosophy wavers dangerously close to what Mogobe Ramose terms colonial "epistemicide," the practice of the degradation of indigenous, black, and non-Western forms of knowledge.[25] According to Ramose,

> colonialism claimed the questionable "right of conquest" over the indigenous conquered peoples. By virtue of this questionable right colonialism imposed unilaterally and by force upon the indigenous conquered peoples its own meaning of experience, knowledge and truth. In this way, indigenous ways of knowing and doing were either forbidden, suppressed or eliminated. Thus colonialism committed epistemicide, the killing of the epistemology

and praxis of the indigenous conquered peoples. It did so in the name of the christianisation and "civilization" of the indigenous conquered peoples.[26]

Van der Walt's attachment to these underlying principles means that some considerations of a postapartheid jurisprudence are left off the table. Ironically considering his criticism of Ronald Dworkin's insistence on "consensus," van der Walt's own proclivities to the Christian, Kantian, or Millsian foundations of Western jurisprudence are also indicative of a "community too in touch with itself."[27]

Motha characterizes van der Walt's theory as one invested in a deeply liberal constitutional project "that ultimately has nothing normative to say about the death of the other."[28] He claims that van der Walt's descent into ontology is part of a wider trend that equates normative claim making with the death of the political. In contrast, Motha argues, following Ramose, that constitutional theory must also "confront the issue of epistemicide."[29] The problem in van der Walt's theory, however, is not his descent into an ontological abstraction that ultimately has no normative position. Rather, the problem arises, in my opinion, due to van der Walt's competing desires to accommodate both an ontological claim to plurality and a theory of law that pivots on the existing constitutional structure. Ultimately, van der Walt's commitment to the latter suffocates the aims and objectives of the former. Consequently, it is not van der Walt's descent into ontology that is the problem, but his attachment to Western law and philosophy. Rather than taking seriously the limits of the sovereign legal subject and its attendant political community, van der Walt endorses its production and its grounding in the foundations of Western liberalism. Attending to legacies of apartheid and colonialism requires a retreatment of such attachments and what imaginations of the political they are put in service of.

THE POTENTIAL OF *UBUNTU*

Drucilla Cornell and Nyoko Muvangua also proffer a theory of postapartheid jurisprudence in the South African context. Rather than scorn the powers and potentials of *ubuntu*, however, these authors take it up as a device with which a more "humane" jurisprudence can be delivered.[30] Their book outlines contemporary theoretical debates about the meaning and possibilities of *ubuntu* and pair it with an exhaustive description of the ways it has been drawn upon in contemporary Constitutional Court cases in South Africa. The result is a fascinating exploration of twenty-three cases and their intersecting themes of restorative justice, socioeconomic rights, and reconciliation. Most importantly, the authors claim that although there is no strict definition of the concept, *ubuntu* encapsulates a distinctly different approach to notions of justice and sociality than those proffered by the Western liberal legal paradigm. Whereas the latter is preoccupied with individual rights and contractual obligations, the former eschews these models based on a fundamentally different worldview, one that refuses to see individuals as separate beings:

> In Western jurisprudence, the social bond is understood as an experiment in the imagination in which we seek to conceive why individuals would concede any of their natural liberty and agree to the limiting of their liberty (whereby liberty is defined as a lack of restraint) by joining together with others to form a legal system [. . . .] uBuntu, alternatively, does not conceive of a social bond as one that precedes through an imagined social contract. uBuntu is both the African principle of transcendence for the individual, and the law of the social bond. [uBuntu emphasizes that] it is only through the engagement and support of others that we are able to realize a true individuality and rise above our biological distinctiveness into a fully developed person whose uniqueness is inseparable from the journey to moral and ethical development.[31]

They claim that *ubuntu*, while certainly a contested concept with no single definition, emphasizes a mutual relation between humans. According to Cornell and Muvangua, this mutual relation in turn demands ethical action between members of humanity.

For the authors, *ubuntu* is distinctly *not* an ontological claim. They claim that to characterize it as such is a mistake. Rather, for them, *ubuntu* is a strategy used within the juridical order to "bring about a humane world."[32] Elsewhere Cornell claims that *ubuntu* provides the *Grundnorm* of the constitution, setting forth a "uniquely African" ethical imperative for dignity.[33] Indeed, Cornell and Muvangua's latest book argues that *ubuntu* has been used over the past sixteen years to transform constitutional and private law in South Africa.

This conception of postapartheid jurisprudence, however, comes close to a formula that equates the political with the mere addition of *ubuntu* into the already existing legal arrangements. Rather than consider what a post-apartheid theory of law might look like at a distance from the demands of the existing legal order and, crucially, how the concept of *ubuntu* might inspire such a distance, Cornell and Muvangua tame their project by transforming its potential into an institutional strategy. While Cornell and Muvangua offer a helpful resource in negotiating where the concept of *ubuntu* has, in many cases, been used to deliver decisions more attuned to an agenda committed to restorative justice, the deployment of a constitutional principle cannot be the only nor the central thrust of a postapartheid jurisprudence. As with van der Walt's contribution, Cornell and Muvangua's theory remains too focused on the constitution as the key tool for the negotiation of political community. Moreover, their theory hinges on an idea that the public good is created when a common world is formed.[34]

Their project is deeply invested in creating a notion of the public good "so that we can harmonize our individual interests."[35] As such, Cornell and Muvanguas' theory is also animated by a theme of assimilation. They claim that *ubuntu* moralizes all social relations and in so doing reveals the need for justice between individuals.[36] But this theory has little to say about plurality and constitutionalism's role in its destruction. Rather, this approach sets plurality's neutralization as its end goal; it exalts the collapsing of difference into the harmony of common interest founded through law.

The sure-footedness of constitutionalism's ability to found a common world where all social relations are moralized is particularly striking given the authors' own commitment to a continued struggle over what justice looks like. Indeed, Cornell and Muvangua claim that "there can never be any end to the dialogue about what justice means in a given context. In South Africa there has been a traumatic rip in the relations between people. [. . .] And thus there is a call to participate in the dialogue of what restorative justice might mean."[37] But this seems antithetical to their approach. Where here they are drawing attention to the infinite project of considering the meaning of justice, their postapartheid theory of law seems more assured in its assertion of what it is, something that will come about through the use of *ubuntu* in the courts. Moreover, their notion of the "public good" raises crucial questions about who the "public" is and what they consider to be "good." Mogobe Ramose certainly does not see the new Constitution as a tool for the production of the public good. Rather, he refers to the monumentalization of the Constitution as part of what he calls, citing J. M. Rantete, the "democratization paradigm."[38]

For Ramose, the democratization paradigm privileges a formal institutional notion of democracy that puts off substantive questions, such as land distribution and the role of contemporary beneficiaries of apartheid and colonialism. Ramose claims that this is what was at play in the negotiations over the content of the 1996 Constitution. In that case, and mirroring the critiques of Madlingozi and Mngxitama in chapter 4, a formal and insubstantial notion of democracy allowed South Africa to appear to move quickly away from apartheid and into the new era of supposed emancipation, led by the African National Congress. This paradigm tells us that there is nothing fundamentally wrong with the 1996 Constitution but, rather, only a few bad policies that need amending, and it erases the ongoing contestation of land and the struggle for redistribution since the end of apartheid. Although this historical reality continues to cement racial inequality for black, colored, and indigenous South Africans, it is structurally sidelined by the exaltation of the liberal constitution as the determining device of the political.

Moreover, Ramose points out that the exaltation of the constitutional arrangement is also part of a racist agenda aimed at doing away with parliamentary supremacy. He argues that the transition from parliamentary supremacy to the lauded constitutional democracy was curiously promoted at a time when the majority of South Africans, formerly disenfranchised black individuals, were given the right to vote:

> [C]ontrary to its rejection of this in the past, the conqueror now urged for the Constitution as the basic law of the country. The essence of the argument here is that the Constitution as the basic and supreme law of the country shall be above the law-making power vested in parliament. The laws enacted by parliament shall, in principle, always be subject to their conformity and consistency with the Constitution. Parliament would therefore be the prisoner of the Constitution whose principles possessed the character of essentiality and immutability.[39]

What is missed in the equation of democracy with the constitution is a deeper consideration about the voices and issues that the legal arrangement stifles. Where Cornell and Muvangua argue that an *ubuntu*-inspired constitutional jurisprudence can offer a path to a shared, common world, Ramose highlights that the South African Constitution actively limits this potential.

Moreover, Ramose's account of *ubuntu* is much less amenable to institutional incorporation. For Ramose, Western law is the opposite of *ubuntu*.

Where law recognizes individuals, *ubuntu* is about recognizing that "the human individual is inextricably linked to the all-encompassing" physical and metaphysical universe.[40] Moreover, it is because of this relationality—not just to humans but to the world—that Ramose claims "it is crucial to reincorporate the principle of sharing [. . .] in the construction of an emancipative mode of politics in contemporary Africa."[41] Ramose's insights go unaccounted for in Cornell and Muvangua's figuration of the compatibility of *ubuntu* and the new Constitution.[42] Instead, Cornell and Muvangua draw largely on the work of Kwame Gyekye[43] and Kwasi Wiredu,[44] who are both used to ultimately endorse the existing constitutional arrangement.

For Cornell and Muvangua, the liberal legal appropriation of *ubuntu* as a constitutional principle is expected to take its effects on the jurisprudence of the Constitutional Court, thereby affecting a larger symbolic shift for the potential of the constitution itself. This approach is not surprising from Cornell, whose commitment to legal reform is based on her commitment to building the "best aesthetic representations of a moral world."[45] For her, it is this project—of making law reflect an image of the world that "we" want—that has the potential to deliver justice.

It is in her book *The Imaginary Domain: Abortion, Pornography, and Sexual Harassment* that Cornell lays out a theory of the subject that is constituted by the symbolic order of law. Cornell uses Lacan's mirror stage to explain how the subject is eternally dependent on an external source of validation for its identification and that, if we take the role of this externality in the constitution of the self seriously, the law may be conceived of as this symbolic Other. In this theory, an individual's perceived reflection in the law forms a constitutive element of the self. Indeed, Cornell claims that the legal system can be thought of as active, as

> a system that does not merely recognize, but constitutes and confirms who is to be valued, who is to matter. Moreover, if the legal system as a symbolic Other is also understood to operate through the future anterior, then its operations are transitive in that they constitute what is recognized.[46]

For Cornell, the symbolic Other of law reflects important social values. For this reason, Cornell argues that those who attempt to reform the law—especially feminists—are justified in doing so as means of achieving more ethical reflections of themselves in the world. In other words, reforms to the legal system mean that the symbolic order, which reflects an image of the subject, can less harmfully represent the female subject (e.g., who may be victimized by patriarchal pornography laws).[47]

A theory of the subject via the mirror stage asserts a temporality fixated on the future whereby the self is continually "coming-into" as it seeks validation from others.[48] According to Lacan's theorization, the self cannot be conceived of as immediately present; it is always a subject to come. Cornell argues that this theory emphasizes the importance of protecting the possibilities of the future anterior subject:

> It is only from within such a psychoanalytic framework that we can see how other-dependent the sense of self is, and why the time frame of its constitution through the future anterior demands the protection of the future self's anticipated continuity and bodily integrity. Without the protection of the future of anticipation, the self cannot project its own continuity.[49]

For Cornell, this "anticipation" is central to both the constitution of the subject as well as her moral and political project of emancipation. It is as a result of this anticipation that the imaginary domain—a universalizable *legal right* to moral and psychic space—can take shape.[50] This is how Cornell's theory of the subject guards against overdetermination. Rather than claiming that the symbolic wholly constitutes the subject, it serves in the protection of a possible future where this subject may come to be.[51] In this way, her theory provides "the politics of utopian possibility."[52] While some may argue that this is an overly optimistic view of the potential of the legal system, she contends that there is no reason to be pessimistic. Cornell claims that the unknowable renders pessimism unjustifiable "because this beyond cannot be shown to be either illusory or fully accessible to us in the present"; we must keep "open the impossibility of knowing what is impossible."[53]

Cornell's theory is deeply rooted in the powers and possibilities of the human individual. Indeed, her theory of the subject, as well as her theory of ethical and political transformation, is predicated on its existence.[54] For her, it is at the level of the individual that the imagination's capacity for emancipation resides, both in its possibility to deliver the potential of the imaginary domain and to imagine an ethical project based on "moral images of freedom":

> The ultimate purpose of human beings, if we are thought of as an end, can only be aesthetic in that it is an act of the imagination in which we project

who and what we might become, and this would include, as I suggested in
The Imaginary Domain, the projection of our somatic freedom.[55]

For Cornell, the law's given place in society plays a role in the shaping of our
individual imaginative capacities.[56] Therefore, it should reflect—and, indeed, has the power to reflect—the "ideal of humanity differently."[57] This
theoretical backdrop provides the foundation for Cornell's contention that
the use of *ubuntu* in constitutional adjudication has the potential to deliver
justice in the South African context. This theory of transformation, however, remains contingent on a theory of the subject that experiences transformation through the potential of the symbolic order of law.

In the first place, Cornell's theory of the subject—even as it is inherently
contingent on an Other—transforms the individual into something distinct
from the world. The notion of a delimited subject tells a lie about this absolute enclosure; it denies its inherent being-in-common. Of course, Cornell
would emphasize that her subject is not entirely individualized but, rather,
in relation to the symbolic order; it is not "there" but always coming-into.[58]
But this postulation continues to hinge on the existence of a subject that is
there first, and only secondly able to look into the Lacanian mirror. Indeed,
Cornell's theory of the subject runs into the similar problem Nancy finds in
Heidegger's concept of being-with (*Mitsein*). Although Heidegger's concept
points toward Being's relationality, it is imagined to come only after the
"originary character of *Dasein*."[59] For Nancy, on the other hand, "it is not the
case that the 'with' is an addition to some prior Being; instead the 'with' is at
the heart of Being."[60] For Cornell, the problem is similar in that her theory of
the subject presupposes a "me" (that is there first) that proceeds to understand itself through others (afterwards).[61]

Nancy makes this very critique of Lacanian psychoanalysis. He argues
that in order for it to function, it must presuppose a subject apart from the
world. In this way, metaphysics is built into its very structure; it cannot get
rid of the subject.[62] As such, psychoanalysis is not concerned with the world
(the infinite sharing of the exposure of existence) but with some *one*. What
psychoanalysis does in its identification and exaltation of the unconscious is
participate in the privation of sense; psychoanalysis delimits the unconscious from the world. In contrast, for Nancy, the symbolic is *nothing*: "before
the symbolic, there is this spacing out which no symbol could symbolize:
there is being-in-common, the world."[63] Therefore, any presupposition of a
distinct subject or world inaugurates a political project in the service of a fu-

ture utopia that suggests that the truth of transformation lies elsewhere. This is an endorsement of the potential of a transcendent to fill a lack or gap in the subject. This assertion of a lack and subsequent promise of an elsewhere, however, denies the truth of the world that is here. It introduces an outside to the world and therefore the potential for some one or some thing to be outside of it. This inclination is a betrayal of being-in-common; the task of justice is not to *make* a world, but to expose the truth of infinite sharing.

The postulation of this primordial subject seems to also run Cornell and Muvangua's decolonial project into a problem. Their aim is to promote non-Western theories of being, but their theory of transformation continues to, albeit mutedly, import the centrality of the individual. This psychoanalytic concept of the subject is the theoretical backdrop that allows Cornell and Muvangua to endorse the potential of *ubuntu* as a liberating constitutional principle. While it may be difficult to conceive of a constitutionalism that refuses or deposes of this individual, a countermonumental constitutionalism insists that the sharing of the world must be written, interrupting the sovereign subject and its attendant community.

A COUNTERMONUMENTAL CONSTITUTIONALISM

The political requires writing the interruption of community. Writing is that "which does not respond to any model whatsoever of the appropriation of significations, that which opens at once relation and, along with relation, significance itself."[64] This is not writing in the service of a cause, unless it is for the cause of undoing sovereignty, but this project cannot collapse into the mere romanticization of nihilism or fragmentation. The self-assured position of nihilism that carries the banner of countermonumentalism emanates all the coherence and veneer of the monumental. In contrast, countermonumental constitutionalism resists the closure by writing the world. This does not mean the delimiting of *a* world but, rather, the interruption of any such delimitation.

Moreover, the act of writing is not *an* articulation but an *incessant* writing of being-in-common. As Devisch and Vandeputte claim, "being exposed to co-existence is the law without law before which we continuously appear. The law without law is the command literally to do justice to the co-existence that is ours, a criterion before all criteria."[65] Further, this exposure reveals the impossibility of community to be absolutely immanent. This task requires an acknowledgment of both being-in-common and its necessary articulation as an interruption of stable conceptions of community; this is the exigency of a countermonumental constitutionalism.

How is this project of writing the interruption of community compatible with the practices of juridical decision making? Indeed, van der Walt, as well as Cornell and Muvangua, are primarily concerned with this question. Although these authors are suspicious of the limiting effects of the law, they agree on the necessity of maintaining a primary role for the constitution. They delicately draw out ways in which it can be tinkered with to make its inevitable force more accountable to legacies of colonialism and apartheid. Both theories attempt to build a future for South Africa through the reform of its Constitution and are therefore trapped in a position of monumentalizing it because of their commitment to it as the key tool in the production of an anticolonial and anti-apartheid political community. As I argue in chapter 1, it is a paradoxical request to ask the constitution to undo itself. Moreover, turning to the potential of a collective subject at the helm of constituent power returns us to problems not all that different to those presented by constitutionalism. Indeed, both hinge on the presence of a definable community at its core. I want to propose, in addition to, rather than as a rejection of the careful jurisprudential thinking of van der Walt and of Cornell and Muvangua, the pursuit of a *countermonumental constitutionalism* that both decenters the constitution in thinking about political community *and* attempts to undo the communing logic at the center of projects oriented by both constituted and constituent power. The countermonumentalizing practices of the educational programming at the District Six Museum offer insight here.

Specifically, the museum offers something not dissimilar to Christodoulidis's civil society. Indeed, the museum is also a site at which imaginations of political community are launched. As such, it, like the activity of civil society, can offer a place from which the limits of constitutionalism can be challenged. But unlike Christodoulidis's collective subject, the museum's countermonumental practices can explicitly focus on *undoing* political community. They can challenge simple formulations of politics based on supposedly innocuous categories of history, class, race, and gender. Rather than carry out an agenda that takes the production of community as its task, for example, the District Six Museum sees the political as the struggle over who and what community is. These practices demonstrate that the interruption of community is not nihilistic, abstract, or unrealistic but, rather, a vital political task.

The museum can thus offer a reflexive resource to the limits of the constitution. While the constitution continues to serve its role in organizing and delimiting the boundaries of political community that inevitably lead to sacrifice, countermonumental memorializing practices at the museum can serve to contest those boundaries. These practices *write the interruption of community* and challenge the logic of communion. Importantly, the museum in this scenario does not serve to augment the constitution but rather works at undoing its organizing force. This countermonumental constitutionalism then simultaneously allows us to mediate human conflict with legal tools, but it also emphatically strives to write "the inscription of our infinite existence."[66] In short, the constitution's role must be deflated, and other sites that can offer critical interruptions of community must be considered at least as equal if not more important for those imagining the process of societal transformation, especially in postconflict and postcolonial societies. Although the constitution continues to play a key role in the existing politico-juridical edifice of the nation-state, its importation of the liberal individual and suffocating proclivities to the truth of being-in-common can be resisted from the site of the museum.

Conclusion: Museums, Constitutions, and the Possibility of (a Different) Politics

Constitutions are imagined to be the supreme and authoritative designators of political community. But museums also tell stories about membership (or lack thereof) in political community. Indeed, both museums and constitutions are sites from which these imaginations are launched, and both are animated by a resolute interest in producing community. This theme recurs even in alternative and critical approaches. While museums and constitutionalism attempt to address critiques of their representational inadequacies, the goal of representing community remains in their strategies of reform. What is at stake in this persistent production of community is a denial of being-in-common. Both museums and constitutionalism conflate their political projects with the representation of communities; they present these projects as synonymous with democracy. As a result, both collapse a notion of politics—the concerns of the everyday practices of population management—with the political—a reconsideration of the primacy of our ontological existence. What is lost in this collapse is an understanding of ourselves as part of a world that is always already sharing and us as beings that are always already sharing. Our imaginations are linked again and again to a liberal individual subject that is assumed to be the primary concern for our political and social hopes and dreams about the past and the future. Moreover, both museums and constitutions deploy anamorphic orientations that help cohere their presentations of the world, such as chronological time. Both draw on this temporal conception to lend authority to their respective conception of the political. Indeed, both participate in the classification of the world.

But museums are also not like constitutions. Although both the museum and the constitution are charged with the task of delimiting community, the constitution, if it is to retain its juridical function, cannot escape the necessity of maintaining these boundaries. The museum is not tied to this same task. Therefore a combination of similarities *and* differences between the museum and the constitution make them productive sites to be brought together. It is only a result of these similarities and differences that the museum, when paired with the constitution, can serve as a crucial resource in the production of alternative imaginations of political community. This pairing of the museum and the constitution can serve in the articulation of a countermonumental constitutionalism, which has key insights for contributing to postcolonial and postapartheid theories of law.

The hegemony of liberal sovereignty is in circulation in the adult interactive educational programs at the British Museum. But these programs also offer examples that demonstrate the ways this power can be subverted, confused, and contested. While museum programming may attempt to interpellate particular subjects into standardized narratives, there is always a chance that such invitations can be misheard and refused, whether accidentally or intentionally. But I argue that, in order for a museum to articulate the exigency that offers the most poignant contribution for postcolonial and postapartheid futures, their programming cannot just be left to accidental interpretation. Rather, museums must embrace an active interest in interrupting stable and steady formulations of community.

The interactive adult educational programming at the District Six Museum shows that there is a clear and crucial political imperative to challenge ideas of community that are subconsciously and consciously inherited from colonialism and apartheid. In response, the staff members there use the museum not as a site from which to concretize notions of community, but to force the very concept into crisis. For staff members, the disruption of community constitutes their political project. Importantly, they develop this approach from their political experiences in South Africa (and internationally) and from other authors and thinkers also writing in that context. The examples from the District Six Museum demonstrate that the project of troubling the concept of community is not abstract idealism but rather an urgent political task.

While the District Six Museum may offer a unique and dynamic example of the possibilities of writing the interruption of community, however, its existence does not erase the persistent demand to speak to the everyday politics of government and constitutional decision making. To highlight

the limitations of the constitutional arrangement and then call for its destruction is too cavalier an approach. Moreover, it misidentifies the constitutional arrangement as the main progenitor of the production of community, thereby neglecting the ways in which discourses of community
circulate elsewhere. Therefore, I want to underscore that I am not ignoring
the continued role of constitutions in the negotiation and navigation of
political community. Rather, the problem is its *centralization as the key tool*
from which to reimagine how to be together in the world, as well as its in-
ability to attend to the project of writing the interruption of community.
Although some constitutional scholars such as Loughlin and Walker attempt to attend to the constitution's limits by drawing attention to its reflexive potential, this reflexivity is impossible. The constitution cannot simultaneously be asked to delimit political community and undo it. Rather
than attempt to make the structure of the constitution turn on itself, the
museum can function as an external site from which such reflexivity can
be fostered. Therefore, although there is reason to critique both the constitution and the museum, they continue to serve as important sites for a
countermonumental constitutionalism.

To be clear, this is not to suggest that the pairing of museums with constitutions should lead to a more representative and inclusive national project. This is not an argument for a more effective management of postcolonial
societies through liberal democratic constitutionalism. The equation of representation with democracy neglects to recognize the limitations of representation. The project of representation assumes that the categories it relies
on are adequate for addressing deep and conflicting issues of colonialism,
apartheid, and our being together in the world. Rather than look to these
strategies within constitutionalism or at the museum, the political task at
hand is to disrupt the ideas of community that animate these institutions as
well as the calls for more and better representation within them.

The disruption of the idea of community is a crucial endeavor for societies confronting legacies of colonialism and apartheid such as the United
Kingdom and South Africa because a reconsideration of community refuses to redeploy the categories of representation derived from the colonial
and apartheid state. The interruption of stable conceptions of community
is also vital for all societies, however, because it challenges the limited
frameworks of modern Western sovereignty that dominate the modern political landscape and maintain our focus on state-based and anthropocentric forms of justice. Imaginations of sovereignty provide a conception of

the world made up of sovereign individuals and sovereign communities and act as a barrier to confronting problems supplied not least by an increasingly warming globe.

This book is invested in unearthing the ways in which our political imaginations are shaped and hindered by pre-existing conceptions of community. These conceptions take the form of nationalisms and antinationalisms, theological and secularist determinations, campaigns for localism, civilizational claims to superiority, and anthropocentrism, among other proclamations of distinct and autonomous communities. The interruption of community holds great potential for confronting long-standing instantiations of peoples who claim superiority, ownership, and righteousness based on their supposed membership of a distinct community. These presuppositions have long fueled vicious battles in the name of land, empire, religion, and revenge.

It may be argued that the project of incessantly interrupting community has little to say about the normative dilemmas of addressing the historical injustices that have already been propagated in the name of community. Skeptics may wonder if we should not also make efforts to redress those who have been particularly violated by violent incarnations of community-oriented thought. Indeed, this is a poignant question in the context of postcolonial and postapartheid societies; is there an obligation to redistribute land, natural resources, and political power to those it was stolen from through colonialism and apartheid? The short answer is yes. But the means and justification of that redistribution should refuse the language of community if it is to avoid returning to the limited logics of representation. Transformation requires a non-liberal imagination of community, one that is more attuned to the reality of the world as being-in-common. This is not to postulate a de-political or race-blind approach to pressing political questions. Let me emphasize the District Six Museum's recognition of racism, and simultaneous commitment to interrogating and contesting notions of community. For them and for me, it is a deep commitment to confronting the racial logics of classification, including formulations of sovereign subjects and sovereign people, that necessitate the incessant interruption of community.

It is possible to recognize the way in which notions of community have been mobilized throughout history to enrich some while impoverishing others and yet resist these notions in our future imaginations. We are not forever chained to ideas and concepts that have only recently animated our political lexicon. It is possible to reimagine our being in the world differently, and the museum can help foster this necessary project. This is a project that must write the essencelessness of relation and that must refuse the anamorphic orientations that smooth and cohere the world. In the vein of Benjamin, this is a task of atomic fission that blasts open the stifling proclivities of frameworks of representations. In the meantime, as we work on rethinking community not as an autonomous and individuated whole but as being-in-common, we can also make demands on existing constitutional arrangements to redress these violent legacies. But constitutional redress cannot be the primary tool; it is a limited device whose very framework sets the production of community as its task. This is why the pairing of the museum and the constitution is crucial for a theory of countermonumental constitutionalism. This approach allows for a simultaneous attention to the demand of everyday politics (through constitutional claims) while also recognizing and resisting its logic (through countermonumental museum practices).

Justice is not found in constitutional rights but, rather, in the exposure of the truth of infinite sharing. Attention to this truth is not simply a postmodern romanticization of plurality; it is a necessary step in unsticking the formidable grasp that the liberal legal subject and its mythological autonomy have on our collective imagination. In this way, this book is deeply concerned with making "real world" contributions to anticolonial legal and political transformation. Strategies based solely on institutional recognition of sovereign selves and sovereign communities, or a rejection of institutional recognition in favor of alternative sovereignties, continue to import one of the biggest barriers to unthinking colonialism: the centrality of sovereignty. While such claims, whether in law or at the museum, may function as stopgap measures in saving lives in the here and now—a reality not to be taken lightly—they cannot and should not exhaust our horizons of intelligibility. We must push beyond the hegemony of sovereignty if we want to live together better.

Notes

Introduction

1. Margaret Atwood, "A Night in the Royal Ontario Museum," in *The Animals in That Country* (New York: Little, Brown, and Company, 1969), 20-22.

2. British Museum, "General History," http://www.britishmuseum.org/about_us/the_museums_story/general_history.aspx, accessed May 17, 2009; David Wilson, *The British Museum: Purpose and Politics* (London: British Museum Publications, 1989), 13.

3. British Museum, "Funding Agreement 2008-11," http://www.britishmuseum.org/pdf/British_Museum_Signed_Funding_Agreement_2008-11.pdf, accessed March 1, 2012; British Museum, "General History." The museum is governed by a board of twenty-five trustees that is empowered by the *British Museum Act* 1963 and the *Museum and Galleries Act* 1992. It is funded by the UK Department for Culture, Media, and Sport on a three-year rolling funding agreement.

4. Lauren Segal, Karen Martin, and Sharon Cort, *Number Four: The Making of Constitution Hill*, ed. Lauren Segal (Johannesburg: Penguin, 2006), 1-30.

5. Constitution Hill, "Tours," http://www. constitutionhill.org.za/tours/, accessed March 12 2012.

6. Donald Preziosi, *The Brain of the Earth's Body: Art, Museums, and the Phantasms of Modernity* (Minneapolis: University of Minnesota, 2003), 34.

7. Ibid., 27.

8. The insistence on equating concerns of political community with constitutionalism has been referred to by Neil Walker as the "constitutional fetish." Neil Walker, "The Idea of Constitutional Pluralism," *The Modern Law Review* 65, no. 3 (2002): 319. Jean and John Comaroff also describe the fetishistic quality of constitutionalism. They claim that "the ways and means of the law—constitutions and contracts, rights and remedies, statutory enactments and procedural rituals—are attributed an almost magical capacity to accomplish order, civility, justice, and empowerment. And to remove inequities of all kinds. Note, in this respect, how many new national constitutions have been promulgated since 1989." Jean Comaroff and John Comaroff, "Reflections on Liberalism, Policulturalism, and ID-ology: Citizenship and Difference in South Africa," *Social Identities: Journal for the Study of Race, Nation and Culture* 9, no. 4 (2003): 457.

9. Hannah Arendt, *The Human Condition*, 2nd ed. (Chicago: University of Chicago Press, 1998); Hannah Arendt, *On Revolution* (London: Penguin, 2006); Jean-Luc Nancy and Phillipe Lacoue-Labarthe, *Retreating the Political*, ed. Simon Sparks (London: Routledge, 1997); Carl Schmitt, *The Concept of the Political*, trans. George Schwab (Chicago: University of Chicago Press, 1996); Claude Lefort, *Democracy and Political Theory*, trans. David Macey (Minneapolis: University of Minnesota Press, 1989).

10. Hannah Arendt, *Between Past and Future: Six Exercises in Political Thought* (New York: Viking Press, 1961); Hannah Arendt, *The Origins of Totalitarianism* (Orlando, FL: Harcourt, 1973); Schmitt, *Concept of the Political*; Carl Schmitt, *Political Theology: Four Chapters on the Concept of Sovereignty*, trans. George Schwab (Chicago: University of Chicago Press, 2005).

11. Arendt, *Origins of Totalitarianism*; Schmitt, *Concept of the Political*.

12. Arendt, *Human Condition*; Jean-Luc Nancy, *The Inoperative Community*, ed. Peter Connor, trans. Simona Sawhney (Minneapolis: University of Minnesota Press, 1991).

13. Gayatri Spivak, "Subaltern Studies: Deconstructing Historiography," in *Other Worlds: Essays in Cultural Politics* (London: Methuen, 1987).

14. Pius Langa, "The Role of the Constitutional Court in the Enforcement and Protection of Human Rights in South Africa," *St. Louis University Law Journal* 18 (1997): 1259–1277; Pius Langa, "Foreword," in *Number Four: The Making of Constitution Hill*, ed. Lauren Segal, Karen Martin, and Sharon Cort (Johannesburg: Penguin, 2006); Thabo Mbeki, "State of the Nation Address of the President of South Africa: Joint Sitting of Parliament," February 8, 2008, South African Government Information, http://www.gov.za/node/537711; Albie Sachs, "South Africa's Unconstitutional Constitution: Transition from Power to Lawful Power," *St. Louis University Law Journal* 41 (1997): 1249–1258; Patti Waldmeir, *Anatomy of a Miracle: The End of Apartheid and the Birth of the New South Africa* (New York: W. W. Norton & Company, 1997).

15. Patrick Bond, "Pretoria's Last Gasp Strategy: South Africa Loses its War on Poverty," *CounterPunch*, August 25, 2010, http://www.counterpunch.org/bond08052010.html; Patrick Bond, "South African Development Goals Will Not Be Met," *ZSpace Commentaries*, September 29, 2010, http://www .zcommunications.org/south-african-development-goals-will-not-be-met-by-patrick-bond; David A. McDonald and John Pape, "Introduction," in *Cost Recovery and the Crisis of Service Delivery in South Africa*, ed. David A. McDonald and John Pape (London: Zed Books, 2002).

16. Tshepo Madlingozi, "Good Victim, Bad Victim: Apartheid's Beneficiaries, Victims and the Struggle for Social Justice," in *Law, Memory, and the Legacy of Apartheid: Ten Years After AZAPO v. President of South Africa*, ed. Wessel le Roux and Karin van Marle (Pretoria: Pretoria University Law Press, 2007); Andile Mngxitama, *Why Steve Biko Would Not Vote* (Johannesburg: New Frank Talk, 2009).

17. Constitution of the Republic of South Africa (1996).

18. Interviews, 2009. All interviews were conducted in confidentiality, and the

names of interviewees are withheld by mutual agreement. See also Christopher Hitchens, *The Elgin Marbles: Should They be Returned to Greece?* (London: Verso, 1997); Wilson, *British Museum*.

19. Interviews, 2009.

20. Claudine Pache, "Content Curators: The DJs of the Web," *Journal of Digital Research and Publishing* (2011): 19-25; *New Oxford American Dictionary*, 3rd ed., s.v. "curate"; Claire Robins, "Engaging with Curating," *International Journal of Art & Design Education* 24, no. 2 (2005): 150.

21. *New Oxford American Dictionary*, 3rd ed, s.v. "curator," emphasis mine.

22. Ibid.

23. Didier Maleuvre, *Museum Memories: History, Technology, Art* (Stanford, CA: Stanford University Press, 1999), 111.

24. Preziosi, *The Brain of the Earth's Body*, 27.

25. Ibid., 41.

26. Ibid., 27.

27. Martin Loughlin and Neil Walker, "Introduction," in *The Paradox of Constitutionalism: Constituent Power and Constitutional Form*, ed. Martin Loughlin and Neil Walker (Oxford: Oxford University Press, 2007), 1.

28. Comaroff and Comaroff, "Liberalism, Policulturalism, and ID-ology," 457; emphasis mine.

29. Jürgen Habermas, "Struggles for Recognition in the Democratic Constitutional State," in *Multiculturalism: Examining the Politics of Recognition*, ed. Charles Taylor and Amy Gutmann (Princeton, NJ: Princeton University Press, 1994), 107.

30. Aletta Norval, *Deconstructing Apartheid Discourse* (London: Verso, 1996), 4.

31. Nancy and Lacoue-Labarthe, *Retreating the Political*.

32. Nancy, *Inoperative Community*, 5.

33. Ibid., 31.

34. Jean-Luc Nancy, *The Sense of the World*, trans. Jeffrey S. Librett (Minneapolis: University of Minnesota Press, 1997), 91.

35. Marie Battiste and James (Sa'ke'j) Youngblood Henderson, *Protecting Indigenous Knowledge and Heritage: A Global Challenge* (Saskatoon: Purich Publishing, 2000).

36. Ibid., 203.

37. Glen Coulthard, "Subjects of Empire: Indigenous Peoples and the 'Politics of Recognition' in Canada," *Contemporary Political Theory* 6, no. 4 (2007): 437-460; Glen Coulthard, *Red Skin, White Masks: Rejecting the Colonial Politics of Recognition* (Minneapolis: University of Minnesota, 2014); Taiaiake Alfred, "Sovereignty," in *A Companion to American Indian History*, ed. Philip J. Deloria and Neal Salisbury (Oxford: Blackwell, 2002), 460-474; Audra Simpson, *Mohawk Interruptus: Political Life Across the Borders of Settler States* (Durham, NC: Duke University Press, 2014); Andrea Smith, "Queer Theory and Native Studies: The Heteronormativity of Settler Colonialism," *GLQ: A Journal of Lesbian and Gay Studies* 16, no. 1-2 (2010): 41-68; John Borrows, *Recovering Canada: The Resurgence of Indigenous Law* (Toronto: University of Toronto Press, 2002). Borrows

lands in a different place but is still starting from the problem of imagined liberal legalism and its narrowly defined subjects and jurisdictions. See also Denise Ferriera da Silva, *Towards a Global Idea of Race* (Minneapolis: University of Minnesota Press, 2007).

38. Mogobe B. Ramose, *African Philosophy Through Ubuntu* (Harare: Mond Books, 1999), 102.

39. Mogobe B. Ramose, "Learning Inspired Education," *Caribbean Journal of Philosophy* 2, no. 1 (2001): 6.

40. Henk Botha, "Constitutionalism and the Politics of Memory: A Response to Professors Rubenfeld and Snyman," *Acta Juridica* (1998): 342-347; Lourens du Plessis, "The South African Constitution as a Memory and Promise," *Stellenbosch Law Review* 3 (2000): 385-394; Wessel le Roux, "War Memorials, the Architecture of the Constitutional Court Building and Counter-monumental Constitutionalism," in *Law, Memory, and the Legacy of Apartheid: Ten Years After AZAPO v. President of South Africa*, ed. Wessel le Roux and Karin van Marle (Pretoria: Pretoria University Law Press, 2007); Johannes Snyman, "Interpretation and the Politics of Memory," *Acta Juridica* (1998): 312-337; Karin van Marle, "Constitution as Archive," in *Law and the Politics of Reconciliation*, ed. Scott Veitch (Aldershot: Ashgate, 2007); Karin van Marle, "The Spectacle of Post-Apartheid Constitutionalism," *Griffith Law Review* 16, no. 2 (2007): 411-429.

41. Le Roux, "War Memorials," 87.

42. Emilios Christodoulidis, "Constitutional Irresolution: Law and the Framing of Civil Society," *European Law Journal* 9, no. 4 (2003): 403.

43. Arendt, *Human Condition*, 237.

44. Nancy, *The Sense of the World*, 119.

45. Christodoulidis, "Constitutional Irresolution," 429.

46. Johan van der Walt, *Law and Sacrifice: Towards a Post-Apartheid Theory of Law* (London: Birkbeck Law Press, 2005); Drucilla Cornell and Nyoko Muvangua, eds., *uBuntu and the Law: African Ideals and Postapartheid Jurisprudence* (New York: Fordham University Press, 2011).

Chapter One

1. Jean-Luc Nancy, *The Sense of the World*, trans. Jeffrey S. Librett (Minneapolis: University of Minnesota Press, 1997), 48.

2. Carl Schmitt, *The Concept of the Political*, trans. George Schwab (Chicago: University of Chicago Press, 1996); Carl Schmitt, *Political Theology: Four Chapters on the Concept of Sovereignty*, trans. George Schwab (Chicago: University of Chicago Press, 2005); Hannah Arendt, *The Human Condition*, 2nd ed. (Chicago: University of Chicago Press, 1998); Hannah Arendt, *On Revolution* (London: Penguin, 2006). For secondary commentary on Schmitt's and Arendt's critique of the depoliticization of the political see, George Schwab, "Introduction," in Carl Schmitt, *The Concept of the Political*, trans. George Schwab (Chicago: University of Chicago Press, 1996), 12-13; Oliver Marchart, *Post-Foundational Political Thought:*

Political Difference in Nancy, Lefort, Badiou and Laclau (Edinburgh: Edinburgh University Press, 2007), 4.

3. Nancy, *Sense of the World*, 102.

4. Jean-Luc Nancy, *The Inoperative Community*, ed. Peter Connor, trans. Simona Sawhney (Minneapolis: University of Minnesota Press, 1991), 14; Jean-Luc Nancy, *Being Singular Plural*, ed. Werner Hamacher and David E. Wellberry, trans. Robert D. Richardson and Annie E. O'Byrne (Stanford, CA: Stanford University Press, 2000), 30-31.

5. See Martin Loughlin and Neil Walker, "Introduction," in *The Paradox of Constitutionalism: Constituent Power and Constitutional Form*, ed. Martin Loughlin and Neil Walker (Oxford: Oxford University Press, 2007); Emilios Christodoulidis and Stephen Tierney, eds., *Public Law and Politics: The Scope and Limits of Constitutionalism* (Hampshire: Ashgate, 2008).

6. Martin Loughlin, *The Idea of Public Law* (Oxford: Oxford University Press, 2003); Martin Loughlin, *The Foundations of Public Law* (Oxford: Oxford University Press, 2010); Neil Walker, "The Idea of Constitutional Pluralism," *The Modern Law Review* 65, no. 3 (2002): 317-359; Neil Walker, "Taking Constitutionalism Beyond the State," *Political Studies* 56, no. 3 (2008): 519-543.

7. Emilios Christodoulidis, *Law and Reflexive Politics* (London: Kluwer Academic Publishers, 1998); Emilios Christodoulidis, "Constitutional Irresolution: Law and the Framing of Civil Society," *European Law Journal* 9, no. 4 (2003): 401-432.

8. Gopal Balakrishnan, *The Enemy: An Intellectual Portrait of Carl Schmitt* (London: Verso, 2000), 190; Joseph Bendersky, *Carl Schmitt: Theorist for the Reich* (Princeton, NJ: Princeton University Press, 1983); Richard Wolin, "Carl Schmitt, Political Existentialism and the Total State," *Theory and Society* 19, no. 4 (1990): 389.

9. Carl Schmitt, *Crisis of Parliamentary Democracy*, trans. Ellen Kennedy (Cambridge, MA: MIT Press, 1988); Schmitt, *Concept of the Political*, 72.

10. Schmitt, *Political Theology*, 65.

11. Schmitt, *Concept of the Political*, 53.

12. Ibid., 45.

13. Ibid., 26.

14. Ibid., 37.

15. Ibid., 26.

16. Ibid., 28-29; William Rasch, "Locating the Political: Schmitt, Mouffe, Luhmann, and the Possibility of Pluralism," *International Review of Sociology* 7, no. 1 (1997): 104.

17. Emilios Christodoulidis, "Public Law as Political Jurisprudence: Loughlin's 'Idea of Public Law,'" in *Public Law and Politics: The Scope and Limits of Constitutionalism*, ed. Emilios Christodoulidis and Stephan Tierney (London: Ashgate, 2008), 42. This reflexivity thesis is also drawn out by Rasch, who claims that "the political, on this view, is not a utopian space of individual or social self-actualization, but an imperfectly human space of infinite negotiation." William

Rasch, *Sovereignty and its Discontents: On the Primacy of Conflict and the Structure of the Political* (London: Routledge, 2004), 99.

18. George Schwab, "Introduction," in *Political Theology: Four Chapters on the Concepts of Sovereignty*, trans. George Schwab (Chicago: University of Chicago Press, 2005), lii; Tracy Strong, "Foreword," in *Political Theology: Four Chapters on the Concept of Sovereignty*, trans. George Schwab (Chicago: University of Chicago Press, 2005), xxv.

19. Andrew Norris, "Jean-Luc Nancy on the Political After Heidegger and Schmitt," *Philosophy and Social Criticism* 37, no. 8 (2011): 904.

20. Rasch, "Locating the Political," 107–108.

21. Hannah Arendt, *The Origins of Totalitarianism* (Orlando, FL: Harcourt, 1973), 141; Arendt, *Human Condition*, 58.

22. Arendt, *Human Condition*, 37.

23. Ibid.

24. Arendt, *Human Condition*, 26–27; Catherine Kellogg, "Freedom After the Law: Arendt and Nancy's Concept of 'The Political,'" in *After Sovereignty: On the Question of Political Beginnings*, ed. Charles Barbour and George Pavlich (London: Routledge, 2010), 71.

25. Arendt, *Human Condition*, 7.

26. Ibid., 28.

27. Arendt, *Origins of Totalitarianism*, 297.

28. Arendt, *Human Condition*, 28.

29. Arendt, *Origins of Totalitarianism*, 54; Arendt, *Human Condition*, 41, 58.

30. Hannah Arendt, *Between Past and Future: Six Exercises in Political Thought* (New York: Viking Press, 1961), 172.

31. Ibid., 174; Andreas Kalyvas, "From the Act to the Decision: Hannah Arendt and the Question of Decisionism." *Political Theory* 32, no. 3 (2004): 326; Kellogg, "Freedom After," 69.

32. Arendt, *Human Condition*, 234; Bonnie Honig, "Arendt, Identity, and Difference." *Political Theory* 16, no. 1 (1988): 85. Yet Arendt was not against revolutions per se. Rather, revolutions offered the chance of a new birth of the political. What was key was that "action, though it may be started in isolation and decided upon by single individuals for very different motives, can be accomplished only by *some joint effort in which the motivation of single individuals* [. . .] *no longer counts*, so that homogeneity of past and origin, the decisive principle of the nation-state, is not required." Arendt, *On Revolution*, 165; emphasis mine.

33. Arendt, *On Revolution*, 191; See also Hannah Arendt, *The Life of the Mind: Volume One: Thinking*, ed. Mary McCarthy (London: Secker and Warburg, 1978), 70; Honig, "Arendt, Identity, and Difference," 85–86; and Bonnie Honig, "Declarations of Independence: Arendt and Derrida on the Problem of Founding a Republic," *American Political Science Review* 85, no. 1 (1991): 98.

34. Arendt, *On Revolution*, 131.

35. Ibid., 134, 145.

36. Arendt, *Between Past and Future*, 174. Dana Villa's work supports this inter-

pretation: "Arendt theorizes action not only as essentially nonstrategic and non-instrumental but as essentially nonsovereign: the peculiar freedom of action cannot be captured by philosophies of action that place autonomous agency at their centre." Dana R. Villa, "Beyond Good and Evil: Arendt, Nietzsche, and the Aestheticization of Political Action," *Political Theory* 21, no. 2 (1992): 275.

37. Arendt, *On Revolution*, 161.

38. Ibid., 161–162.

39. Arendt, *Human Condition*, 237.

40. Ibid., 244.

41. Ibid., 245.

42. Arendt, *On Revolution*, 206.

43. Ibid., 202.

44. Arendt, *Between Past and Future*, 157; and Arendt, *On Revolution*, 191.

45. Arendt, *On Revolution*, 194. Honig claims that "since on Arendt's account, the practice of authority consists largely in this commitment to resistibility, the practice of authority turns out to be, paradoxically enough, a practice of deauthorization." Honig, "Declarations of Independence," 111.

46. Arendt, *Between Past and Future*, 153–154; Arendt, *On Revolution*, 191.

47. Andrew Schaap, "Enacting the Right to Have Rights: Jacques Rancière's Critique of Hannah Arendt," *European Journal of Political Theory* 10, no. 1 (2011): 27. Arendt's notion of the intersection of space and the political is articulated in the section titled "Power and the Space of Appearance" in *The Human Condition*. Arendt, *Human Condition*, 199.

48. Arendt, *Human Condition*, 237.

49. Roberto Esposito, *Communitas: The Origin and Destiny of Community*, trans. Timothy C. Campbell (Stanford, CA: Stanford University Press, 2010), 81, quoting Jean-François Lyotard, "The Survivor," in *Towards the Postmodern*, trans. Robert Harvey and Mark S. Roberts (New York: Humanity Books, 1999), 151.

50. For an extended defense of Arendt's concept of politics over Nancy's theory of the "sharing of the world," see Howard Caygill, "The Sharing of the World: Philosophy, Violence, and Freedom," in *On Jean-Luc Nancy: The Sense of Philosophy*, ed. Darren Shepard, Simon Sparks, and Colin Thomas (London: Routledge, 1997), 19–31.

51. Jean-Luc Nancy and Phillipe Lacoue-Labarthe, *Retreating the Political*, ed. Simon Sparks (London: Routledge, 1997).

52. See Ignaas Devisch and Kathleen Vandeputte, "Responsibility and Spatiality: Or Can Jean-Luc Nancy Sit on a Bench in Hannah Arendt's Public Space?" *Lumina* 22, no. 2 (2011): 6.

53. Nancy, *Inoperative Community*, 1–9.

54. Ibid., 4–5. See also Georges Bataille, *Inner Experience*, trans. Leslie Anne Boldt (Albany: State University of New York Press, 1988), 109.

55. Nancy, *Inoperative Community*, 4.

56. Ibid., 5.

57. Ibid., 30–31. Nancy refers to this as the "heteronomy of the relation." See

also Jean-Luc Nancy, *The Experience of Freedom*, trans. Bridget McDonald (Stanford, CA: Stanford University Press, 1993), 68–72.

58. Nancy, *Inoperative Community*, 11.

59. Ibid., 18, 31.

60. Nancy, *Inoperative Community*, 14; Nancy, *Being Singular Plural*, 27, 30–31, 93.

61. Alison Ross emphasizes that "instead of the subject being the site or source of meaning, meaning is exteriorized; its "origin" is being-in-common, between bodies." Alison Ross, *The Aesthetic Paths of Philosophy: Presentation in Kant, Heidegger, Lacoue-Labarthe, and Nancy* (Stanford, CA: Stanford University Press, 2007), 149.

62. Nancy, *Inoperative Community*, 35.

63. Ibid., 18.

64. Nancy, *Sense of the World*, 89, 93. See also Nancy, *Being Singular Plural*, 186.

65. Nancy, *Inoperative Community*, 44–46.

66. Ibid., 57.

67. Ibid.

68. Nancy, *Sense of the World*, 89.

69. Nancy, *Inoperative Community*, 57.

70. Andreas Wagner, "Jean-Luc Nancy: A Negative Politics?" *Philosophy & Social Criticism* 31, no.1 (2006): 89–109; Norris, "After Heidegger and Schmitt."

71. Nancy, *Sense of the World*, 79, 125.

72. Ibid., 111–112. However, Derrida takes aim at Nancy's use of the concept "fraternity." Derrida claims that in addition to the obvious gendered implications of the term it is too entangled with ideas of "birth" and "above all, the word privileges some 'virility.'" Jacques Derrida, *On Touching—Jean-Luc Nancy*, trans. Christine Irizarry (Stanford, CA: Stanford University Press, 2005), 22. Caygill builds on this in his critique, claiming that Nancy's sharing resonates all too closely with the Freudian fraternity of brothers that commune after the killing of the father. Caygill, "Sharing of the World," 29. While there is a place for this critique (at times Nancy returns to curious gender binaries in other texts), *The Experience of Freedom* was published in French in 1988, while most of Nancy's other works were not published until 1992 and later. Therefore, any misconception about an attachment to fraternal republicanism, humanism, or vitalism would have likely been dispelled by Nancy's later work. Derrida concedes as much in his Foreword to *On Touching*, indicating that his critique is now "dated [. . .] but also increasingly deficient, faltering, or obsolete." Derrida, *On Touching*, x. By "curious gender binaries" I mean places where Nancy seems to deploy a strict gender binary, which consistently strikes me as odd given his task of undoing subjectivity. Jean-Luc Nancy, *Birth to Presence*, trans. Brian Holmes (Stanford, CA: Stanford University Press, 1993), 30–33; Jean-Luc Nancy, *The Truth of Democracy*, trans. Pascale-Anne Brault and Michael Naas (New York: Fordham University Press, 2010), 11–12.

73. Judith Butler, "Contingent Foundations: Feminism and the Question of

'Postmodernism,'" in *Feminists Theorize the Political*, ed. Judith Butler and Joan W. Scott (London: Routledge, 1992), 7; emphasis hers.

74. Loughlin, *Idea of Public Law*, 33–35, 52.

75. Ibid., 37–38.

76. Ibid., 42.

77. Ibid., 52.

78. Jacques Derrida, "Declarations of Independence," trans. Thomas Keenan and Thomas Pepper, *New Political Science* 15 (1986): 10.

79. Martin Loughlin, *The Foundations of Public Law* (Oxford: Oxford University Press, 2010), 311.

80. Loughlin, *Foundations*, 2.

81. Loughlin, *Foundations*, 112.

82. Martin Loughlin, "Reflections on the Idea of Public Law," in *Public Law and Politics: The Scope and Limits of Constitutionalism*, ed. Emilios Christodoulidis and Stephan Tierney (Aldershot: Ashgate, 2008), 60. Significantly, however, Loughlin claims that he too is suspicious of the "contractual metaphor." Loughlin, *Foundations*, 310. But while Loughlin's theory may seek to minimize the role of the contract, he does not entirely dispense with it.

83. Christodoulidis also critiques Loughlin on this point. See Christodoulidis, "Public Law," 41–42. Although Loughlin explicitly argues in response that his three orders are not meant to be continuous, what Christodoulidis calls the "continuity thesis" persists as a theme in Loughlin's latest work. See Loughlin, "Reflections," 61.

84. Loughlin, *Foundations*, 7–8.

85. Ibid., 49.

86. Loughlin has been accused of evacuating the political before. See Christodoulidis, "Public Law," 43, as well as Loughlin's response to that accusation in Loughlin, "Reflections," 62.

87. Loughlin, "Reflections," 60; Loughlin, *Foundations*, 231.

88. Loughlin, *Foundations*, 12.

89. Ibid.

90. Loughlin, "Reflections," 49.

91. Walker, "Taking Constitutionalism."

92. Walker, "The Idea of Constitutional Pluralism," 337.

93. Ibid., 358.

94. Walker, "Taking Constitutionalism," 519.

95. Ibid., 525–536. Walker argues that this constitutional imaginary can be conceived of through a series of five reinforcing frames: the juridical, political-institutional, self-authorizing, social, and discursive.

96. Walker, "Taking Constitutionalism," 524; Neil Walker, "Constitutionalism and the Incompleteness of Democracy: A Reply to Four Critics," *Rechtsfilosofie & Rechtstheorie* 39, no. 3 (2010): 206–207. This is not to imply that Walker naïvely understands constitutionalism as necessarily delivering all of the aims and objec-

tives of democracy. He concedes that this is not the case and that their relationship should be conceived of as "ceaselessly controversial." Walker, "Constitutionalism," 285–286.

97. Walker, "The Idea of Constitutional Pluralism," 324.

98. Ibid., 319.

99. Ibid., 324.

100. Ibid., 327.

101. Ibid., 331.

102. Ibid., 339.

103. Ibid., 335.

104. Blaise Pascal, *Pensée*, trans. A. J. Krailsheimer (London: Penguin, 1966), 124.

105. Walker, "Constitutionalism," 284.

106. Walker, "The Idea of Constitutional Pluralism," 319, 327.

107. Christodoulidis, *Law and Reflexive Politics*, xiv.

108. Ibid., xvii.

109. Ibid., xiv.

110. Christodoulidis, "Constitutional Irresolution," 411.

111. Ibid., 413.

112. Ibid.

113. Ibid., 415.

114. Emilios Christodoulidis, "Against Substitution: The Constitutional Thinking of Dissensus," in *The Paradox of Constitutionalism: Constituent Power and Constitutional Form,* ed. Martin Loughlin and Neil Walker (Oxford: Oxford University Press, 2007).

115. Christodoulidis, "Constitutional Irresolution," 428. For further elaboration on the Italian Autonomist movement, see Sylvere Lotringer and Christian Marazzi, *Autonomia: Post-Political Politics* (Los Angeles: Semiotext(e), 2007); Steve Wright, *Storming Heaven: Class Composition and Struggle in Italian Autonomist Marxism* (London: Pluto Press, 2002).

116. Christodoulidis, "Constitutional Irresolution," 429.

117. Ibid. Here Christodoulidis is drawing on Antonio Negri, *Savage Anomaly: The Power of Spinoza's Metaphysics and Politics,* trans. Michael Hardt (Minneapolis: University of Minnesota Press, 1991); as well as Giorgio Agamben, *Potentialities: Collected Essays in Philosophy,* trans. and ed. Daniel Heller-Roazen (Stanford, CA: Stanford University Press, 1999).

118. Christodoulidis, "Constitutional Irresolution," 427.

119. Ibid., 431; emphasis his.

120. Ibid., 427.

121. Christodoulidis, *Law and Reflexive Politics*, xiv.

122. Christodoulidis makes this claim of Loughlin in another essay, Christodoulidis, "Public Law," 44.

123. Christodoulidis, *Law and Reflexive Politics*, 138.

124. Ross, *Aesthetic Paths*, 147–148.

125. Nancy, *Sense of the World*, 111–112.

126. Nancy, *Being Singular Plural*, 185.

127. Jean-Luc Nancy, *The Creation of the World, or Globalization*, trans. François Raffoul and David Pettigrew (Albany: State University of New York Press, 2007), 37.

128. Nancy, *Sense of the World*, 157.

129. Nancy, *Being Singular Plural*, 185.

130. Nancy, *Creation of the World*, 43; See also François Raffoul and David Pettigrew, "Translators' Introduction," in *The Creation of the World, or Globalization* (Albany: State University of New York Press, 2007), 4.

131. Nancy, *Being Singular Plural*, 186; Pascale-Anne Brault and Michael Naas, "Translator's Note," in *The Truth of Democracy* (New York: Fordham University Press, 2010), xi.

132. For another use of Nancy to critique the limits of juridical representation—in this case a critique of human rights discourse—see Illan Wall, *Human Rights and Constituent Power: Without Model or Warranty* (New York: Routledge, 2012).

133. Nancy, *Sense of the World*, 91.

134. Nancy, *Inoperative Community*, 80-81.

135. Nancy, *Sense of the World*, 122.

136. Ibid., 119; Nancy, *Inoperative Community*, 81.

Chapter Two

1. Donald Preziosi and Claire Farago, "What Are Museums For?" in *Grasping the World: The Idea of the Museum*, ed. Donald Preziosi and Claire Farago (Aldershot: Ashgate, 2004), 4.

2. Jens Andermann and Silke Arnold-de Simine, "Memory, Community and the New Museum," *Theory, Culture & Society* 29, no. 1 (2012): 3-13; Hilde Stern Hein, "Redressing the Museum in Feminist Theory," *Museum Management and Curatorship*, 22, no. 1 (2007): 29-42; Victoria Newhouse, *Towards a New Museum* (New York, Monacelli Press, 1998).

3. Elizabeth Edwards, Chris Gosden, and Ruth B. Phillips, eds., *Sensible Objects: Colonialism, Museums, and Material Culture* (New York: Berg, 2006); Amy Lonetree, *Decolonizing Museums: Representing Native America in National and Tribal Museums* (Chapel Hill: University of North Carolina Press, 2012); Moira G. Simpson, *Making Representations: Museums in the Post-Colonial Era* (London: Routledge, 2001); Susan Sleeper-Smith, *Contesting Knowledge: Museums and Indigenous Perspectives* (Lincoln: University of Nebraska Press, 2009).

4. Gail Anderson, *Reinventing the Museum: Historical and Contemporary Perspectives on the Paradigm Shift* (Oxford: Altamira Press, 2004); Douglas Crimp, *On the Museum's Ruins* (London: MIT Press, 1995); Newhouse, *Towards a New Museum*; Peter Vergo, ed., *The New Museology* (London: Reaktion, 1989).

5. Andrew Barry, "On Interactivity: Consumers, Citizens, and Culture," in *The Politics of Display*, ed. Sharon MacDonald (London: Routledge, 1998); Mi-

randa Brady, "Governmentality and the National Museum of the American Indian: Understanding the Indigenous Museum in Settler Society," *Social Identities: Journal for the Study of Race, Nation and Culture* 14, no. 6 (2008): 763–773; Wendy Brown, "Tolerance as a Museum Object: The Simon Wiesenthal Centre Museum of Tolerance," in *Regulating Aversion: Tolerance in the Age of Identity and Empire* (Princeton, NJ: Princeton University Press, 2006), 107–148; Carol Duncan, *Civilizing Rituals: Inside Public Art Museums* (London: Routledge, 1995); Patrick Hughes, "Making Science 'Family Fun': The Fetish of the Interactive Exhibit," *Museum Management and Curatorship* 19, no. 2 (2001): 175–185; Kylie Message, *New Museums and the Making of Culture* (New York: Berg, 2006); Roger Simon, "The Terrible Gift: Museums and the Possibility of Hope Without Consolation," *Museum Management and Curatorship* 21, no. 3 (2006): 187–204; Hein, "Redressing the Museum."

6. Graham Black, *The Engaging Museum: Developing Museums for Visitor Involvement* (London: Routledge, 2005); Tim Caulton, *Hands-On Exhibitions: Managing Interactive Museums and Science Centres* (London: Routledge, 1998); Kylie Message, "Multiplying Sites of Sovereignty Through Community and Constituent Services at the National Museum of the American Indian?" *Museum and Society* 7, no. 1 (2009): 50–67; Nina Simon, *The Participatory Museum* (Santa Cruz, CA: Museum 2.0, 2010).

7. Didier Maleuvre, *Museum Memories: History, Technology, Art* (Stanford, CA: Stanford University Press, 1999), 10.

8. Jean-Luc Nancy, *The Inoperative Community*, ed. Peter Connor, trans. Simona Sawhney (Minneapolis: University of Minnesota Press, 1991), 81.

9. Donald Preziosi, *Brain of the Earth's Body: Art, Museums, and the Phantasms of Modernity* (Minneapolis: University of Minnesota Press, 2003), 34.

10. Duncan, *Civilizing Rituals*, 8.

11. Ibid., 2.

12. The concept of the "destinal figure" comes from Nancy. Jean-Luc Nancy, *The Creation of the World, or Globalization*, trans. François Raffoul and David Pettigrew (Albany: State University of New York Press, 2007), 94.

13. Paula Findlen, "The Museum: Its Classical Etymology and Renaissance Genealogy," *Journal of the History of Collections* 1, no. 1 (1989): 59–78. The word "museum" comes from the Greek *mouseion* meaning "seat of the muses," the muses being the nine daughters of Zeus and Mnemosyne that hold jurisdiction over the arts and sciences. See Jonah Siegel, *The Emergence of the Modern Museum: An Anthology of Nineteenth-Century Sources* (Oxford: Oxford University Press, 2008), 3; and Jeffrey Abt, "The Origins of the Public Museum," in *A Companion to Museums Studies*, ed. Sharon MacDonald (Oxford: Blackwell, 2006), 117–119.

14. William B. Ashworth Jr., "Natural History and the Emblematic World View," in *Grasping the World: The Idea of the Museum*, ed. Donald Preziosi and Claire Farago (Aldershot: Ashgate, 2004), 144–158; Findlen, "The Museum."

15. Ashworth, "Natural History," 146.

16. Findlen, "The Museum," 68; See also Paul Hirst, "Power/Knowledge: Con-

structed Space and the Subject," in *Grasping the World: The Idea of the Museum*, ed. Donald Preziosi and Claire Farago (Aldershot: Ashgate, 2004), 385–386.

17. Ashworth, "Natural History," 149; Michel Foucault, *The Order of Things: An Archaeology of the Human Sciences* (London: Routledge, 1970), 140–143.

18. Giuseppe Olmi, "Science-Honour-Metaphor: Italian Cabinets of the Sixteenth and Seventeeth Centuries" in *Grasping the World: The Idea of the Museum*, ed. Donald Preziosi and Claire Farago (Aldershot: Ashgate, 2004), 129–130. Cosimo I and Francesco I de' Medici, successive grand dukes of Tuscany from the Medici family (father and son respectively), both held private studios in their places of residence that were for private viewing only. Francesco eventually gave his collection to the Uffizi. Findlen, "The Museum," 70–71; Olmi, "Science-Honour-Metaphor," 135.

19. The Renaissance naturalists largely kept their collections in rooms close to or directly connected to their bedrooms for ease of study. Correspondingly, the term "cabinet," "as it evolved in seventeenth-century French, connoted the closet beyond the main bed-chamber." Findlen, "The Museum," 69.

20. Olmi, "Science-Honour-Metaphor," 135; Tony Bennett, *The Birth of the Museum: History, Theory, Politics* (London: Routledge, 1995), 36.

21. Eilean Hooper-Greenhill, *Museums and the Shaping of Knowledge* (London: Routledge, 1992), 106.

22. Tony Bennett, "Civic Seeing: Museums and the Organization of Vision," in *A Companion to Museums Studies*, ed. Sharon MacDonald (Oxford: Blackwell, 2006), 267; Olmi, "Science-Honour-Metaphor," 135. See also Thomas DaCosta Kaufmann, "Remarks on the Collection of Rudolf II: The *Kunsthammer* as a Form of *Representatio*," *The Art Journal* 38 (1978): 22–28.

23. Colonialism, imperialism, and world travel increased the number of new objects and people coming in and out of Italy, and the Reformation shook up existing social, political, and religious institutions. Renaissance naturalists and monarchs were thus challenged to come up with new systems of classification that explained what they perceived as an increasingly "illogical and pluralistic world." Findlen, "The Museum," 66, 68.

24. Findlen, "The Museum," 68. According to Findlen, collections became more public with the decline of privacy as a result of the rise of print and the growing literacy of the public. For further elaboration on the connection between the rise of print (the Gutenberg printing press was invented around 1436), the corresponding rejection of monarchical rule, and expansion of nationalism, see Benedict Anderson, *Imagined Communities* (London: Verso, 2006) and Marshall McLuhan, *The Gutenberg Galaxy: The Making of Typographic Man* (Toronto: University of Toronto Press, 1962).

25. Duncan, *Civilizing Rituals*, 26. The concept of what counts as "public" with regards to the museum is fraught with difficulties, as the dividing line between public and private has shifted greatly since the sixteenth century. Bennett, *Birth of the Museum*, 35; Findlen, "The Museum," 70. This difficulty extends to any attempt to designate the first public European museums, but some of the first

museum-like institutions that were open to the public in Europe were the Ash-molean Museum in Oxford (1683), the Capitoline in Rome (1734), the British Museum in London (1759), the Uffizi in Florence (1769), the Pio-Clementio at the Vatican (1771), and the Louvre in Paris (1793). Siegel, *Emergence*, 6; Abt, "Origins", 117; Findlen, "The Museum," 71.

26. Carol Duncan and Alan Wallach, "The Universal Survey Museum," *Art History* 3, no. 4 (1980): 454; Hooper-Greenhill, *Museums and the Shaping of Knowledge*, 168; Bennett, *Birth of the Museum*, 36–37.

27. Siegel, *Emergence*.

28. Neil MacGregor and Jonathan Williams, "The Encyclopaedic Museum: Enlightenment Ideals, Contemporary Realities," *Public Archaeology* 4, no. 1 (2005): 57–59; British Museum, "General History," accessed May 17, 2009, http://www.britishmuseum.org/about_us/the_museums_story/general_history.aspx. Although the British Museum was founded by The British Museum Act of 1753, it was not opened to the public until 1759. David Wilson, *The British Museum: Purpose and Politics* (London: British Museum Publications, 1989), 13; British Museum, "General History." Even when opened to the public, restrictions on the museum's entrance policy ensured that it was not open to *all* studious and curious persons. For its first hundred years the British Museum was only open during daytime hours (when working-class people were unable to attend). Moreover, groups could be no larger than fifteen and every individual had to have their credentials inspected. Bennett, *Birth of the Museum*, 170. In fact, visitors had to apply for a ticket. Wilson, *British Museum*, 19. After decades of debate in the House of Commons, the museum's opening hours were eventually extended to the evening in 1883. Bennett, *Birth of the Museum*, 71.

29. Bennett, *Birth of the Museum*, 36–37; Duncan, *Civilizing Rituals*, 21; Hooper-Greenhill, *Museums and the Shaping of Knowledge*, 168. Although the French royal collection was nationalized and declared public in 1793 (after the Revolution) the institutional plans for the museum that had been drawn up by the monarchy remained the same under official decree by the revolutionary Assemblée Nationale. Bennett, *Birth of the Museum*, 37; Duncan, *Civilizing Rituals*, 35.

30. Bennett, *Birth of the Museum*, 38; Hooper-Greenhill, *Museums and the Shaping of Knowledge*, 168.

31. Bennett, *Birth of the Museum*, 37; Hooper-Greenhill, *Museums and the Shaping of Knowledge*, 168; Duncan and Wallach, "Universal Survey Museum," 456.

32. Hannah Arendt, *On Revolution* (London: Penguin, 2006), 147.

33. Bennett, *Birth of the Museum*, 38.

34. Duncan and Wallach, "Universal Survey Museum," 456. See also Duncan, *Civilizing Rituals*, 27.

35. Here the gendered inflection is intended. As several authors indicate, many of the eighteenth- and nineteenth-century museums perpetuated gendered narratives of progress and evolution that consistently located women at least one step behind their masculine counterparts. Bennett, *Birth of the Museum*, 201–209; Hein, "Redressing the Museum."

36. Stuart Hall, "The State In Question," in *The Idea of the Modern State*, ed. Gregor McLennan, David Held and Stuart Hall (Milton Keynes: Open University Press, 1984), 19–24; John Rawls, *Political Liberalism* (New York: Columbia University Press, 1996), xxvi; and Paul Kahn, *Putting Liberalism in its Place* (Princeton, NJ: Princeton University Press, 2005), 84, also make the link between the wars against the arbitrary power of religious monarchies and the rise of political liberalism.

37. Carl Schmitt, *Political Theology: Four Chapters on the Concept of Sovereignty*, trans. George Schwab (Chicago: University of Chicago Press, 2005), 36.

38. For further elaboration on the complication of a clear delineation between a "religious" and a "secular" age, see Talal Asad, *Formations of the Secular: Christianity, Islam, Modernity* (Stanford, CA: Stanford University Press, 2003); Hent de Vries and Lawrence Sullivan, ed., *Political Theologies: Public Religions in a Post-Secular World* (New York: Fordham University Press, 2006); and Jean-Luc Nancy, "Church, State, Resistance," *Journal of Law and Society* 34, no. 1 (2007): 3–13.

39. Foucault, *Order of Things*, xxiii–xiv.

40. Ibid., 140.

41. Ibid., 142.

42. Bennett, *Birth of the Museum*, 96; Foucault, *Order of Things*, 143.

43. Foucault, *Order of Things*, 144.

44. Ibid., 154.

45. Foucault, *Order of Things*, 158; Mary Beth Mader, "Modern Living and Vital Race: Foucault and the Science of Life," *Foucault Studies* 12 (2011): 100.

46. Michel Foucault, *Society Must Be Defended: Lectures at the Collège De France 1975–76*, ed. Mauro Bertani and Alessandro Fontana, trans. David Macey (New York: Picador, 2003), 243–245.

47. Foucault, *Society Must be Defended*, 242.

48. Bennett, *Birth of the Museum*, 192.

49. Donna Haraway, "Teddy Bear Patriarchy in the Garden of Eden, New York City, 1908–1936," in *Primate Visions: Gender, Race, and Nature in the World of Modern Science* (London: Routledge, 1989), 30; Krzysztof Pomian, *Collectors and Curiosities: Paris and Venice, 1500–1800*, trans. Elizabeth Wiles-Porter (Cambridge: Polity Press, 1990), 77–78; Bennett, "Civic Seeing," 270.

50. Bennett, *Birth of the Museum*, 47. See also Toby Miller, *The Well-Tempered Self: Citizenship, Culture, and the Postmodern Subject* (Baltimore: John Hopkins University Press, 1993).

51. Bennett, *Birth of the Museum*, 100. According to Bennett, it was also at this time that the discourse of class mobility gained increasing currency. As a result, the bourgeoisie "pose[d] itself as an organism in continuous movement, capable of absorbing the entire society, assimilating [the working class] to its own cultural and moral level." Bennett, *Birth of the Museum*, 98.

52. Bennett, *Birth of the Museum*, 70–71, 100, 169; Duncan, *Civilizing Rituals*, 109; Wilson, *British Museum*, 19.

53. Annie Coombes, "Museums and the Formation of National and Cultural

Identities," in *Grasping the World: The Idea of the Museum*, ed. Donald Preziosi and Claire Farago (Aldershot: Ashgate, 2004), 289.

54. Bennett, *Birth of the Museum*, 79.

55. Coombes, "Museums," 290–293. See also footnote 73.

56. Bennett, *Birth of the Museum*, 90.

57. Ibid., 97.

58. Ibid., 90.

59. Maleuvre, *Museum Memories*, 3.

60. Ibid., 10.

61. Ibid., 111.

62. Preziosi, *Brain of the Earth's Body*, 48.

63. Ibid., 20.

64. Ibid., 41.

65. Ibid., 98.

66. Tim Barringer and Tom Flynn, eds. *Colonialism and the Object: Empire, Material Culture, and the Museum* (London: Routledge, 1998); Craig Clunas, "China in Britain: The Imperial Collection" in *Colonialism and the Object: Empire, Material Culture and the Museum*, ed. Tim Barringer and Tom Flynn (London: Routledge, 1998), 41–51.; Newhouse, *Towards a New Museum*; Simpson, *Making Representations*; Sleeper-Smith, *Contesting Knowledge*.

67. Simpson, *Making Representations*; Sleeper-Smith, *Contesting Knowledge*.

68. Simpson, *Making Representations*, 35.

69. Edwards, Gosden, and Phillips, *Sensible Objects*; Sleeper-Smith, *Contesting Knowledge*; Wilson, *British Museum*.

70. Olmi, "Science-Honour-Metaphor," 135; Bennett, *Birth of the Museum*, 36.

71. There is a strong sentiment among directors of the British Museum and various Lords that objects in the British Museum should not be repatriated. For example, in a BBC television interview in 1986, then director of the British Museum, Sir David Wilson, asserts that those who call for the restitution of the marbles back to Greece are "cultural fascists" and likens them to Adolf Hitler and Benito Mussolini. He claims that such talk is "nationalism and it's cultural danger. Enormous cultural danger. If you start to destroy great intellectual institutions, you are culturally fascist." Christopher Hitchens, *The Elgin Marbles: Should They Be Returned to Greece?* (London: Verso, 1997), 85. In another example, Hitchens cites Lord Boyd Carpenter as he begs his colleagues to "bear in mind that the survival of these lovely creations results from their being taken over by this country and that it is therefore very important that they should remain here." Hitchens, *Elgin Marbles*, vii. The current director, Neil MacGregor, argues that "controversy over ownership of [the museum's] treasures obscures the British Museum's purpose." Neil MacGregor, "The Whole World in Our Hands," *The Guardian*, July 24, 2004, https://www.theguardian.com/artanddesign/2004/jul/24/heritage.art. These sentiments are codified in the British Museum Act, 1963, which prevents the museum trustees from repatriating objects from the museum without express authorization from parliament. *Attorney General v. Trustees of the British Museum*, EWHC 1089 (2005).

72. Simpson, *Making Representations*, 253–264.

73. Ibid., 215–246.

74. Ibid., 107–134.

75. Marie Battiste and James (Sa'ke'j) Youngblood Henderson, *Protecting Indigenous Knowledge and Heritage: A Global Challenge* (Saskatoon: Purich, 2000); Sleeper-Smith, *Contesting Knowledge*; Simon, "Terrible Gift."

76. Janet Marstine, *New Museum Theory and Practice: An Introduction* (Oxford: Blackwell, 2006), 5.

77. Battiste and Henderson, *Protecting Indigenous Knowledge*; Brady, "Governmentality."

78. Andrea Smith also vocalizes a concern with the articulation of the truth of community. Smith links these demands for authenticity in discourses of sovereignty and governmental policy to the practices of colonial anthropologists. She claims that "the very quest for full subjecthood implicit in the ethnographic project to tell our "truth" is already premised on a logic that requires us to be objects to be discovered." Andrea Smith, "Queer Theory and Native Studies: The Heteronormativity of Settler Colonialism," *GLQ: A Journal of Lesbian and Gay Studies* 16, no. 1–2 (2010): 42.

79. Amy Lonetree, "Missed Opportunities: Reflections on the NMAI," *American Indian Quarterly* 30, no. 3–4 (2006): 632–645. See also Lonetree, *Decolonizing Museums*.

80. Ibid., 640–641.

81. Mark Rifkin, *The Erotics of Sovereignty: Queer Native Writing in the Era of Self-Determination* (Minneapolis: University of Minnesota Press, 2012), 264.

82. Viv Golding, "Learning at the Museum Frontiers: Democracy, Identity and Difference," in *Museum Revolutions: How Museums Change and Are Changed*, ed. Simon J. Knell, Suzanne MacLeod, and Sheila E. R. Watson (London: Routledge, 2007), 316.

83. Golding, "Learning at the Museum Frontiers," 316.

84. Ibid.

85. Ibid., 325.

86. Ibid.

87. Ibid., 324.

88. Ibid., 325.

89. Anthony Anghie argues that the United Nations, as it emerged from the League of Nations, was and continues to be fundamentally tied to the legacies of Western colonialism and imperialism. Anthony Anghie, *Imperialism, Sovereignty and the Making of International Law* (Cambridge: Cambridge University Press, 2005).

90. James Clifford, *Routes: Travel and Translation in the Late Twentieth Century* (Cambridge, MA: Harvard University Press, 1997), 192; Mary Louise Pratt, *Imperial Eyes: Travel Writing and Transculturation* (London: Routledge, 1992), 7.

91. Clifford, *Routes*, 192.

92. Clifford, *Routes*, 192, quoting Pratt, *Imperial Eyes*, 7.

93. Ken Arnold, "Presenting Science as Product or as Process: Museums and the

Making of Science," in *Exploring Science in Museums*, ed. Susan Pearce (London: Athlone Press, 1996); Black, *The Engaging Museum*.

94. Brady, "Governmentality"; Brown, "Tolerance"; Amy M. Tyson, "Crafting Emotional Comfort: Interpreting the Painful Past at Living History Museums in the New Economy," *Museums and Society* 6, no. 3 (2008): 246–262.

95. Hughes, "Making Science"; Scott Paris, "How Can Museums Attract Visitors in the Twenty-First Century?" in *Museum Philosophy for the Twenty-First Century*, ed. Hugh H. Genoways (Lanham, MD: Altamira Press, 2006), 255–266.

96. Kevin Hetherington, "The Unsightly: Touching the Parthenon Frieze," *Theory, Culture and Society* 19, no. 5–6 (2002): 194.

97. Bennett, *Birth of the Museum*, 104–105; Black, *The Engaging Museum*.

98. Bennett, "Civic Seeing," 276–277.

99. George Hein, *Learning in the Museum: Museum Meanings* (London: Routledge, 1998); Terry Russell, "The Enquiring Visitor: Useable Learning Theory for Museum Contexts," *Journal of Education in Museums* 15 (1994): 19–21.

100. Hein, *Learning in the Museum*, 25.

101. Ibid., 29.

102. Ibid., 30–31.

103. Ibid., 32.

104. Sharon MacDonald, *Behind the Scenes at the Science Museum* (Oxford: Berg, 2002); Barry, "On Interactivity."

105. Bennett, "Civic Seeing"; Joshua Lepawsky, "A Museum, the City, and a Nation," *Cultural Geographies* 15, no. 1 (2008): 119–142.

106. Paula Findlen, *Possessing Nature: Museums, Collecting, and Scientific Culture in Early Modern Italy* (London: University of California Press, 1996), 205.

107. Nancy, *Creation of the World*, 50.

108. Jean-Luc Nancy, *Being Singular Plural*, ed. Werner Hamacher and David E. Wellbery, trans. Robert D. Richardson and Annie E. O'Byrne (Stanford, CA: Stanford University Press, 2000), 189.

109. Preziosi, *Brain of the Earth's Body*, 19.

110. Michel Foucault, "Text/Context: Of Other Places," *Diacritics* 16, no. 1 (1986): 26.

111. Donald Preziosi, "Art History and Museology: Rending the Visible Legible," in *A Companion to Museum Studies*, ed. Sharon MacDonald (Oxford: Blackwell, 2006), 50; emphasis his.

Chapter Three

1. British Museum, "General History," accessed May 17, 2009, http://www.british museum.org/about_us/the_museums_story/general_history.aspx.

2. President Nelson Mandela, Inaugural Speech, May 9, 1994, http://www.info. gov.za/speeches/1994/990319514p1007.htm.

3. Carl Schmitt, *Political Theology: Four Chapters on the Concept of Sovereignty*, trans. George Schwab (Chicago: University of Chicago Press, 2005), 36–52.

4. Carl Schmitt, *The Concept of the Political*, trans. George Schwab (Chicago: University of Chicago Press, 1996), 61, 72.

5. Schmitt, *Political Theology*, 38.

6. Walter Benjamin, *The Arcades Project*, trans. Howard Eiland and Kevin McLoughlin (London: Belknap Press, 1999), 863.

7. Walter Benjamin, "On the Critique of Violence," in *One-Way Street and Other Writings*, trans. J. A. Underwood (London: Penguin, 2009). Werner Hamacher cites this use of "deposing" in "On the Critique of Violence" from the original German version of Benjamin's *Selected Writings [Gesammelte Schriften]*. Quoting and translating Benjamin, he writes, "upon the breaking of this cycle, upon the deposing [*Entsetzung*] of law with all the forces on which it depends as they depend on it, finally therefore upon the abolition of state forces, a new historical age is founded." Werner Hamacher, "Afformative, Strike: Benjamin's 'Critique of Violence,'" in *Walter Benjamin's Philosophy: Destruction and Experience*, ed. Andrew Benjamin and Peter Osborne, trans. Dana Hollander (New York: Routledge, 1994), 114.

8. Walter Benjamin, "On the Concept of History," in *Walter Benjamin Selected Writings, Volume Four, 1938–1940*, ed. Howard Eiland and Michael Jennings, trans. Edmund Jephcott, Howard Eiland et al (London: Belknap Press, 2002); Benjamin, "On the Critique of Violence."

9. George Hein, *Learning in the Museum: Museum Meanings* (London: Routledge, 1998), 32.

10. Ernst Kantorowicz, *The King's Two Bodies: A Study in Medieval Political Theology* (Princeton, NJ: Princeton University Press, 1957), 276.

11. Carol Greenhouse also traces this genealogy of linear time through the Middle Ages. She claims that "linear time became the constant marker of the contingent and incomplete nature of human society and of every individual's life. The advancement of time, always toward Judgment Day, represented the advancement of human perfectibility, always relative to the perfect completeness of God." Carol J. Greenhouse, "Just in Time: Temporality and the Cultural Legitimation of Law," *Yale Law Journal* 98, (1988–1989): 1635.

12. Kantorowicz, *The King's Two Bodies*; Reinhart Koselleck, *Futures Past: On the Semantics of Historical Time*, trans. Keith Tribe (New York: Columbia University Press, 2004). Reinhart Koselleck also makes this argument, buy he claims that the shift did not come until the sixteenth century. Koselleck, *Futures Past*, 11–12. He argues that the shift occurred as the Church's previous monopoly on prophets (i.e., those who could see "into the future") began to dwindle, especially as a result of the Reformation. Furthermore, Koselleck cites the rise of interest in astrology and its purported ability to predict the future as another factor that contributed to the gradual decline of a fixed conception of time. Koselleck, *Futures Past*, 15.

13. Kantorowicz, *The King's Two Bodies*, 277. Koselleck argues that the Church used a system of approval to control who was considered an authorized prophet and who was not. He claims that a "ruling principle (*Herrschaftsprinzip*) of the

Roman Church was that all visionaries had to be brought under its control. Proclaiming a vision of the future presupposed that it has first received the authorization of the Church (as decided at the Fifth Lathern Council, 1512–1517)." Koselleck, *Futures Past*, 13. This system ensured that the Church always managed the imagined future.

14. Kantorowicz, *The King's Two Bodies*, 281. Jennifer Rust argues that this shift, rather than being new, was actually a return to the earlier confluence of "man" with the "divine" that took the form of the Eucharist. She claims, drawing on the work of Henri Lubac, *Corpus Mysticum: The Eucharist and the Church in the Middle Ages*, ed. Laurence Paul Hemming and Susan Frank Parsons, trans. Gemma Simmonds, with Richard Price and Christopher Stephens (Notre Dame, IN: University of Notre Dame Press, 2007), also a source of Kantorowicz's, that this sharing of Christ's body represented a social bond that also made "the people" an immanent part of the sacred. She states that "in the pre-modern Mass, the 'people' (the laity as much as the clergy) constitute the Body of Christ as a mystical body; in their immanent participation in the ritual, they are infused with the 'sublime' substance of the divine made flesh." Jennifer Rust, "Political Theology: Sacred Flesh and Social Form," *Journal for Cultural and Religious Theory* 12, no. 1 (2012): 7.

15. Kantorowicz, *The King's Two Bodies*, 275–276; Koselleck, *Futures Past*, 11; Keith Tribe, "Introduction," in *Futures Past: On the Semantics of Historical Time*, trans. Keith Tribe (New York: Columbia University Press, 2004), xviii. Many others agree on what Kantorowicz identifies as this general shift in time, including Lior Barshack, "Time and the Constitution," *International Journal of Constitutional Law* 7, no. 4 (2009): 553–576; James Martel, *Divine Violence: Walter Benjamin and the Eschatology of Sovereignty* (London: Routledge); Lubac, *Corpus Mysticum*; and Rust, "Political Theology." While Quentin Skinner claims that Kantorowicz focuses too much on the concept of the "state" (a concept, he argues, which was not in wide usage during that era), and David Norbrook contests Kantorowicz's theory of "the king's two bodies," neither take direct aim at his theory of the rise of continuous time. Quentin Skinner, "The State," in *Political Innovation and Conceptual Change*, ed. Terence Ball, James Farr, and L. Hanson (Cambridge: Cambridge University Press, 1989), 96; David Norbrook, "The Emperor's New Body? Richard II, Ernst Kantorowicz, and the Politics of Shakespeare Criticism," *Textual Practice* 10, no. 2 (1996): 329–357.

16. Martel, *Divine Violence*, 21. Koselleck echoes this sentiment. He claims that "it was the philosophy of historical process which first detached early modernity from its past and, with a new future, inaugurated our modernity. A consciousness of time and the future begins to develop in the shadows of absolutist politics, first in secret, later openly, sustained by an audacious combination of politics and prophecy." Koselleck, *Futures Past*, 21. See also Karl Löwith, *Meaning in History: The Theological Implications of the Philosophy of History* (Chicago: University of Chicago Press, 1949).

17. Daniel Engster, *Divine Sovereignty: The Origins of Modern State Power* (DeKalb:

Northern Illinois University Press, 2001), 10. Lior Barshack also argues that the authority of the state comes from its intimate connection to a notion of perpetual time. Barshack, "Time and the Constitution," 562.

18. Schmitt, *Political Theology*, 15.

19. Schmitt, *Concept of the Political*, 61, 72.

20. Schmitt, *Political Theology*, 5.

21. As Kathleen Davis eloquently expresses, "Schmitt wishes the state to recognize and act upon its theological form, rather than repress this inherent sovereign structure." Kathleen Davis, *Periodization and Sovereignty: How Ideas of Feudalism and Secularization Govern the Politics of Time* (Philadelphia: University of Pennsylvania Press, 2008), 81.

22. Charles Barbour, "Sovereign Times: Acts of Creation," *Law, Culture, and the Humanities* 6, no. 2 (2010), 149.

23. Benjamin and Schmitt were in correspondence in the early 1920s in Germany and drew on (and departed significantly from) each other's work on the topic of political theology and the "state of exception." Agamben goes so far as to intimate that Schmitt's theory of sovereignty in *Political Theology* (originally published in 1922) is an undeclared reply to Benjamin's "On the Critique of Violence" (originally published in 1921), and that Benjamin's *Origin of German Tragic Drama* (originally published in 1925) is a response to Schmitt's concept of sovereign decisionism. Giorgio Agamben, *The State of Exception*, trans. Kevin Attell (Chicago: University of Chicago Press, 2005), 52–64, 284–297. For more on their relationship see Martel, *Divine Violence*, 54–62, and Robert Sinnerbrink, "Violence, Deconstruction, and Sovereignty: Derrida and Agamben on Benjamin's 'Critique of Violence,'" in *Walter Benjamin and the Architecture of Modernity*, ed. Andrew Benjamin and Charles Rice (Melbourne: re.press, 2009), 77–78.

24. In his eleventh and thirteenth theses in "On the Concept of History," Benjamin criticizes the Social Democratic Party of Germany for being conformists who uncritically endorsed the notion of historical progress. He argues that this led to the "illusion that the factory work ostensibly furthering technological progress constituted a political achievement." Benjamin, "Concept of History," 393–394. His essay "On the Critique of Violence" further chastises leftist revolutionaries who contribute to law-preserving violence in their failure to recognize the structure of the means-end relationship. Benjamin, "Critique of Violence," 7–12. Werner Hamacher claims that Benjamin's criticism in this part of the text speaks directly to the social democratic government of Weimar's repression of communist uprisings in early 1920. Hamacher, "Afformative," 113.

25. Benjamin, "Critique of Violence," 2–3.

26. George Sorel, *Reflections on Violence*, trans. T. E. Hulma and J. Roth (London: Allen and Unwin, 1950).

27. Benjamin, "Critique of Violence," 17.

28. Ibid., 18. For supporting interpretations of this distinction see Hamacher, "Afformative," 119–120; Ari Hirvonen, "The Politics of Revolt: On Benjamin and Critique of Law," *Law and Critique* 22 (2011): 110; and Massimiliano Tomba, "An-

other Kind of *Gewalt*: Beyond Law, Re-reading Walter Benjamin," *Historical Materialism* 17 (2009): 139.

29. Hamacher, "Afformative," 121. This is also the key point that Agamben takes from Benjamin and that he articulates through his use of Herman Melville's short story *Bartleby the Scrivener*. Giorgio Agamben, *The Coming Community*, trans. Michael Hardt (Minneapolis: University of Minnesota Press, 2003), 37. For further elaboration on Agamben, Bartleby, and law, see Jessica Whyte, "'I Would Prefer Not To': Giorgio Agamben, Bartleby and the Potentiality of the Law," *Law and Critique* 12 (2009): 309–324.

30. Benjamin, "Critique of Violence," 21.

31. Ibid., 22–23.

32. Benjamin, *Arcades*, 863.

33. Benjamin, "On the Concept of History," 392.

34. Benjamin, "Critique of Violence," 24. In this essay, Benjamin demonstrates the difference between the two types of violence with two different mythical tales, the legend of Niobe from Greek mythology and the story of Korah cited in the religious traditions of Christianity, Islam, and Judaism. The legend of Niobe serves as an example of mythic violence because it is not a story of complete destruction. Instead, Artemis and Apollo's actions establish a new law, intended to impose guilt and remorse. In the story of God's punishment of Korah and his followers, however, God opens up the earth to have them all swallowed. This act does not create a new law; it is an act empty of the utilitarian means/ends logic. Benjamin, "Critique of Violence," 21–22, 24. See also Sinnerbrink, "Violence, Deconstruction, and Sovereignty," 83–84; and Hirvonen, "Politics of Revolt," 107.

35. Benjamin, "Critique of Violence," 28. See also Davis, *Periodization and Sovereignty*, 82.

36. Walter Benjamin, *The Origin of German Tragic Drama*, trans. John Osborne (New York: Verso, 1998).

37. Martel, *Divine Violence*, 54–59.

38. Benjamin, *Origin of German Tragic Drama*, 50–51.

39. Ibid., 232; Martel, *Divine Violence*, 54–59. Benjamin claims that it is "precisely visions of the frenzy of destruction, in which all earthly things collapse into a heap of ruins, which reveal the limit set upon allegorical contemplation, rather than its ideal quality." Benjamin, *Origin of German Tragic Drama*, 232.

40. Benjamin, "On the Concept of History," 392.

41. Ibid., 391.

42. Amy Kapczynski writes about Benjamin's work in relation to what she calls "constitutional historicism" in the context of the United States. She claims that constitutional scholars and practitioners draw on the teleological sense of time that Benjamin was writing against, thereby lending "both authority and restraint to constitutionalism, and the particular practice of judicial review." She proposes an alternative approach she calls "constitutional redemptivism," which would eschew the heavy weight of historicism, thereby making room for the manifold

histories that orient the present. Amy Kapczynski, "Historicism, Progress, and the Redemptive Constitution," *Cardozo Law Review* 26 (2004–2005): 1060.

43. Benjamin, "Concept of History," 395.

44. Walter Benjamin, "Surrealism," in *One-Way Street and Other Writings*, trans. J. A. Underwood (London: Penguin, 2009), 157.

45. Benjamin, "Surrealism," 148.

46. Ibid., 160.

47. Benjamin, "Concept of History," 396.

48. Benjamin, "Surrealism," 237.

49. Susan Buck-Morss, *The Dialectics of Seeing Walter Benjamin and the Arcades Project* (Cambridge, MA: MIT Press, 1995), 121–123, 149–154.

50. Benjamin, *Arcades*, 463.

51. For further proof of temporality's tenacious grip on political imaginations, one only need look to the General Assembly of the French Revolution. In their reimagining of a revolutionary France, Robespierre and his comrades rejected the modern Western standard temporal reference in an attempt at a total symbolic transformation for the new nation. In place of the calendar of the *Ancien Régime*, "the Revolutionary Calendar was introduced in an age which advocated the total obliteration of the old order in the name of progress and modernity: the beginning of the new Republican Era marked the total discontinuity between past and present." Eviatar Zerubavel, "The French Republican Calendar: A Case Study in the Sociology of Time," *American Sociological Review* 42, no. 6 (1977): 871. This nationalist project, however, carried with it the zest of a righteously secular and modernist agenda that merely replaced the symbol at the center of the calendar. In the old calendar it was the birthday of Jesus that stood as the marker of the passing of time, whereas the revolutionary calendar used the birth of the republic as its symbol for commemoration. Thus the thrust of progress remained in the new temporal order. This persistence of progress leads Koselleck to state that for Robespierre, "the acceleration of time is a human task, presaging an epoch of freedom and happiness, the golden future. Both positions, insofar as the French Revolution descended from the Reformation, mark the beginning and end of our period." Koselleck, *Futures Past*, 12–13.

52. Skills for Life Improvement Programme, "Learning and Skills Improvement Service," accessed February 15, 2012, http://sflip.excellencegateway.org.uk; Hilary Metcalf et al., "Evaluation of the Impact of *Skills for Life* Learning: Longitudinal Survey of Adult Learners on College-Based Literacy and Numeracy Courses," National Institute of Economic and Social Research and BMRB Social Research, http://www.skillsforlifenetwork.com/?mod=1&dok=1592, accessed February 15, 2012. The *Skills for Life* program was introduced following the publication of the Moser Report, which found that one in five adults in the United Kingdom are "not functionally literate and far more people have problems with numeracy." Sir Claus Moser, "Fresh Start: Improving Literacy and Numeracy," A Fresh Start: Improving Literacy and Numeracy, Department for Education and Skills, http://www.lifelonglearning.co.uk/mosergroup/, 1, accessed November 10, 2011.

53. Interviews, 2009. Other studies confirm the staff's view that white middle-class and middle-aged populations are overrepresented in the British Museum audience. Research published by MORI and the Museums, Libraries, and Archives Council (MLA) based on data from 1999 to 2004 found that "the higher an individual's social class, household income and education, the more likely they are to visit museums and art galleries." MORI/MLA, "Visitors to Museums and Galleries," http://www.mla.gov.uk/documents/mori _hub_exit_survey.doc, accessed February 17, 2012,; Stuart Davies, "Still Popular: Museums and Their Visitors 1994–2004," *Cultural Trends* 14, no. 1 (2005): 96.

54. Miranda Brady claims that multiculturalism is used as a tool that visitors can identify with to mark themselves as proper citizens. She claims that at the American Museum of the American Indian (AMAI), "multiculturalism is considered a form of civility, and the successful cultural citizen [. . .] is one who effectively engages with sites that can help them signify multicultural understanding." Miranda J. Brady, "Governmentality and the National Museum of the American Indian: Understanding the Indigenous Museum in a Settler Society," *Social Identities: Journal for the Study of Race, Nation and Culture* 14, no. 6 (2008): 768.

55. Interviews, 2009. All information in this section is from interviews except where noted.

56. Benjamin, *Arcades* ; Kantorowicz, *The King's Two Bodies*; Koselleck, *Futures Past*; Martel, *Divine Violence*; Schmitt, *Political Theology*.

57. Interviews, 2009. All information in this section is from interviews except where noted.

58. Crain Soudien, "Memory and Critical Education: Approaches in the District Six Museum," in *City-Site-Museum: Reviewing Memory Practices at the District Six Museum*, ed. Bonita Bennett, Chrischené Julius, and Crain Soudien (Cape Town: District Six Museum, 2008), 120.

59. Mandy Sanger, "Education Work in the District Six Museum: Layering in New Voices and Interpretations," in *City-Site-Museum: Reviewing Memory Practices at the District Six Museum*, ed. Bonita Bennett, Chrischené Julius, and Crain Soudien, (Cape Town: District Six Museum, 2008), 102.

60. Interviews, 2009. All information in this section is from interviews except where noted.

Chapter Four

1. Thabo Mbeki, "State of the Nation Address of the President of South Africa: Joint Sitting of Parliament," South African Government Information, http://www.gov.za/node/537711, accessed October 15, 2009.

2. NOPE! is an activist group based in South Africa that launched a campaign critical of parliamentary democracy and its use as a tool to bring about change in South Africa. Touting the slogan, "Our dreams don't fit on your ballots!" the group had an active web presence with videos and pamphlets. Their choice of

language (i.e., the use of the term "being-in-common" and "manifestering" as opposed to "manifesto") suggests that members were drawing on continental philosophy, such as the work of Martin Heidegger and Jean-Luc Nancy, to articulate their concerns with the equation of democracy with voting. Mngxitama cites them in his work, claiming that although he subscribes to the ideas they promote in their "manifestering" (e.g., "Fuck Voting!"), he distances himself from the group because it has been "hijacked by a group of rich white activists." Andile Mngxitama, *Why Steve Biko Would Not Vote* (Johannesburg: New Frank Talk, 2009), 23. The group is no longer active and, as of May 2012, their website (formerly www.nope.org.za) no longer exists.

3. For one elaboration of the PAC's critique of the 1996 Constitution, see their 2009 manifesto. "Election Manifesto," Pan Africanist Congress of Azania, http://www.pac.org.za/2009-Election-Manifesto.pdf, accessed September 1, 2012.

4. Mngxitama, *Why Steve Biko*, 17.

5. Tshepo Madlingozi, "Good Victim, Bad Victim: Apartheid's Beneficiaries, Victims and the Struggle for Social Justice," in *Law, Memory, and the Legacy of Apartheid: Ten Years After AZAPO v. President of South Africa*, ed. Wessel le Roux and Karin van Marle (Pretoria: Pretoria University Law Press, 2007), 124.

6. *Soobramoney v. Minister of Health, KwaZulu-Natal*, CCT32 ZACC, 17 (1997).

7. *Soobramoney*, 28, 31. Section 27(2) of the Constitution of the Republic of South Africa, § 27, cl. 2, states that "the state must take reasonable legislative and other measures, *within its available resources*, to achieve the progressive realization of each of these rights"; emphasis mine.

8. Lourens du Plessis, "The South African Constitution as Memory and Promise," *Stellenbosch Law Review* 3 (2000): 391.

9. Mngxitama, *Why Steve Biko*, 22.

10. Patrick Bond, "South African Development Goals Will Not Be Met," *ZSpace Commentaries*, September 29, 2010, http://www.zcommunications.org/south-african-development-goals-will-not-be-met-by-patrick-bond; Patrick Bond, *Elite Transition: From Apartheid to Neoliberalism in South Africa* (Johannesburg: Wits University Press, 2000); Patrick Bond, "Pretoria's Last Gasp Strategy: South Africa Loses its War on Poverty," *CounterPunch*, August 25, 2010, http://www.counterpunch.org/bond08052010.html. McDonald and Pape argue that the dilemma has arisen largely out of the infrastructure boom that immediately followed the end of apartheid that was then too expensive for the government to maintain without resorting to neoliberal cost-recovery mechanisms. As a result, much of the service infrastructure that was implemented in the second half of the 1990s is now out of service due to lack of maintenance or vandalism. David A. McDonald and John Pape, "Introduction," in *Cost Recovery and the Crisis of Service Delivery in South Africa*, ed. David A. McDonald and John Pape (London: Zed Books, 2002), 4; Peter Wellman, "Sustainability of South Africa's Water Miracle Questioned," *African Eye News Service*, May 9, 1999, www.thewaterpage.com/SAWSProblems.html. For further elaboration on the problems of cost-recovery in contemporary South Africa see Patrick Bond, *Talk Left,*

Walk Right: South Africa's Frustrated Global Reforms (Scottsville, SA: University of Kwazulu-Natal Press, 2006); Grace Khunou, "'Massive Cutoffs': Cost Recovery and Electricity Service in Diepkloof, Soweto," in *Cost Recovery and the Crisis of Service Delivery in South Africa,* ed. David A. McDonald and John Pape (London: Zed Books, 2002), 61–80; David McDonald, "The Theory and Practice of Cost Recovery in South Africa," in *Cost Recovery and the Crisis of Service Delivery in South Africa,* ed. David A. McDonald and John Pape (London: Zed Books, 2002), 17–40; and Mthetho Xali, "'They Are Killing Us Alive': A Case Study of the Impact of Cost Recovery on Service Provision in Makhaza Section, Khayelitsha," in *Cost Recovery and the Crisis of Service Delivery in South Africa,* ed. David A. McDonald and John Pape (London: Zed Books, 2002).

11. Mngxitama, *Why Steve Biko,* 22. See also Dennis Brutus, "Preface," in *Cost Recovery and the Crisis of Service Delivery in South Africa,* ed. David A. McDonald and John Pape (London: Zed Books, 2002), vii.

12. du Plessis, "The South African Constitution"; Wessel le Roux, "War Memorials, the Architecture of the Constitutional Court Building and Counter-monumental Constitutionalism," in *Law, Memory, and the Legacy of Apartheid: Ten Years After AZAPO v. President of South Africa,* ed. Wessel le Roux and Karin van Marle (Pretoria: Pretoria University Law Press, 2007); Johannes Snyman, "Interpretation and the Politics of Memory," *Acta Juridica* (1998): 312–337; Karin van Marle, "Law's Time, Particularity and Slowness," in *Law, Memory, and the Legacy of Apartheid: Ten Years After AZAPO v. President of South Africa,* ed. Wessel le Roux and Karin van Marle (Pretoria: Pretoria University Law Press, 2007), 11–32; Karin van Marle, "The Spectacle of Post-Apartheid Constitutionalism," *Griffith Law Review* 16, no. 2 (2007): 411–429.

13. Karl Klare, "Legal Culture and Transformative Constitutionalism," *South African Journal on Human Rights* 14 (1998): 151.

14. du Plessis, "The South African Constitution," 390. Ultimately, however, he argues that it was exactly monumentalization that covered up the urgent need to think through the complexities of capital punishment and democracy. Although the death penalty was declared unconstitutional, large portions of the population remain sympathetic to it. Du Plessis suggests that the court too easily used the Constitution as a monument to "consign the death penalty to oblivion" and contemplates whether a constitutional "memorialism" could have better highlighted the historical political abuse of capital punishment by the state during apartheid, as a reminder to the nation of its mythical associations with justice. du Plessis, "The South African Constitution," 391.

15. Drucilla Cornell and Karin van Marle, "Exploring *Ubuntu*: Tentative Reflections," *African Human Rights Law Journal* 5, no. 2 (2005): 219.

16. I cited this quote from Christodoulidis in chapter 1. Emilios Christodoulidis, "Constitutional Irresolution: Law and the Framing of Civil Society," *European Law Journal* 9, no. 4 (2003): 415.

17. Hannah Arendt, *The Human Condition,* 2nd ed. (Chicago: University of Chicago Press, 1998), 245. See also Bonnie Honig, "Declarations of Independence:

Arendt and Derrida on the Problem of Founding a Republic," *American Political Science Review* 85, no. 1 (1991): 99–100.

18. Hannah Arendt, *On Revolution* (London: Penguin, 2006), 173.

19. Antonio Negri, *Insurgencies: Constituent Power and the Modern State*, trans. Maurizia Boscagli (Minneapolis: University of Minnesota Press, 1999), 8, 14. The uppercase "P" on transcendent Power (relating to *potere*) and lowercase "p" on immanent power (relating to *potenza*) is intentional. It is a technique used by Negri. Elsewhere Hardt and Negri translate the terms into Latin, using *potestas* to refer to constituted power and *potentia* to refer to constituent power. Antonio Negri, *The Savage Anomaly: The Power of Spinoza's Metaphysics and Politics*, trans. Michael Hardt (Minneapolis: University of Minnesota Press, 1991).

20. Negri, *Insurgencies*, 322.

21. Ibid., 333.

22. For more on the relationship between Arendt and Negri, see Miguel Vatter, "Legality and Resistance: Arendt and Negri on Constituent Power," in *The Philosophy of Antonio Negri: Volume Two*, ed. Timothy S. Murphy and Adbul-Karim Mutapha (London: Pluto Press, 2007), 54.

23. According to Michael Hardt, "multitude" describes "the collective social subject that is unified inasmuch as it manifests common desires through common social behavior. Through the passion and intelligence of the multitude, power is constantly engaged in inventing new social relations." Michael Hardt, "Foreword," in Antonio Negri, *The Savage Anomaly: The Power of Spinoza's Metaphysics and Politics*, trans. Michael Hardt (Minneapolis: University of Minnesota Press, 1991), xv.

24. Negri, *Insurgencies*, 18.

25. Ibid., 14.

26. Ibid., 13.

27. Ibid., 4–10.

28. Alex Callinicos and Étienne Balibar intimate that Negri's ontology resonates with vitalism. Alex Callinicos, *The Resources of Critique* (Cambridge: Polity Press, 2006), 144; Balibar, cited in Brett Neilson, "Potenza Nuda? Sovereignty, Biopolitics, Capitalism," *Contretemps* 5 (2004): 69. Alberto Toscano, however, argues that "the vitalist *thanatos* is alien to Negri's democratic Spinozist vision." Alberto Toscano, "Always Already Only Now: Negri and the Biopolitical," in *The Philosophy of Antonio Negri: Volume Two*, ed. Timothy S. Murphy and Abdul-Karim Mustapha (London: Pluto Press, 2007), 126. Using a definition of totalitarianism from Foucault, Toscano claims that Negri's work does not fetishize the category of life as an independent principle or "mystical force in its own right"; rather, it is always linked to a materialist construction of labor, bodies, and cooperation. Toscano, "Always Already Only Now," 126. Negri himself explicitly claims that his theory is not totalitarian: "[T]he constituent absolute and the democratic absolute have nothing to do with the totalitarian conception of life and politics." Negri, *Insurgencies*, 29.

29. Michael Hardt and Antonio Negri, *Empire* (Cambridge, MA: Harvard Uni-

versity Press, 2000), 358. Hardt and Negri claim that biopolitical becoming generates the world: "biopower—a horizon of the hybridization of the natural and the artificial, needs and machines, desire and the collective organization of the economic and the social—must continually regenerate itself in order to exist." Hardt and Negri, *Empire*, 389.

    30. Hardt, "Foreword," xiv.

    31. Negri, *Savage Anomaly*, 207.

    32. Negri, *Insurgencies*, 28.

    33. Ibid., 23.

    34. Ibid., 29.

    35. Ibid., 35.

    36. Ibid., 30.

    37. Christodoulidis, "Constitutional Irresolution," 429.

    38. Jean-Luc Nancy, *The Inoperative Community*, ed. Peter Connor, trans. Simona Sawhney (Minneapolis: University of Minnesota Press, 1991), 3.

    39. Negri, *Insurgencies*, 318.

    40. Ibid., 12.

    41. Christodoulidis, "Constitutional Irresolution," 426.

    42. Peter Fitzpatrick, "The Immanence of Empire," in *Empire's New Clothes: Reading Hardt and Negri,* ed. Paul A. Passavant and Jodi Dean (London: Routledge, 2004), 32.

    43. Feminist scholars such as Silvia Federici and Donatella Alessandrini have also criticized the muted particularity of Hardt and Negri's supposedly universal multitude. Silvia Federici, "Precarious Labour: A Feminist Perspective," *The Journal of Aesthetics and Protest* (2008): 1–9, http://inthemiddleofthewhirlwind.wordpress .com/precarious-labor-a-feminist-viewpoint/; Donatella Alessandrini, "Immaterial Labour and Alternative Valorisation Process in Italian Feminist Debates: (Re)Exploring the 'Commons' of Re-production," *feminists@law* 1, no. 2 (2011).

    44. Antonio Negri, "Letter to a Tunisian Friend," *Negri in English* (blog), trans. Nate Lavey, accessed February 14, 2011, http://antonionegriinenglish.wordpress. com/2011/02/14/negri-letter-to-a-tunisian-friend/.

    45. Ignaas Devisch and Kathleen Vandeputte, "Responsibility and Spatiality: Or Can Jean-Luc Nancy Sit on a Bench in Hannah Arendt's Public Space?" *Lumina* 22, no. 2 (2011): 8.

    46. Christodoulidis, "Constitutional Irresolution."

    47. In making this distinction Snyman draws on Arthur C. Danto's *The State of the Art*. Arthur C. Danto, *The State of the Art* (New York: Prentice Hall, 1987).

    48. Snyman, "Interpretation and the Politics of Memory," 317–318.

    49. Ibid., 318.

    50. Cornell and van Marle, "Exploring *Ubuntu*," 202. See also Karin van Marle, "Constitution as Archive," in *Law and the Politics of Reconciliation*, ed. Scott Veitch (Aldershot: Ashgate, 2007), 226; and le Roux, "War Memorials," 68.

    51. Snyman is not the first to use this term. For one of the earliest English articles to take up the concept of the "counter-monument," see James Young, "The

Counter-Monument: Memory against Itself in Germany Today," *Critical Inquiry* 18, no. 2 (1992): 267–296.

52. Snyman, "Interpretation and the Politics of Memory," 318.

53. Le Roux, "War Memorials," 69–70.

54. Jochen Gerz and Esther Shalev-Gerz, "Monument against Fascism, Artist's Statement," http://www.gerz.fr, accessed September 1, 2009.

55. See Pierre de Vos, "A Bridge Too Far? History As Context in the Interpretation of the South African Constitution," *South African Journal of Human Rights* 17, no. 1 (2001): 10.

56. Constitution Hill, visitor brochure (Johannesburg: 2009); Lauren Segal, Karen Martin, and Sharon Cort, *Number Four: The Making of Constitution Hill*, ed. Lauren Segal (Johannesburg: Penguin, 2006), 1, 19.

57. Constitution Hill, visitor brochure.

58. This spatialization of constitutional monumentalism resonates with André van der Walt's observation: "[T]he assumption is that apartheid is a place, a position, and that constitutional democracy is another place, a different position, the two being separated by the divide of transition from the one to the other." André van der Walt, "Dancing With Codes: Protecting, Developing and Deconstructing Property Rights in a Constitutional State," *South African Law Journal* 118 (2001): 294–295.

59. Senior staff members at the museum claim that the tours are fairly structured so that each one is "more or less the same." Interviews, 2009. As I demonstrate below, this is in contrast to the tours on offer at the District Six Museum.

60. de Vos, "A Bridge Too Far," 24.

61. Le Roux, "War Memorials," 79–80.

62. Ibid., 66.

63. Ibid., 85. Daniel Herwitz makes a similar argument about dynamic architecture of the Constitutional Court serving as a countermonument. Daniel Herwitz, "Monument, Ruin, and Redress in South African Heritage," *The Germanic Review: Literature, Culture, Theory* 86, no. 4 (2011): 241.

64. For example, researchers King and Flynn argue in their study of Constitution Hill that the site's focus on heritage is "part of legitimizing the new South Africa and especially its democratic dispensation based on the constitutional rule of law. As such, the site's redevelopment is an important example of how the state is using heritage as an overt nation-building tool." Tony King and M. K. Flynn, "Heritage and the Post-Apartheid City: Constitution Hill, Johannesburg," *International Journal of Heritage Studies* 18, no. 1 (2012): 69. They argue that this focus is beneficial because it avoids the traps of particularism. In other words, King and Flynn equate the rule of law with universality and exalt it for its ability to include "everyone" in South Africa. King and Flynn, "Heritage," 71.

65. Interviews, 2009. See also Bonita Bennett and Chrischené Julius, "Where Is District Six? Between Landscape, Site and Museum," in *City-Site-Museum: Reviewing Memory Practices at the District Six Museum*, ed. Bonita Bennett, Chrischené Julius, and Crain Soudien (Cape Town: District Six Museum, 2008), 53.

66. Crain Soudien, "Memory in the Re-making of Cape Town," in *City-Site-Museum: Reviewing Memory Practices at the District Six Museum*, ed. Bonita Bennett, Chrischené Julius, and Crain Soudien (Cape Town: District Six Museum, 2008), 29.

67. Staff members emphasize the lasting effects of apartheid-inspired conceptions of race in South Africa. They claim that "'whiteness,' 'blackness,' 'colouredness,' or 'Indianness' was rigidly and racially policed and so reproduced [. . .] Short as this period was, 'community' and the boundaries drawn around it came to be accessible virtually only through the discourse of race." Soudien, "Memory in the Remaking," 22. Sociologist Deborah Posel similarly argues that apartheid notions of race continue to animate the South African social, political, and economic landscape. She claims that "after decades of apartheid's racial reasoning, the idea that South African society comprises four distinct races—'whites,' 'Coloureds,' 'Indians,' and 'Africans'—has become a habit of thought and experience, a facet of popular 'common sense' still widely in evidence." Deborah Posel, "What's In a Name: Racial Categorisations Under Apartheid and Their Afterlife," *Transformation* 47 (2001): 52. See also Deborah Posel, "Race As Common Sense: Racial Classification in Twentieth-Century South Africa," *African Studies Review* 44, no. 2 (2001): 87–113; Sarah Nuttal, "Subjectivities of Whiteness," *African Studies Review* 44, no. 2 (2001): 115–140; and Achille Mbembe, "Ways of Seeing: Beyond the New Nativism," *African Studies Review* 44, no. 2 (2001): 1–14.

68. Soudien, "Memory in the Re-making of Cape Town," 28.

69. Mandy Sanger, "Education Work in the District Six Museum: Layering in New Voices and Interpretations," in *Cite-Site-Museum: Reviewing Memory Practices at the District Six Museum*, ed. Bonita Bennett, Chrischené Julius, and Crain Soudien (Cape Town: District Six Museum, 2008), 102.

70. The identity of those found in the mass grave continues to be in dispute. Soudien, "Memory in the Re-making of Cape Town," 26; Michael Weeder, "Topographies of the Forgotten: Prestwich and Cape Town's Nineteenth Century Cemeteries," in *City-Site-Museum: Reviewing Memory Practices at the District Six Museum*, ed. Bonita Bennett, Chrischené Julius, and Crain Soudien (Cape Town: District Six Museum, 2008), 32–37. Due to the high density of bodies in a small, unmarked space, however, it is thought that they are either the remains of former slaves and paupers or victims of an epidemic such as smallpox. Weeder, "Topographies of the Forgotten," 35.

71. Soudien, "Memory in the Re-making of Cape Town," 26; Weeder, "Topographies of the Forgotten," 32.

72. Soudien, "Memory in the Re-making of Cape Town," 26.

73. Sanger, "Education Work," 107.

74. Nazir Carrim, *Exploring Human Rights Education: Framework, Approaches, and Techniques* (Cape Town: British Council of South Africa, 2006), 52.

75. Soudien, "Meemory in the Re-making of Cape Town," 23.

76. Ibid.

77. Interviews, 2009.

78. Madlingozi, "Good Victim, Bad Victim," 112. Mahmood Mamdani also emphasizes the importance of recognizing the role of the beneficiaries of apartheid (i.e., rather than only the victims). Mahmood Mamdani, *Citizen and Subject* (Princeton, NJ: Princeton University Press, 1996); Mahmood Mamdani, "When Does Reconciliation Turn Into a Denial of Justice? *Sam Molutshungu Memorial Lectures, Volume 1* (Pretoria: Human Sciences Research Council Publishers, 1998).

79. Bonita Bennett, "Introduction," in *City-Site-Museum: Reviewing Memory Practices at the District Six Museum*, ed. Bonita Bennett, Chrischené Julius, and Crain Soudien (Cape Town: District Six Museum, 2008), 2; Soudien, "Memory in the Re-making of Cape Town," 18.

80. Soudien, "Memory in the Re-making of Cape Town," 24.

Chapter Five

1. Crain Soudien, "Memory and Critical Education: Approaches in the District Six Museum," in *City-Site-Museum: Reviewing Memory Practices at the District Six Museum*, ed. Bonita Bennett, Chrischené Julius, and Crain Soudien (Cape Town: District Six Museum, 2008), 24.

2. Jean-Luc Nancy, *The Inoperative Community*, ed. Peter Connor, trans. Simona Sawhney (Minneapolis: University of Minnesota Press, 1991), 63.

3. Jean-Luc Nancy, *The Sense of the World*, trans. Jeffrey S. Librett (Minneapolis: University of Minnesota Press, 1997), 117.

4. Johan van der Walt, *Law and Sacrifice: Towards a Post-Apartheid Theory of Law* (London: Birkbeck Law Press, 2005), 11.

5. Ibid., 8.

6. Ibid., 7. Heidegger uses the concept of *lēthe* to refer to "the concealment of Being which gives rise to the illusion that there is no such thing as Being." Martin Heidegger, *Nietzsche: Volumes One and Two*, trans. David Farrell Krell (San Francisco: Harper Collins, 1991), 194. I do not pursue a close reading of Heidegger's concept here but, rather, take van der Walt's definition of it. For more on the concept of *lēthe* in relation to law, see Emilios Christodoulidis and Scott Veitch, "Introduction," in *Lethe's Law: Justice, Law, and the Ethics of Reconciliation*, ed. Emilios Christodoulidis and Scott Veitch (Oxford: Hart Publishing, 2001), and Thanos Zartaloudis, "Without Negative Origins and Absolute Ends: A Jurisprudence of the Singular," *Law and Critique* 13 (2002): 197–230.

7. van der Walt, *Law and Sacrifice*, 7.

8. Ibid., 15. Van der Walt is careful to point out that his theory is not one that returns the lost plurality. He argues that this can never be done. But what can be salvaged is a *trace of the potential of plurality*, or the ruins of the lost plurality. He claims that "the alongside will never capture or salvage plurality from its retreat, from the destruction of plurality that takes place with every judicial decision. It will simply open up a space within the judicial decision for an oblique or crossed-out plurality, a space that will be marked by the ruins of the plurality destroyed by the decision." Ibid., 17.

9. Ibid., 15. Frank Michelman launches a critique of van der Walt for an article he wrote with Henk Botha. Frank I. Michelman, "Postmodernism, Proceduralism, and Constitutional Justice: A Comment on van der Walt and Botha," *Constellations* 9, no. 2 (2002): 246–262; Johan van der Walt and Henk Botha, "Democracy and Rights in South Africa: Beyond a Constitutional Culture of Justification," *Constellations* 7, no. 3 (2000): 341–362. In his critique, Michelman claims that he does not see how van der Walt and Botha's theory—one of recognizing the sacrificial logic of every legal decision—differs from political liberals' theories. He likens their approach to Rawls's. He argues that Rawls "takes his stand on the perception that the possibility of political justification, in modern pluralist conditions, among participants reciprocally recognized as free and equal, depends on everyone's acceptance of a commitment to give reasons for their constitutional interpretations—their human rights interpretations—that they in all sincerity believe can be found reasonable by reasonable and rational, free and equal others." Michelman, "Postmodernism, Proceduralism," 259–260. Van der Walt responds to this critique seven years later in a piece in the same journal by claiming "we never claimed to share with political liberals their definition of justice. Nothing therefore prohibited us from endorsing the typical liberal concern with justification in public discourse, but nevertheless refusing to accept that such justification constitutes justice." Johan van der Walt, "Rawls and Derrida on the Historicity of Constitutional Democracy and International Justice," *Constellations* 16, no. 1 (2009): 25.

10. van der Walt, *Law and Sacrifice*, 73–74.

11. Ibid., 74.

12. Ibid., 49.

13. Ibid., 49.

14. Ibid., 52. Although van der Walt is trying to retrieve a small part of this moment—the oath of allegiance—it is crucial to note the dangers of a romantic memory of the values of the French Revolution that glosses over its myriad hierarchies and exclusions and that mythologizes it as a smooth, lateral space of universality. This mythological instantiation fails to recognize the inherent values of rationality and self-sufficiency that animated the revolutionary moment, not to mention its contemporary republican incarnations. These inherent values, far from instituting a program of universal emancipation, continued to act as the justification for the exclusion of members who did not accord to the standards of civility set out. As Gary Wilder states in his book on French colonialism, "the republican order thus created categories of persons such as minors, domestic servants, the indigent and propertyless [*sic*], women and (former) slaves. The point is that new forms of inequality were enabled and entwined with republican principles; they expressed rather than violated the new political universalism." Gary Wilder, *The French Imperial Nation-State: Negritude and Colonial Humanism Between the Wars* (Chicago: University of Chicago Press, 2005), 16.

15. van der Walt, *Law and Sacrifice*, 17.

16. Ibid., 196; emphasis mine.

17. Ibid., 245.

18. Ibid., 246.

19. Ibid., 245.

20. Jean-Luc Nancy, *The Experience of Freedom*, trans. Bridget McDonald (Stanford, CA: Stanford University Press, 2003), 75. For more on Nancy's thinking of sacrifice, see Nancy, *Inoperative Community*, 17; Jean-Luc Nancy, "The Unsacrificeable," trans. Richard Livingston, *Yale French Studies* no. 17 (1991): 55–77; and Miguel de Beistegui, "Sacrifice Revisited," in *On Jean-Luc Nancy: The Sense of Philosophy*, ed. Darren Sheppard, Simon Sparks, and Colin Thomas (London: Routledge, 1997).

21. van der Walt claims that he is not a liberal (van der Walt, "Historicity of Constitutional Democracy," 25) nor a republican (Johan van der Walt, "Piracy, Property and Plurality: Re-Reading the Foundations of Modern Law," *Tydskrif vir die Suid-Afrikaanse reg (TSAR)/ Journal for South African Law* 3 (2001): 524), nor is he a "naïve revolutionary or an anarchist" (van der Walt, "Piracy, Property and Plurality," 525). Although he is critical of the law, he is not arguing for a wholesale change of the legal system and, according to him, "may even be said to endorse [the] criminality of the law." Ibid., 525. He claims he is a reformist who desires a more "completely egalitarian global society" but that he does not think such change will come about through a "wholesale or immediate redistribution of wealth." Ibid., 525.

22. van der Walt, *Law and Sacrifice*, 111.

23. Ibid.

24. Stewart Motha, "Archiving Colonial Sovereignty: From Ubuntu to a Jurisprudence of Sacrifice," *SA Publiekreg/ Public Law* 24 (2009): 320.

25. Mogobe B. Ramose, "In Memoriam: Sovereignty and the New South Africa," *Griffith Law Review* 16, no. 2 (2007): 318.

26. Mogobe B. Ramose, "Learning Inspired Education," *Caribbean Journal of Philosophy* 2, no. 1 (2010): 7.

27. van der Walt, "Piracy, Property and Plurality," 545–546. Van der Walt criticizes Dworkin's approach because, he argues, Dworkin's constitutional review demands ultimate consensus. Moreover, this consensus is based on values already determined by the community as "proper." Van der Walt argues that Dworkin's theory therefore results in the necessary disciplining and assimilation of difference and the subsequent loss of plurality. See also van der Walt, *Law and Sacrifice*, 141.

28. Motha, "Archiving Colonial Sovereignty," 314, 317.

29. Ibid., 317.

30. Drucilla Cornell and Nyoko Muvangua, eds., *uBuntu and the Law: African Ideals and Postapartheid Jurisprudence* (New York: Fordham University Press, 2011), 6. While I use lowercase italics when spelling "*ubuntu*," Cornell and Muvangua do not italicize it and use an uppercase "B" in their spelling. When quoting them, I keep the term as it appears in their text.

31. Ibid., 2–3.

32. Ibid., 6. These claims to humanism are surprising coming from Cornell, as she speaks dismissively of it in some of her other work by, for example, referring to it as "naïve." Drucilla Cornell, *Moral Images of Freedom: A Future for Critical Theory* (New York: Rowman & Littlefield, 2008), 76. Yet the appeal to the "humane" appears multiple times in the 2011 text.

33. Drucilla Cornell, "uBuntu, Plurality and the Responsibility of Legal Academics in the New South Africa," *Law and Critique* 20, no. 1 (2009): 57.

34. Wendy Brown claims that "Cornell's critical yet ultimately utopian rapprochements with rights discourse . . . is a tacit confession [. . .] of the historical limits of our political imagination." For Brown, endorsements of the potential of liberal rights fail to recognize the deeply complicated and contradictory outcome of appealing to this discourse. Wendy Brown, "Suffering the Paradoxes of Rights" in *Left Legalism/Left Critique*, ed. Wendy Brown and Janet Halley (Durham, NC: Duke University Press, 2002), 421.

35. Cornell and Muvangua, *ubuntu and the Law*, 10.

36. Ibid., 8, 10, 11, 13, 25.

37. Ibid., 27.

38. Mogobe Ramose, "An African Perspective on Justice and Race," *Polylog: Forum for Intercultural Philosophy* 3 (2001): 14. See also J. M. Rantete, *The African National Congress and the Negotiated Settlement in South Africa* (Pretoria: J. L. van Schaik, 1998): xv–xix.

39. Ramose, "African Perspective," 18. For another articulation of this argument see Alfred Cockrell, "The South African Bill of Rights and the 'Duck/Rabbit,'" *Modern Law Review* 60, no. 4 (1997): 513–537.

40. Mogobe B. Ramose, *African Philosophy Through Ubuntu* (Harare: Mond Books, 1999), 80. Although both Nancy and Ramose contest the atomization of the individual, it is crucial to note that, ultimately, their theories do not align. Where Nancy meticulously challenges the channeling of being-in-common into a stable figure, Ramose's conception of *ubuntu* rests on an assuredness about reality as an "indivisible wholeness." Ibid., 50–57, 103, 106. Ramose posits being as one-ness, whereas Nancy's thought speaks to the incessant sharing, infinite exposure, and trembling contours of singularities. Ramose, *African Philosophy Through Ubuntu*, 50; Jean-Luc Nancy, *Being Singular Plural*, ed. Werner Hamacher and David E. Wellbery, trans. Robert D. Richardson and Annie E. O'Byrne (Stanford, CA: Stanford University Press, 2000), 186.

41. Ramose, *African Philosophy Through Ubuntu*, 144.

42. The only mention of Ramose in the book comes in a small reference in Narnia Bohler-Müller's article "Some Thoughts on the ubuntu Jurisprudence of the Constitutional Court." Narnia Bohler-Müller, "Some Thoughts on the uBuntu Jurisprudence of the Constitutional Court," in *Ubuntu and the Law: African Ideals and Postapartheid Jurisprudence*, ed. Drucilla Cornell and Nyoko Muvangua (New York: Fordham University Press, 2011), 372. Cornell and van Marle, however, do take up Valentin Yves Mudimbe's concept of "*gnosis*" to interrogate how colonial-

ism has shaped who "has been given the right and credentials to write, describe, and produce opinions of what is African philosophy." Drucilla Cornell and Karin van Marle, "Exploring *Ubuntu:* Tentative Reflections," in *Ubuntu and the Law: African Ideals and Postapartheid Jurisprudence,* ed. Drucilla Cornell and Nyoko Muvangua (New York: Fordham University Press, 2011), 345–346. In this way, Mudimbe's *"gnosis"* resonates with Ramose's concept of "epistemicide" and the urgent task of confronting the continuing colonization of African philosophy.

43. Cornell and Muvangua draw on Gyekye after he is cited by Justice Langa in *MEC for Education: Kwazulu-Natal and Others v. Pillay,* CCT 51/06 21 (2007): 53. A longer look at Gyekye's philosophy, however, demonstrates a commitment to a stable notion of the individual that resonates with a traditional liberal approach. He endorses what he calls "moderate communitarianism" that postulates that the individual is partly (not entirely) defined by the community. Kwame Gyekye, *Tradition and Modernity* (New York: Oxford University Press, 1997), 52–53; Bernard Matolino, "Radicals versus Moderates: A Critique of Gyekye's Moderate Communitarianism," *South African Journal of Philosophy* 28, no. 2 (2009): 168. J. O. Famakinwa argues that "in Gyekye's view, moderate communitarianism will not oppose the doctrine of individual rights for the reason that the individual and the community, while closely interacting, must maintain their unique spheres." J. O. Famakinwa, "How Moderate Is Kwama Gyekye's Moderate Communitarianism?" *Thought and Practice: A Journal of the Philosophical Association of Kenya* 2, no. 2 (2010): 68.

44. It is not surprising that given Cornell's proclivities to Kantian ethics she is compelled by Wiredu's concept. Wiredu himself likens his approach to the categorical imperative, claiming that the two elements of his concept of "sympathetic impartiality"—"sympathy" and "impartiality"—reflect Kant's moral framework: "[I]t is one thing to act in accordance with a moral rule and quite another to act out of respect for it [. . .] only the latter has moral worth." Kwasi Wiredu, *Cultural Universals and Particulars: An African Perspective* (Bloomington: Indiana University Press, 1996), 31. Moreover, Wiredu's conception of personhood is based on an ability to act freely (and morally). In fact, for Wiredu, personhood is *gained* by an ability to demonstrate this morally motivated free will. Ibid., 6; Kwasi Wiredu, "An Oral Philosophy of Personhood," *Research in African Literatures* 40, no. 1 (2009): 15–16. But Wiredu does articulate a critique of existing political structures, an element not touched upon by Cornell and Muvangua. Wiredu acknowledges the difficulties of overcoming a "conceptually colonized mentality" for the future of African philosophy and politics, and he advocates the composition of a nonparty representative system based on consensus (as opposed to what he calls the European-inspired multiparty system). Kwasi Wiredu, "Democracy and Consensus in African Traditional Politics," *Polylog: Forum for Intercultural Philosophy* 2 (2000); Ademola Kazeem Fayemi, "A Critique of Consensual Democracy and Human Rights in Wiredu's Philosophy," *Lumina* 12, no. 1 (2010): 1–13.

45. Cornell and Muvangua, *uBuntu and the Law*, 6.

46. Drucilla Cornell, *The Imaginary Domain: Abortion, Pornography and Sexual Harassment* (New York: Routledge, 1995), 42.

47. Ibid., 10. Her theory rests on a central commitment to the necessary individuation of women from their constructed dependency on men and entails three conditions: "1) bodily integrity, 2) access to symbolic forms sufficient to achieve linguistic skills permitting the differentiation of oneself from others, and 3) the protection of the imaginary domain itself." Ibid., 4. This notion of equality does not "begin with an end to gender inequality, but instead with the *realization* of that freedom [of individuals to represent their own sexuate being]." Drucilla Cornell, *At the Heart of Freedom: Feminism, Sex, and Equality* (Princeton, NJ: Princeton University Press, 1998), 91. Importantly, Cornell does not see "man" and "woman" as distinct, biologically defined categories but rather as categories predicated on an *assumed* sexual difference. Cornell, *Imaginary Domain*, 4, 232.

48. Cornell, *Imaginary Domain*, 40, 232.

49. Ibid., 43.

50. Cornell, *Moral Images*, 12–13; Drucilla Cornell, "Revisiting *Beyond Accommodation* After Twenty Years." *feminists@law* 1, no. 1 (2011): 1–13. http://journals. kent.ac.uk/index.php/feministsatlaw/article /view/13/40, 3; emphasis mine. The imaginary domain is the place where we can orient "ourselves to our sexuate being." Cornell, *Heart of Freedom*, 8. Sexuate being refers to the fact that "we are all sexual creatures, [and that] there are as many different possible forms to our sexuate being as there are people. Once this basic insight into our sexuate being is grasped, our claim to our person has to include our right to be legally and politically recognized as the legitimate source of meaning and representation of our existence as corporal, sexuate beings [. . . .] This place of free exploration and sexual representations, and personas, is the imaginary domain." Ibid., 8.

51. Cornell, "Revisiting *Beyond Accommodation*," 6.

52. Drucilla Cornell, "Rethinking Legal Ideals After Deconstruction" in *Law's Madness*, ed. Austin Sarat, Lawrence Douglas, and Martha Merrill Umphrey (Ann Arbor: University of Michigan Press, 2003), 149.

53. Cornell, *Moral Images*, 6.

54. See also Adam Thurschwell, "Radical Feminist Liberalism," in *Imagining Law: On Drucilla Cornell*, ed. Renée Heberle and Benjamin Pryor (Albany: State University of New York Press, 2008), 40.

55. Cornell, *Moral Images*, 32.

56. This assertion of law's function surfaces long-standing debates among feminist critics about the potential of law to attend to these (even when qualified) aspirations for justice. See Brown, "Suffering the Paradoxes of Rights"; Davina Cooper, *Challenging Diversity: Rethinking Equality and the Value of Difference* (Cambridge: Cambridge University Press, 2004); and Vanessa Munro and Carl F. Stychin, eds., *Sexuality and the Law: Feminist Engagements* (New York: Routledge, 2007).

57. Cornell, *Moral Images*, 35.

58. Cornell, *Imaginary Domain*, 40.

59. Nancy, *Being Singular Plural*, 31.

60. Ibid., 30.

61. The divide between Heidegger and Cornell is related to the debates between Heidegger himself and Ernst Cassirer (a neo-Kantian). Indeed, Cornell follows Cassirer in her emphasis on the importance of the symbolic order: "[T]here is no human experience outside our symbolic systems." Cornell, *Moral Images*, 81. She claims that "Heidegger's philosophy cannot yield the respect for the plurality of symbolic forms that is at the very heart of Cassirer's philosophy." Ibid., 99. The primary difference between Cassirer and Nancy is where the former claims that "there is nothing outside of the word," Ibid., 86; the latter claims that there is nothing outside of the *world*. Nancy, *Sense of the World*, 56. For more on the debate between Heidegger and Cassirer, see Martin Heidegger, "The Davos Disputation Between Ernst Cassirer and Martin Heidegger," in *Kant and the Problem of Metaphysics*, 5th ed., trans. Richard Taft (Indianapolis: Indiana University Press, 1997).

62. Nancy and Lacouthe-Labarthe devote an entire book to a critique of Lacanian psychoanalysis in 1973 (translated to English in 1992). The main thrust of this critique is what they identify as a paradoxical presence and absence of the subject. They claim that according to Lacan the subject is *impossible* "but the signifying order is not *possible* without it." Jean-Luc Nancy and Phillipe Lacoue-Labarthe, *The Title of the Letter: A Reading of Lacan*, trans. François Raffoul and David Pettigrew (Albany: State University of New York Press, 1992), 116; emphasis theirs. See also François Raffoul and David Pettigrew, "Translator's Preface," in *The Title of the Letter: A Reading of Lacan*, trans. François Raffoul and David Pettigrew (Albany: State University of New York Press, 1992), xvii.

63. Nancy, *Sense of the World*, 48.

64. Nancy, *Sense of the World*, 118.

65. Ignaas Devisch and Kathleen Vandeputte, "Sense, Existence and Justice, or, How to Live in a Secular World?" *Synthesis Philosophica* 25, no. 1 (2010), 158.

66. Nancy, *Inoperative Community*, 81.

Bibliography

Abt, Jeffrey. "The Origins of the Public Museum." In *A Companion to Museum Studies*, edited by Sharon MacDonald, 115–134. Oxford: Blackwell, 2006.

Ackerman, Bruce. "Constitutional Politics/Constitutional Law." *Yale Law Journal* 99, no. 3 (1989): 453–547.

Agamben, Giorgio. *The Coming Community*. Translated by Michael Hardt. Minneapolis: University of Minnesota Press, 2003.

Agamben, Giorgio. *Homo Sacer: Sovereign Power and Bare Life*. Translated by Daniel Heller-Roazen. Stanford, CA: Stanford University Press, 1998.

Agamben, Giorgio. *Potentialities: Collected Essays in Philosophy*. Translated and edited by Daniel Heller-Roazen. Stanford, CA: Stanford University Press, 1999.

Agamben, Giorgio. *The State of Exception*. Translated by Kevin Attell. Chicago: University of Chicago Press, 2005.

Agamben, Giorgio. *The Time That Remains: A Commentary on the Letter to the Romans*. Translated by Patricia Dailey. Stanford, CA: Stanford University Press, 2005.

Ahmed, Sara. *Strange Encounters: Embodied Others in Post-Coloniality*. London: Routledge, 2000.

Aldrich, Robert. "Colonial Museums in a Postcolonial Europe." *African and Black Diaspora: An International Journal* 2, no. 2 (2009): 137–156.

Alessandrini, Donatella. "Immaterial Labour and Alternative Valorisation Processes in Italian Feminist Debates: (Re)Exploring the 'Commons' of Reproduction." *feminists@law* 1, no. 2 (2011).

Alfred, Taiaiake, "Sovereignty." In *A Companion to American Indian History*, edited by Philip J. Deloria and Neal Salisbury, 460–474. Oxford: Blackwell, 2002.

Althusser, Louis. "Ideology and Ideological State Apparatuses." In *Lenin and Philosophy and Other Essays*, translated by Ben Brewster, 127–188. London: Monthly Review Press, 1971.

Andermann, Jens. "Returning to the Site of Horror: On the Reclaiming of Clandestine Concentration Camps in Argentina." *Theory, Culture and Society* 29, no. 1 (2010): 76–98.

Andermann, Jens, and Silke Arnold-de Simine. "Memory, Community and the New Museum." *Theory, Culture & Society* 29, no. 1 (2012): 3–13.

Anderson, Benedict. *Imagined Communities: Reflections on the Origin and Spread of Nationalism.* New Edition. London: Verso, 2006.

Anderson, Gail. *Reinventing the Museum: Historical and Contemporary Perspectives on the Paradigm Shift.* Oxford: Altamira Press, 2004.

Anderson, Gavin. *Human Rights After Globalisation.* Oxford: Hart, 2005.

Andrews, Molly, Shelley Day Sclater, Michael Rustin, Corinne Squire, and Amal Treacher. "Introduction." In *The Uses of Narrative: Explorations in Sociology, Psychology, and Cultural Studies,* edited by Molly Andrews, Shelley Day Sclater, Michael Rustin, Corinne Squire, and Amal Treacher, 1–10. New York: Routledge, 2000.

Anghie, Anthony. *Imperialism, Sovereignty and the Making of International Law.* Cambridge: Cambridge University Press, 2005.

Antaki, Mark. "The Book and the Bridge: Metaphors for Transformative Constitutionalism." Unpublished paper, 2011.

Apartheid Museum. "A Place of Healing," http://www.apartheidmuseum.org/place-healing, accessed November 17, 2011.

Arditi, Benjamin. "Politics, Publicness and Difference." PhD diss., University of Essex, 1995.

Arendt, Hannah. *Between Past and Future: Six Exercises in Political Thought.* New York: Viking Press, 1961.

Arendt, Hannah. *The Human Condition.* 2nd edition. Chicago: University of Chicago Press, 1998.

Arendt, Hannah. *The Life of the Mind: Volume One: Thinking.* Edited by Mary McCarthy. London: Secker and Warburg, 1978. Arendt, Hannah. *On Revolution.* London: Penguin, 2006.

Arendt, Hannah. *The Origins of Totalitarianism.* Orlando, FL: Harcourt, 1973.

Arnold, Ken. "Presenting Science as Product or as Process: Museums and the Making of Science," In *Exploring Science in Museums,* edited by Susan Pearce. London: Athlone Press, 1996.

Asad, Talal. *Formations of the Secular: Christianity, Islam, Modernity.* Stanford, CA: Stanford University Press, 2003.

Ashworth, William B. Jr. "Natural History and the Emblematic World View." In *Grasping the World: The Idea of the Museum,* edited by Donald Preziosi and Claire Farago, 144–158. Aldershot: Ashgate, 2004.

Atwood, Margaret. "A Night in the Royal Ontario Museum." In *The Animals in That Country,* 20–22. New York: Little, Brown, and Company, 1969.

Badiou, Alain. *Metapolitics.* Translated by Jason Barker. London: Verso, 2005.

Bal, Mieke. "Exposing the Public." In *A Companion to Museum Studies,* edited by Sharon MacDonald, 525–542. Oxford: Blackwell, 2006.

Balakrishnan, Gopal. *The Enemy: An Intellectual Portrait of Carl Schmitt.* London: Verso, 2000.

Bamford, Helen. "Cracks Appear in District Six Dream." *Cape Argus,* February 20,

2011. http://www.iol.co.za/news/south-africa/western-cape/cracks-appear-in-district-six-dream-1.1029272.

Barbour, Charles. "Sovereign Times: Acts of Creation." *Law, Culture, and the Humanities* 6, no. 2 (2010): 142–152.

Barker, Jason. Translator's introduction to Alain Badou, *Metapolitics*, vii–xxx. Translated by Jason Barker. London: Verso, 2005.

Barringer, Tim, and Tom Flynn, eds. *Colonialism and the Object: Empire, Material Culture, and the Museum*. London: Routledge, 1998.

Barry, Andrew. "On Interactivity: Consumers, Citizens, and Culture." In *The Politics of Display*, edited by Sharon MacDonald, 98–117. London: Routledge, 1998.

Barshack, Lior. "The Constituent Power of Architecture." *Law, Culture, and the Humanities* 7, no. 2 (2010): 217–243.

Barshack, Lior. "Time and the Constitution." *International Journal of Constitutional Law* 7, no. 4 (2009): 553–576.

Bataille, Georges. *Inner Experience*. Translated by Leslie Anne Boldt. Albany: State University of New York Press, 1988.

Battiste, Marie, and James (Sa'ke'j) Youngblood Henderson. *Protecting Indigenous Knowledge and Heritage: A Global Challenge*. Saskatoon: Purich, 2000.

Beistegui, Miguel de. "Sacrifice Revisited." In *On Jean-Luc Nancy: The Sense of Philosophy*, edited by Darren Sheppard, Simon Sparks, and Colin Thomas, 157–173. London: Routledge, 1997.

Bendersky, Joseph. *Carl Schmitt: Theorist for the Reich*. Princeton, NJ: Princeton University Press, 1983.

Benjamin, Walter. *The Arcades Project*. Translated by Howard Eiland and Kevin McLoughlin. London: Belknap Press, 1999.

Benjamin, Walter. "Eduard Fuchs: Collector and Historian." In *The Essential Frankfurt School Reader*, edited by Andrew Arato and Eike Gebhardt, 225–253. New York: Urizen Books, 1978.

Benjamin, Walter. "On the Concept of History." In *Walter Benjamin Selected Writings, Volume Four, 1938–1940*, edited by Howard Eiland and Michael Jennings, translated by Edmund Jephcott, Howard Eiland, and others, 389–400. Cambridge, MA: Harvard University Press, 2002.

Benjamin, Walter. "On the Critique of Violence." In *One-Way Street and Other Writings*, translated by J. A. Underwood, 1–28. London: Penguin, 2009.

Benjamin, Walter. *The Origin of German Tragic Drama*. Translated by John Osborne. New York: Verso, 1998.

Benjamin, Walter. "Surrealism." In *One-Way Street and Other Writings*, translated by J. A. Underwood, 143–160. London: Penguin, 2009.

Benjamin, Walter. "Theological-Political Fragment." In *Walter Benjamin Selected Writings, Volume Three, 1935–1938*, edited by Howard Eiland and Michael Jennings, translated by Edmund Jephcott, Howard Eiland, and others, 305–306. Cambridge, MA: Harvard University Press, 2002.

Bennett, Bonita, ed. "Introduction." In *City-Site-Museum: Reviewing Memory Prac-

tices at the District Six Museum, edited by Bonita Bennett, Chrischené Julius, and Crain Soudien, 4–5. Cape Town: District Six Museum, 2008.

Bennett, Bonita, ed. *Reflections on the Conference, Hands On District Six: Landscapes of Postcolonial Memorialisation*. Cape Town: District Six Museum, 2007.

Bennett, Bonita, and Chrischené Julius. "Where Is District Six? Between Landscape, Site and Museum." In *City-Site-Museum: Reviewing Memory Practices at the District Six Museum*, edited by Bonita Bennett, Chrischené Julius, and Crain Soudien, 52–67. Cape Town: District Six Museum, 2008.

Bennett, Tony. *The Birth of the Museum: History, Theory, Politics*. London: Routledge, 1995.

Bennett, Tony. "Civic Seeing: Museums and the Organization of Vision." In *A Companion to Museum Studies*, edited by Sharon MacDonald, 263–281. Oxford: Blackwell, 2006.

Bennett, Tony. *Culture: A Reformer's Science*. London: Sage, 1998.

Benson, Robert L., Ralph E. Giesey, and Margaret B. Sevcenko. "Defending Kantorowicz: Reply to Robert Bartlett." *The New York Review of Books*, May 14, 1992. http://www.nybooks.com/articles/archives/1992/aug/13/defending-kantorowicz/?pagination=false.

Berlant, Lauren. "The Subject of True Feeling: Pain, Privacy, and Politics." In *Left Legalism/Left Critique*, edited by Wendy Brown and Janet Halley, 105–133. Durham, NC: Duke University Press, 2002.

Beyers, Christiaan. "The Contentious Politics of Integrated Urban Development in District Six." *Social Dynamics* 34, no. 1 (2008): 86–100.

Bhabha, Homi. "Freedom's Basis in the Indeterminate." *October* 61 (1992): 46–57.

Birnbaum, Antonia. "To Exist Is to Exit the Point." In *Corpus*, translated by Richard A. Rand, 145–149. New York: Fordham University Press, 2008.

Black, Graham. *The Engaging Museum: Developing Museums for Visitor Involvement*. London: Routledge, 2005.

Boast, Robin. "Neocolonial Collaboration: Museum as Contact Zone Revisited." *Museum Anthropology* 34, no. 1 (2011): 56–70.

Bohler-Müller, Narnia. "Some Thoughts on the ubuntu Jurisprudence of the Constitutional Court." In *Ubuntu and the Law: African Ideals and Postapartheid Jurisprudence*, edited by Drucilla Cornell and Nyoko Muvangua, 367–376. New York: Fordham University Press, 2011.

Bond, Patrick. *Elite Transition: From Apartheid to Neoliberalism in South Africa*. Johannesburg: Wits University Press, 2000. Bond, Patrick. "Pretoria's Last Gasp Strategy: South Africa Loses Its War on Poverty." *CounterPunch*, August 25, 2010. http://www.counterpunch .org/bond08052010.html.

Bond, Patrick. "Pretoria's Last Gasp Strategy: South Africa Loses Its War on Poverty." *CounterPunch*, August 25, 2010, http://www.counterpunch.org/bond 08052010.html.

Bond, Patrick. "South African Development Goals Will Not Be Met." *ZSpace Commentaries*, September 29, 2010. http://www.zcommunications.org/south-african development-goals-will-not-be-met-by-patrick-bond.

Bond, Patrick. *Talk Left, Walk Right: South Africa's Frustrated Global Reforms*. Scottsville, SA: University of Kwazulu-Natal Press, 2006.

Borges, Jorge Luis. *Dreamtigers*. New York: Dutton, 1970.

Borrows, John. *Recovering Canada: The Resurgence of Indigenous Law*. Toronto: University of Toronto Press, 2002.

Botha, Henk. "Constitutionalism and the Politics of Memory: A Response to Professors Rubenfeld and Snyman." *Acta Juridica* (1998): 342–347.

Bourdieu, Pierre. *Distinction: A Social Critique of the Judgement of Taste*. Translated
by Richard Nice. Oxford: Polity Press, 1987.

Brady, Miranda J. "Governmentality and the National Museum of the American Indian: Understanding the Indigenous Museum in a Settler Society." *Social Identities: Journal for the Study of Race, Nation and Culture* 14, no. 6 (2008): 763–773.

Brault, Pascale-Anne, and Michael Naas. Translator's note to Jean-Luc Nancy, *The
Truth of Democracy*, ix–xii. New York: Fordham University Press, 2010.

British Museum. "Adult Learner's Week Pre-workshop Materials." British Museum. 2009.

British Museum. "Architecture." British Museum. http://www.britishmuseum.
org/about_us/the_museums_story/architecture.aspx, accessed May 17, 2009.

British Museum. "Funding Agreement 2008–11." British Museum. . http://www.
britishmuseum.org/pdf/British_Museum_Signed_Funding_Agreement
_2008–11.pdf, accessed March 1, 2012.

British Museum. "General History." http://www.britishmuseum.org/about_us/
the_museums_story/general_history.aspx, accessed May 17, 2009.

British Empire and Commonwealth Museum. "About Us." British Empire and
Commonwealth Museum. http://www.empiremuseum .co.uk, accessed June
1, 2012.

Brown, Wendy, ed. "Freedom's Silences." In *Edgework: Critical Essays on Knowledge
and Politics*, 83–97. Princeton, NJ: Princeton University Press, 2005.

Brown, Wendy, ed. "Suffering the Paradoxes of Rights." In *Left Legalism/Left Critique*, edited by Wendy Brown and Janet Halley, 420–434. Durham, NC: Duke
University Press, 2002.

Brown, Wendy, ed. "Tolerance as Museum Object: The Simon Wiesenthal Centre
Museum of Tolerance." In *Regulating Aversion: Tolerance in the Age of Identity
and Empire*, 107–148. Princeton, NJ: Princeton University Press, 2006.

Buck-Morss, Susan. *The Dialectics of Seeing Walter Benjamin and the Arcades Project*.
Cambridge, MA: MIT Press, 1995.

Buck-Morss, Susan. *The Origin of Negative Dialectics*. New York: The Free Press,
1979.

Brutus, Dennis. "Preface." In *Cost Recovery and the Crisis of Service Delivery in South
Africa*, edited by David A. McDonald and John Pape, vii. London: Zed Books,
2002.

Butler, Judith. "Contingent Foundations: Feminism and the Question of 'Postmodernism.'" In *Feminists Theorize the Political*, edited by Judith Butler and
Joan W. Scott, 3–21. London: Routledge, 1992.

Callinicos, Alex. *The Resources of Critique*. Cambridge: Polity Press, 2006.

Campbell, Timothy. "Translator's Introduction." In *Bios: Biopolitics and Philosophy*, edited by Roberto Esposito, vii–xlii. Minneapolis: University of Minnesota, 2008.

Cantle, Ted. *Community Cohesion: A New Framework for Race and Diversity*. London: Palgrave Macmillan, 2005.

Cantor, Norman. *Inventing the Middle Ages: The Lives, Works, and Ideas of the Great Medievalists of the Twentieth Century*. New York: W. Morrow, 1991.

Carrim, Nazir. *Exploring Human Rights Education: Framework, Approaches, and Techniques*. Cape Town: British Council of South Africa, 2006.

Caulton, Tim. *Hands-On Exhibitions: Managing Interactive Museums and Science Centres*. London: Routledge, 1998.

Caygill, Howard. "The Sharing of the World: Philosophy, Violence, Freedom." In *On Jean-Luc Nancy: The Sense of Philosophy*, edited by Darren Shepard, Simon Sparks, and Colin Thomas, 19–31. London: Routledge, 1997.

Caygill, Howard. "Walter Benjamin's Concept of Cultural History." In *The Cambridge Companion to Walter Benjamin*, edited by David S. Ferris, 73–96. Cambridge University Press, 2004.

Christodoulidis, Emilios. "Against Substitution: The Constitutional Thinking of Dissensus." In *The Paradox of Constitutionalism: Constituent Power and Constitutional Form*, edited by Martin Loughlin and Neil Walker, 189–210. Oxford: Oxford University Press, 2007.

Christodoulidis, Emilios. "Constitutional Irresolution: Law and the Framing of Civil Society." *European Law Journal* 9, no. 4 (2003): 401–432.

Christodoulidis, Emilios. "Depoliticizing Poverty: Arendt in South Africa." *Stellenbosch Law Review* 22, no. 3 (2011): 501–520.

Christodoulidis, Emilios. *Law and Reflexive Politics*. London: Kluwer Academic Publishers, 1998.

Christodoulidis, Emilios. "Public Law as Political Jurisprudence: Loughlin's 'Idea of Public Law.'" In *Public Law and Politics: The Scope and Limits of Constitutionalism*, edited by Emilios Christodoulidis and Stephen Tierney, 35–46. London: Ashgate, 2008.

Christodoulidis, Emilios. "Strategies of Rupture." *Law and Critique* 20, no. 1 (2009): 3–26.

Christodoulidis, Emilios, and Ruth Dukes. "Labour, Constitution and a Sense of Measure: A Debate with Alain Supiot." *International Union Rights Journal* 18, no. 4 (2010): 20–21.

Christodoulidis, Emilios, and Stephen Tierney, eds. *Public Law and Politics: The Scope and Limits of Constitutionalism*. Hampshire: Ashgate, 2008.

Christodoulidis, Emilios, and Scott Veitch. "Introduction." In *Lethe's Law: Justice, Law, and the Ethics of Reconciliation*, edited by Emilios Christodoulidis and Scott Veitch, ix–xv. Oxford: Hart Publishing, 2001.

City of Johannesburg. "Investing in Joburg." http://www.joburg.org.za/index. php?option=com_content&task=view&id=993&Itemid=58, accessed June 2, 2012.

Clifford, James. *Routes: Travel and Translation in the Late Twentieth Century*. Cambridge, MA: Harvard University Press, 1997.

Clunas, Craig. "China in Britain: The Imperial Collection." In *Colonialism and the Object: Empire, Material Culture and the Museum*, edited by Tim Barringer and Tom Flynn, 41–51. London: Routledge, 1998.

Cockrell, Alfred. "The South African Bill of Rights and the 'Duck/Rabbit.'" *Modern Law Review* 60, no. 4 (1997): 513–537.

Cohen, Jean. "Whose Sovereignty? Empire Versus International Law." *Ethics and International Affairs* 18, no. 3 (2004): 1–24.

Comaroff, Jean, and John Comaroff. "Reflections on Liberalism, Policulturalism, and ID-ology: Citizenship and Difference in South Africa." *Social Identities: Journal for the Study of Race, Nation and Culture* 9, no. 4 (2003): 445–473.

Constitution Hill. "Tours." http://www.constitutionhill.org.za/tours/, Accessed March 10, 2012.

Constitution Hill. "Visitor Brochure." 2009.

Coombes, Annie E. *History After Apartheid: Visual Culture and Public Memory in a Democratic South Africa*. Durham, NC: Duke University Press, 2003.

Coombes, Annie E. "Museums and the Formation of National and Cultural Identities." In *Grasping the World: The Idea of the Museum*, edited by Donald Preziosi and Claire Farago, 278–297. Aldershot: Ashgate, 2004.

Cooper, Davina. *Challenging Diversity: Rethinking Equality and the Value of Difference*. Cambridge: Cambridge University Press, 2004.

Cooper, Davina. "Opening Up Ownership: Community, Belonging, Belongings, and the Productive Life of Property." *Law & Social Inquiry* 32, no. 3 (2007): 625–664.

Cornell, Drucilla. *At the Heart of Freedom: Feminism, Sex, and Equality*. Princeton, NJ: Princeton University Press, 1998.

Cornell, Drucilla. *The Imaginary Domain: Abortion, Pornography and Sexual Harassment*. New York: Routledge, 1995.

Cornell, Drucilla. *Moral Images of Freedom: A Future for Critical Theory*. New York: Rowman and Littlefield, Inc., 2008.

Cornell, Drucilla. *The Philosophy of the Limit*. London: Routledge, 1992.

Cornell, Drucilla. "Rethinking Legal Ideals After Deconstruction." In *Law's Madness*, edited by Austin Sarat, Lawrence Douglas, and Martha Merrill Umphrey, 147–168. Ann Arbor: University of Michigan Press, 2003.

Cornell, Drucilla. "Revisiting *Beyond Accommodation* After Twenty Years." *feminists@law* 1, no. 1 (2011): 1–13. http://journals.kent.ac.uk/index.php/feministsatlaw/article /view/13/40.

Cornell, Drucilla. "uBuntu, Pluralism and the Responsibility of Legal Academics in the New South Africa." *Law and Critique* 20, no. 1 (2009): 43–58.

Cornell, Drucilla and Nyoko Muvangua, eds. *uBuntu and the Law: African Ideals and Postapartheid Jurisprudence*. New York: Fordham University Press, 2011.

Cornell, Drucilla, and Karin van Marle. "Exploring *Ubuntu*: Tentative Reflections." *African Human Rights Law Journal* 5, no. 2 (2005): 195–220.

Cornell, Drucilla, and Karin van Marle. "Exploring *Ubuntu*: Tentative Reflections." In *Ubuntu and the Law: African Ideals and Postapartheid Jurisprudence*, edited by Drucilla Cornell and Nyoko Muvangua, 344–366. New York: Fordham University Press, 2011.

Coulthard, Glen. *Red Skin, White Masks: Rejecting the Colonial Politics of Recognition*. Minneapolis: University of Minnesota, 2014.

Coulthard, Glen. "Subjects of Empire: Indigenous Peoples and the 'Politics of Recognition' in Canada." *Contemporary Political Theory* 6, no. 4 (2007): 437–460.

Crimp, Douglas. *On the Museum's Ruins*. Cambridge, MA: MIT Press, 1995.

Crow, Dennis. "My Friends in Low Places: Building Identity for Place and Community." *Environment and Planning D: Society and Space* 12, no. 4 (1994): 403–419.

Curley, Edward. *The Collected Works of Spinoza: Volume 1*. Princeton, NJ: Princeton University Press, 1985.

DaCosta Kaufmann, Thomas. "Remarks on the Collection of Rudolf II: The *Kuntshammer* as a Form of *Representatio*." *The Art Journal* 38, no. 1 (1978): 22–28.

Danto, Arthur C. *The State of the Art*. New York: Prentice Hall, 1987.

Davies, Margaret. "Beyond Unity." In *Sexuality and the Law: Feminist Engagements*, edited by Vanessa Munro and Carl F. Stychin, 151–170. New York: Routledge, 2007.

Davies, Stuart. "Still Popular: Museums and Their Visitors 1994–2004." *Cultural Trends* 14, no. 1 (2005): 67–105.

Davis, Kathleen. *Periodization and Sovereignty: How Ideas of Feudalism and Secularization Govern the Politics of Time*. Philadelphia: University of Pennsylvania Press, 2008.

De La Durantay, Leland. *Giorgio Agamben: A Critical Introduction*. Stanford, CA: Stanford University Press, 2009.

de Souza Briggs, Xavier. "Doing Democracy Up-Close: Culture, Power, and Communication in Community Building." *Journal of Planning and Education and Research* 18, no. 1 (1998): 1–13.

De Sousa Santos, Boaventura. "Law: A Map of Misreading. Toward a Postmodern Conception of Law." *Journal of Law and Society* 14, no. 3 (1987): 279–302.

De Ville, Jacques. "Sovereignty Without Sovereignty: Derrida's Declarations of Independence." In *After Sovereignty: On the Question of Political Beginnings*, edited by Charles Barbour and George Pavlich, 54–67. London: Routledge, 2010.

de Vos, Pierre. "A Bridge Too Far? History As Context in the Interpretation of the South African Constitution." *South African Journal of Human Rights* 17, no. 1 (2001): 1–33.

de Vries, Hent, and Lawrence E. Sullivan, eds. *Political Theologies: Public Religions in a Post-Secular World*. New York: Fordham University Press, 2006.

Delport, Peggy. "'No Matter Where We Are, We Are Here.' Beginnings: The Fresco Wall of the District Six Museum." In *City-Site-Museum: Reviewing Memory Practices at the District Six Museum*, edited by Bonita Bennett, Chrischené Julius, and Crain Soudien, 130–151. Cape Town: District Six Museum, 2008.

Derrida, Jacques. "Declarations of Independence." Translated by Thomas Keenan and Thomas Pepper. *New Political Science* 15 (1986): 7–15.

Derrida, Jacques. "Force of Law: The 'Mystical Foundation of Authority.'" Translated by M. Quaintance. *Cardozo Law Review* 11, no. 5–6 (1990): 919–1045.

Derrida, Jacques. *On Touching—Jean-Luc Nancy*. Translated by Christine Irizarry. Stanford, CA: Stanford University Press, 2005.

Derrida, Jacques. *Rogues: Two Essays On Reason*. Translated by Pascale-Anne Brault and Michael Naas. Stanford, CA: Stanford University Press, 2005.

Derrida, Jacques. "Signature Event Context." In *Margins of Philosophy*, translated by Alan Bass, 309–330. Chicago: University of Chicago Press, 1982.

Devisch, Ignaas. "Nancian Virtual Doubts About 'Leformal' Democracy: Or How to Deal with Contemporary Political Configuration in an Uneasy Way?" *Philosophy and Social Criticism* 37, no. 9 (2011): 999–1010.

Devisch, Ignaas, and Kathleen Vandeputte. "Responsibility and Spatiality: Or Can Jean-Luc Nancy Sit on a Bench in Hannah Arendt's Public Space?" *Lumina* 22, no. 2 (2011): 1–10.

Devisch, Ignaas and Kathleen Vandeputte. "Sense, Existence and Justice, or, How to Live in a Secular World?" *Synthesis Philosophica* 25, no. 1 (2010): 149–160.

District Six Museum. "About Us." The District Six Museum Foundation. http://www.districtsix.co.za/aboutus.htm, accessed September 10, 2009.

District Six Museum. "Annual Report 2007/08." The District Six Museum Foundation. http://www.districtsix.co.za/D6-ANN%20REPORT%20final.pdf, accessed November 17, 2010.

Douzinas, Costas. *The End of Human Rights: Critical Legal Thought at the Turn of the Century*. Oxford: Hart Publishing, 2000.

Drakopoulou, Maria. "The Ethic of Care, Female Subjectivity and Feminist Legal Scholarship." *Feminist Legal Studies* 8 (2000): 199–226.

du Plessis, Lourens. "AZAPO: Monument, Memorial . . . or Mistake?" In *Law, Memory, and the Legacy of Apartheid: Ten Years After AZAPO v. President of South Africa*, edited by Wessel LeRoux and Karin van Marle, 51–64. Pretoria: Pretoria University Law Press, 2007.

du Plessis, Lourens. "The South African Constitution as Memory and Promise." *Stellenbosch Law Review* 3 (2000): 385–394.

Dubin, Steven C. *Transforming Museums: Mounting Queen Victoria in a Democratic South Africa*. New York: Palgrave Macmillan, 2006.

Duncan, Carol. *Civilizing Rituals: Inside Public Art Museums*. London: Routledge, 1995.

Duncan, Carol, and Alan Wallach. "The Universal Survey Museum." *Art History* 3, no. 4 (1980): 448–469.

Dyzenhaus, David. "Introduction: Why Carl Schmitt?" In *Law as Politics: Carl Schmitt's Critique of Liberalism*, edited by David Dyzenhaus, 1–22. Durham, NC: Duke University Press, 1998.

Edwards, Elizabeth, Chris Gosden, and Ruth B. Phillips, eds. *Sensible Objects: Colonialism, Museums, and Material Culture*. New York: Berg, 2006.

Eichstedt, Jennifer. "Museums and (In)Justice." In *Museum Philosophy for the Twenty-First Century*, edited by Hugh H. Genoways, 127–137. Lanham, MD: Altamira Press, 2006.

Engster, Daniel. *Divine Sovereignty: The Origins of Modern State Power*. DeKalb: Northern Illinois University Press, 2001.

Ernst, Wolfgang. "Archi(ve)textures of Museology." In *Museums and Memory*, edited by Susan Crane, 17–34. Stanford, CA: Stanford University Press, 2000.

Esposito, Roberto. *Bios: Biopolitics and Philosophy*. Translated by Timothy Campbell. Minneapolis: University of Minnesota, 2008.

Esposito, Roberto. *Communitas: The Origin and Destiny of Community*. Translated by Timothy C. Campbell. Stanford, CA: Stanford University Press, 2010.

Famakinwa, J. O. "How Moderate Is Kwame Gyekye's Moderate Communitarianism?" *Thought and Practice: A Journal of the Philosophical Association of Kenya* 2, no. 2 (2010): 65–77.

Fanon, Frantz. *The Wretched of the Earth*. New York: Grove Press, 1961.

Fassbender, Bardo. "'We the Peoples of the United Nations': Constituent Power and Constitutional Form in International Law." In *The Paradox of Constitutionalism: Constituent Power and Constitutional Form*, edited by Martin Loughlin and Neil Walker, 269–290. Oxford: Oxford University Press, 2007.

Fayemi, Ademola Kazeem. "A Critique of Consensual Democracy and Human Rights in Wiredu's Philosophy." *Lumina* 21, no. 1 (2010): 1–13.

Federici, Silvia. "Precarious Labour: A Feminist Perspective." *The Journal of Aesthetics and Protest* (2008): 1–9. http://inthemiddleofthewhirlwind.wordpress.com/precarious-labor-a-feminist-viewpoint/.

Ferreira da Silva, Denise. *Towards a Global Idea of Race*. Minneapolis: University of Minnesota Press, 2007.

Findlen, Paula. "The Museum: Its Classical Etymology and Renaissance Genealogy." *Journal of the History of Collections* 1, no. 1 (1989): 59–78.

Findlen, Paula. *Possessing Nature: Museums, Collecting, and Scientific Culture in Early Modern Italy*. Berkeley: University of California Press, 1996.

Fitzpatrick, Peter. "The Immanence of Empire." In *Empire's New Clothes: Reading Hardt and Negri*, edited by Paul A. Passavant and Jodi Dean, 31–55. London: Routledge, 2004.

Fitzpatrick, Peter. "Leveraging Leviathan." In *After Sovereignty: On the Question of Political Beginnings*, edited by Charles Barbour and George Pavlich, 12–21. London: Routledge, 2010.

Fitzpatrick, Peter. *The Mythology of Modern Law*. London: Routledge, 1992.

Fitzpatrick, Peter. "'No Higher Duty': *Mabo* and the Failure of Legal Foundation." *Law and Critique* 13, no. 3 (2002): 233–252.

Foucault, Michel. "About the Beginning of the Hermeneutics of the Self." *Political Theory* 21, no. 2 (1993): 198–227.

Foucault, Michel. *The History of Sexuality: An Introduction, Volume 1*. Translated by Robert Hurley. New York: Vintage Books, 1990.

Foucault, Michel. *The Order of Things: An Archaeology of the Human Sciences.* London: Routledge, 1970.

Foucault, Michel. *Society Must Be Defended: Lectures at the Collège De France 1975–76.* Edited by Mauro Bertani and Alessandro Fontana. Translated by David Macey. New York: Picador, 2003.

Foucault, Michel. "Texts/Contexts: Of Other Places." *Diacritics* 16, no. 1 (1986): 22–27.

Fowler, Don D. "A Natural History of Man: Reflections on Anthropology, Museums, and Science." *Fieldiana: Anthropology* 36 (2003): 11–21.

Gerz, Jochen, and Esther Shalev-Gerz. "Monument against Fascism. Artists' Statement." http://www.gerz.fr, accessed September 1, 2009.

Giebelhausen, Michaela. "The Architecture Is the Museum." In *New Museum Theory and Practice: An Introduction,* edited by Janet Marstine, 41–63. Oxford: Blackwell, 2006.

Gilroy, Paul. *After Empire: Melancholia or Convivial Culture.* Oxford: Routledge, 2004.

Gilroy, Paul. *Postcolonial Melancholia.* New York: Columbia University Press, 2005.

Golding, Viv. "Learning at the Museum Frontiers: Democracy, Identity and Difference." In *Museum Revolutions: How Museums Change and Are Changed,* edited by Simon J. Knell, Suzanne Macleod, and Sheila E. R. Watson, 315–329. London: Routledge, 2007.

Greenhouse, Carol J. "Just in Time: Temporality and the Cultural Legitimation of Law." *Yale Law Journal* 98 (1988–1989): 1631–1651.

Guéroult, Martial. *Spinoza: Dieu.* Paris: Aubier-Montaigne, 1968.

Gyekye, Kwame. *Tradition and Modernity.* New York: Oxford University Press, 1997.

Habermas, Jürgen. *Between Facts and Norms: Contributions to a Discourse Theory of Law and Democracy.* Translated by William Rehg. Cambridge, MA: MIT Press, 1996.

Habermas, Jürgen. "Struggles for Recognition in the Democratic Constitutional State." In *Multiculturalism: Examining the Politics of Recognition,* edited by Charles Taylor and Amy Gutmann, 107–148. Princeton, NJ: Princeton University Press, 1994.

Habermas, Jürgen. *The Structural Transformation of the Public Sphere: An Inquiry into a Category of Bourgeois Society.* Translated by Thomas Burger. Cambridge, MA: MIT Press, 1991.

Hall, Catherine. "Introduction: Thinking the Postcolonial, Thinking the Empire." In *Cultures of Empire: Colonizers in Britain and the Empire in the Nineteenth and Twentieth Centuries,* edited by Catherine Hall, 1–36. Manchester: Manchester University Press, 2000.

Hall, Catherine. *White, Male And Middle-Class: Explorations In Feminism and History.* London: Routledge, 1992.

Hall, Stuart. "The State In Question." In *The Idea of the Modern State*, edited by Gregor McLennan, David Held, and Stuart Hall, 1–28. Milton Keynes: Open University Press, 1984.

Hamacher, Werner. "Afformative, Strike: Benjamin's 'Critique of Violence.'" In *Walter Benjamin's Philosophy: Destruction and Experience*, edited by Andrew Benjamin and Peter Osborne, translated by Dana Hollander, 110–138. New York: Routledge, 1994.

Haraway, Donna. "Teddy Bear Patriarchy in the Garden of Eden, New York City, 1908–1936." In *Primate Visions: Gender, Race, and Nature in the World of Modern Science*, 26–58. London: Routledge, 1989.

Hardt, Michael. "Foreword." In Antonio Negri, *The Savage Anomaly*, xi–xvi. Translated by Michael Hardt. Minneapolis: University of Minnesota Press, 1991.

Hardt, Michael, and Antonio Negri. *Empire*. Cambridge, MA: Harvard University Press, 2000.

Harris, Neil. "Museums, Merchandising, and Popular Taste: The Struggle for Influence." In *Material Culture and the Study of American Life*, edited by Ian M. Quimby, 141–149. New York: Norton, 1978.

Hart, H. L. A. *The Concept of Law*. Oxford: Oxford University Press, 1961.

Heberle, Renée. "Introduction." In *Imagining Law: On Drucilla Cornell*, edited by Renée Heberle and Benjamin Pryor, 1–10. Albany: State University of New York Press, 2008.

Heidegger, Martin. *Nietzsche: Volumes One and Two*. Translated by David Farrell Krell. San Francisco: Harper Collins, 1991.

Heidegger, Martin. "The Davos Disputation Between Ernst Cassirer and Martin Heidegger." In *Kant and the Problem of Metaphysics*, 5th ed., translated by Richard Taft, 193–207. Bloomington: Indiana University Press, 1997.

Hein, George. *Learning in the Museum: Museum Meanings*. London: Routledge, 1998.

Hein, Hilde Stern. "Redressing the Museum in Feminist Theory." *Museum Management and Curatorship* 22, no. 1 (2007): 29–42.

Held, David. *Cosmopolitanism: Ideals and Realities*. Cambridge: Polity Press, 2010.

Herwitz, Daniel. "Monument, Ruin, and Redress in South African Heritage." *The Germanic Review: Literature, Culture, Theory* 86, no. 4 (2011): 232–248.

Hetherington, Kevin. "Museum." *Theory, Culture and Society* 23, no. 2–3 (2006): 597–603.

Hetherington, Kevin. "The Unsightly: Touching the Parthenon Frieze." *Theory, Culture and Society* 19, no. 5–6 (2002): 187–205.

Hiddleston, Jane. "Nancy, Globalization and Postcolonial Humanity." In *Jean-Luc Nancy: Justice, Legality and World*, edited by B. C. Hutchens, 146–160. New York: Continuum, 2010.

Hirst, Paul Q. "Power/Knowledge: Constructed Space and the Subject." In *Grasping the World: The Idea of the Museum*, edited by Donald Preziosi and Claire Farago, 380–400. Aldershot: Ashgate, 2004.

Hirvonen, Ari. "The Politics of Revolt: On Benjamin and Critique of Law." *Law and Critique* 22, no. 2 (2011): 101–118.

Hitchens, Christopher. *The Elgin Marbles: Should They Be Returned to Greece?* London: Verso, 1997.

Hobbes, Thomas. *Leviathan.* Edited by J. C. A. Gaskin. Oxford: Oxford University Press. 2008.

Honig, Bonnie. "Arendt, Identity, and Difference." *Political Theory* 16, no. 1 (1988): 77–98.

Honig, Bonnie. "Declarations of Independence: Arendt and Derrida on the Problem of Founding a Republic." *American Political Science Review* 85, no. 1 (1991): 97–113.

Hooper-Greenhill, Eilean. *Museums and the Shaping of Knowledge.* London: Routledge, 1992.

Hughes, Patrick. "Making Science 'Family Fun': The Fetish of the Interactive Exhibit." *Museum Management and Curatorship* 19, no. 2 (2001): 175–185.

Huyssen, Andreas. *Twilight Memories: Marking Time in a Culture of Amnesia.* New York: Routledge, 1995.

International Coalition of Sites of Conscience. "About Us." http://www.sitesofconscience.org, accessed December 10, 2010.

Interviews, 2009.

Johannesburg Development Agency. "What We Do." http://www.jda.org.za/what-we-do, accessed June 20, 2012.

Joyce, Richard. "Sovereignty After Sovereignty." In *After Sovereignty: On the Question of Political Beginnings,* edited by Charles Barbour and George Pavlich, 37–53. London: Routledge, 2010.

Kadalie, Rhoda. "District Six 'Restitution' Efforts a Disgrace." *Die Berger,* April 11, 2012. http://www.politicsweb.co.za/politicsweb/view/politicsweb/en/page71639?oid=292133&sn=Detail&pid=71639.

Kahn, Paul. *Putting Liberalism in its Place.* Princeton, NJ: Princeton University Press, 2005.

Kalyvas, Andreas. "From the Act to the Decision: Hannah Arendt and the Question of Decisionism." *Political Theory* 32, no. 3 (2004): 320–346.

Kantorowicz, Ernst H. *The King's Two Bodies: A Study in Medieval Political Theology.* Princeton, NJ: Princeton University Press, 1957.

Kapczynski, Amy. "Historicism, Progress, and the Redemptive Constitution." *Cardozo Law Review* 26 (2004–2005): 1041–1117.

Kaplan, Flora S. *Museums and the Making of Ourselves: The Role of Objects in National Identity.* London: Continuum, 1996.

Kavanagh, Aileen. "Constitutionalism, Counter-Terrorism and the Courts: Changes in the British Constitutional Landscape." *International Journal of Constitutional Law* 9, no. 1 (2011): 172–199.

Kellogg, Catherine. "Freedom After the Law: Arendt and Nancy's Concept of 'The Political.'" In *After Sovereignty: On the Question of Political Beginnings,* edited by Charles Barbour and George Pavlich, 68–82. London: Routledge, 2010.

Kelly, Mark. *The Political Philosophy of Michel Foucault,* Abingdon: Routledge, 2009.

Kennedy, Duncan. *A Critique of Adjudication: Fin de Siècle.* Cambridge, MA: Harvard University Press, 1998.

Khunou, Grace. "'Massive Cutoffs': Cost Recovery and Electricity Service in Diep-kloof, Soweto." In *Cost Recovery and the Crisis of Service Delivery in South Africa*, edited by David A. McDonald and John Pape, 61–80. London: Zed Books, 2002.

King, Tony, and M. K. Flynn. "Heritage and the Post-Apartheid City: Constitution Hill, Johannesburg." *International Journal of Heritage Studies* 18, no. 1 (2012): 65–82.

Klare, Karl. "Legal Culture and Transformative Constitutionalism." *South African Journal on Human Rights* 14 (1998): 146–188.

Klare, Karl. "The Politics of Duncan Kennedy's Critique." *Cardozo Law Review* 22, no. 3–4 (2001): 1073–1104.

Koselleck, Reinhart. *Futures Past: On the Semantics of Historical Time*. Translated by Keith Tribe. New York: Columbia University Press, 2004.

Krisch, Nico. *Beyond Constitutionalism: The Pluralist Structure of Postnational Law*. Oxford: Oxford University Press, 2010.

Kymlicka, Will. "Liberalism and Communitarianism." *Canadian Journal of Philosophy* 18, no. 2 (1988): 181–203.

Langa, Pius. "Foreword." In *Number Four: The Making of Constitution Hill*, edited by Lauren Segal, Karen Martin, and Sharon Cort, vii. Johannesburg: Penguin, 2006.

Langa, Pius. "The Role of the Constitutional Court in the Enforcement and Protection of Human Rights in South Africa." *St. Louis University Law Journal* 41 (1997): 1259–1277.

Layne, Valmont. "The District Six Museum: An Ordinary People's Place." *The Public Historian* 30, no. 1 (2008): 53–62.

le Grange, Lucien. "Rebuilding District Six." In *City-Site-Museum: Reviewing Memory Practices at the District Six Museum*, edited by Bonita Bennett, Chrischené Julius, and Crain Soudien, 8–17. Cape Town: District Six Museum, 2008.

le Roux, Wessel. "War Memorials, the Architecture of the Constitutional Court Building and Counter-monumental Constitutionalism." In *Law, Memory, and the Legacy of Apartheid: Ten Years After AZAPO v. President of South Africa*, edited by Wessel le Roux and Karin van Marle, 65–92. Pretoria: Pretoria University Law Press, 2007.

Learning and Skills Improvement Service. "Skills for Life Improvement Programme." http://sflip.excellencegateway.org.uk/, accessed February 15, 2012.

Lefort, Claude. *Democracy and Political Theory*. Translated by David Macey. Minneapolis: University of Minnesota Press, 1989.

Lefort, Claude. *The Political Forms of Modern Society*. Edited by John B. Thompson. Cambridge, MA: MIT Press, 1986.

Lemke, Thomas. "The Birth of Bio-Politics: Michel Foucault's Lecture at the Collège de France on Neo-Liberal Governmentality." *Economy and Society* 20, no. 2 (2001): 190–207.

Lepawsky, Joshua. "A Museum, the City, and a Nation." *Cultural Geographies* 15, no. 1 (2008): 119–142.

Lepofsky, Jonathan, and James C. Fraser. "Building Community Citizens: Claiming the Right to Place-making in the City." *Urban Studies* 40, no. 1 (2003): 127–142.

Lerner, Robert E. "'Meritorious Academic Service': Kantorowicz and Frankfurt." In *Ernst Kantorowicz: Erträge der Doppeltagung Institute for Advanced Study, Princeton, Johann Wolfgang Goethe-Universität, Frankfurt*, edited by Robert Louis Benson and Johannes Fried, 14–32. Stuttgart: F. Steiner, 1997.

Lindahl, Hans. "Constituent Power and Reflexive Identity: Towards an Ontology of Collective Selfhood." In *The Paradox of Constitutionalism: Constituent Power and Constitutional Form*, edited by Martin Loughlin and Neil Walker, 9–26. Oxford: Oxford University Press, 2007.

Lindahl, Hans. "Democracy, Political Reflexivity and Bounded Dialogues: Reconsidering the Monism-Pluralism Debate." In *Public Law and Politics: The Scope and Limits of Constitutionalism*, edited by Emilios Christodoulidis and Stephen Tierney, 103–116. London: Ashgate, 2008.

Lindroos, Kia. "Scattering Community: Benjamin on Experience, Narrative and History." *Philosophy Social Criticism* 27, no. 6 (2001): 19–41.

Lonetree, Amy. *Decolonizing Museums: Representing Native America in National and Tribal Museums* (Chapel Hill: University of North Carolina Press, 2012).

Lonetree, Amy. "Missed Opportunities: Reflections on the NMAI." *American Indian Quarterly* 30, no. 3–4 (2006): 632–645.

Lotringer, Sylvere, and Christian Marazzi. *Autonomia: Post-Political Politics*. Los Angeles: Semiotext(e), 2007.

Loughlin, Martin. *The Idea of Public Law*. Oxford: Oxford University Press, 2003.

Loughlin, Martin. *The Foundations of Public Law*. Oxford: Oxford University Press, 2010.

Loughlin, Martin. "Reflections on *The Idea of Public Law*." In *Public Law and Politics: The Scope and Limits of Constitutionalism*, edited by Emilios Christodoulidis and Stephen Tierney, 47–68. Aldershot: Ashgate, 2008.Loughlin, Martin, and Neil Walker. "Introduction." In *The Paradox of Constitutionalism: Constituent Power and Constitutional Form*, edited by Martin Loughlin and Neil Walker, 1–8. Oxford: Oxford University Press, 2007.

Löwith, Karl. *Meaning in History: The Theological Implications of the Philosophy of History*. Chicago: University of Chicago Press, 1949.

Lubac, Henri. *Corpus Mysticum: The Eucharist and the Church in the Middle Ages*. Edited by Laurence Paul Hemming and Susan Frank Parsons. Translated by Gemma Simmonds, with Richard Price and Christopher Stephens. Notre Dame, IN: University of Notre Dame Press, 2007.

Luhmann, Niklas. *Ecological Communication*. Translated by John Bednarz Jr. Chicago: University of Chicago Press, 1989.

Lyotard, Jean-François. "The Survivor." In *Toward the Postmodern*. Edited by Robert Harvey. Translated by Robert Harvey and Mark S. Roberts, 144–163. New York: Humanity Books, 1999.

MacDonald, Sharon. *Behind the Scenes at the Science Museum*. Oxford: Berg, 2002.

MacGregor, Neil. "To Shape the Citizens of 'That Great City, the World.'" In *Whose Culture? The Promise of Museums and the Debate Over Antiquities*, edited by James Cuno, 39–54. Princeton, NJ: Princeton University Press, 2009.

MacGregor, Neil. "The Whole World in Our Hands." *The Guardian*, July 24, 2004. https://www.theguardian.com/artanddesign/2004/jul/24/heritage.art.

MacGregor, Neil, and Jonathan Williams. "The Encyclopaedic Museum: Enlightenment Ideals, Contemporary Realities." *Public Archaeology* 4, no. 1 (2005): 57–59.

Mackey, Eva. *The House of Difference: Cultural Politics and National Identity in Canada*. New York: Routledge, 1999.

MacPherson, C. B. *The Political Theory of Possessive Individualism: Hobbes to Locke*. Oxford: Clarendon Press, 1962.

Mader, Mary Beth. "Modern Living and Vital Race: Foucault and the Science of Life." *Foucault Studies* 12 (2011): 97–112.

Madikida, Churchill, Lauren Segal, and Clive Van Den Berg. "The Reconstruction of Memory at Constitution Hill." *The Public Historian* 30, no. 1 (2008): 17–25.

Madlingozi, Tshepo. "Good Victim, Bad Victim: Apartheid's Beneficiaries, Victims and the Struggle for Social Justice." In *Law, Memory, and the Legacy of Apartheid: Ten Years After AZAPO v. President of South Africa*, edited by Wessel le Roux and Karin van Marle, 107–126. Pretoria: Pretoria University Law Press, 2007.

Mahlong, Audra. "AG Slams Blue IQ." *ITWeb*, September 25, 2009. http://www.itweb.co.za/index.php?option=com_content&view=article&id=26587.

Maleuvre, Didier. *Museum Memories: History, Technology, Art*. Stanford, CA: Stanford University Press, 1999.

Mamdani, Mahmood. *Citizen and Subject*. Princeton, NJ: Princeton University Press, 1996.

Mamdani, Mahmood. "When Does Reconciliation Turn Into a Denial of Justice?" *Sam Molutshungu Memorial Lectures, Volume 1*. Pretoria: Human Sciences Research Council Publishers, 1998.

Mandela, Nelson. "Inaugural Speech." South African Government Information, May 9, 1994. http://www.info.gov.za/speeches/1994/990319514p1007.htm.

Mansfield, Elizabeth. *Art History and its Institutions: Foundations of a Discipline*. London: Routledge, 2002.

Marchart, Oliver. "Being With Against: Jean-Luc Nancy on Justice, Politics and the Democratic Horizon." In *Jean-Luc Nancy: Justice, Legality and World*, edited by B. C. Hutchens, 172–185. New York: Continuum, 2010.

Marchart, Oliver. *Post-Foundational Political Thought: Political Difference in Nancy, Lefort, Badiou and Laclau*. Edinburgh: Edinburgh University Press, 2007.

Marstine, Janet. *New Museum Theory and Practice: An Introduction*. Oxford: Blackwell, 2006.

Martel, James. "Can There Be Politics Without Sovereignty? Arendt, Derrida and the Question of Sovereign Inevitability." *Law, Culture, and the Humanities* 6, no. 2 (2010): 153–166.

Martel, James. *Divine Violence: Walter Benjamin and the Eschatology of Sovereignty.* London: Routledge, 2012.

Martel, James. *Subverting the Leviathan: Reading Thomas Hobbes as a Radical Democrat.* New York: Columbia University Press, 2007.

Mathur, Saloni. "Museums and Globalization." *Anthropological Quarterly* 78, no. 3 (2005): 697–708.

Matolino, Bernard. "Radicals versus Moderates: A Critique of Gyekye's Moderate Communitarianism." *South African Journal of Philosophy* 28, no. 2 (2009): 161–170.

Mbeki, Thabo. "State of the Nation Address of the President of South Africa: Joint Sitting of Parliament." South African Government Information. http://www.gov.za/node/537711, accessed October 15, 2009.

Mbembe, Achille. "Ways of Seeing: Beyond the New Nativism." *African Studies Review* 44, no. 2 (2001): 1–14.

McCarthy, Thomas. "The Philosophy of the Limit and its Other." *Constellations* 2, no. 2 (1995): 175–188.

McClintock, Anne. "The Angel of Progress: Pitfalls of the Term 'Post-Colonialism.'" *Social Text*, no. 31–32 (1992): 84–98.

McDonald, David A. "The Theory and Practice of Cost Recovery in South Africa." In *Cost Recovery and the Crisis of Service Delivery in South Africa*, edited by David A. McDonald and John Pape, 17–40. London: Zed Books, 2002.

McDonald, David A., and John Pape. "Introduction." In *Cost Recovery and the Crisis of Service Delivery in South Africa*, edited by David A. McDonald and John Pape, 1–16. London: Zed Books, 2002.

McGregor, Katherine. "Time, Memory and Historical Justice: An Introduction." *Time and Society* 21, no. 1 (2012): 5–20.

McLuhan, Marshall. *The Gutenberg Galaxy: The Making of Typographic Man.* Toronto: University of Toronto Press, 1962.

Melville, Herman. *Bartleby the Scrivener.* Gloucester: Dodo Press, 2006.

Message, Kylie. "Multiplying Sites of Sovereignty Through Community and Constituent Services at the National Museum of the American Indian?" *Museum and Society* 7, no. 1 (2009): 50–67.

Message, Kylie. *New Museums and the Making of Culture.* New York: Berg, 2006.

Metcalf, Hilary, Pamela Meadows, Heather Rolfe, and Amar Dhudwar, with Nick Coleman, Jo Wapshott, and Hannah Carpenter. "Evaluation of the Impact of *Skills for Life* Learning: Longitudinal Survey of Adult Learners on College-Based Literacy and Numeracy Courses. Final Report." National Institute of Economic and Social Research and BMRB Social Research. http://www.skillsforlifenetwork.com/?mod=1&dok=1592, accessed February 15, 2012.

Michelman, Frank I. "Postmodernism, Proceduralism, and Constitutional Justice: A Comment on van der Walt and Botha." *Constellations* 9, no. 2 (2002): 246–262.

Miller, Toby. *The Well-Tempered Self: Citizenship, Culture, and the Postmodern Subject.* Baltimore: Johns Hopkins University Press, 1993.

Mngxitama, Andile. *Why Steve Biko Would Not Vote*. Johannesburg: New Frank Talk, 2009.

MORI/Museums, Libraries, and Archives Council. "Visitors to Museums and Galleries, 2004." http://www.mla.gov.uk/documents/mori_hub_exit_sur vey.doc, accessed February 17, 2012.

Moser, Sir Claus. "Fresh Start: Improving Literacy and Numeracy. Basic Skills Agency." Department for Education and Skills. http://www.lifelonglearning. co.uk/mosergroup/, accessed November 10, 2011.

Motha, Stewart. "Archiving Colonial Sovereignty: From Ubuntu to a Jurisprudence of Sacrifice." *SA Publiekreg/Public Law* 24 (2009): 297–327.

Mouffe, Chantal. "Carl Schmitt and the Paradox of Liberal Democracy." In *Law as Politics: Carl Schmitt's Critique of Liberalism*, edited by David Dyzenhaus, 159–178. Durham, NC: Duke University Press, 1998.

Munro, Vanessa, and Carl F. Stychin, eds. *Sexuality and the Law: Feminist Engagements*. New York: Routledge, 2007.

Mureinik, Etienne. "A Bridge to Where? Introducing the Interim Bill of Rights." *South African Journal on Human Rights* 10 (1994): 31–48.

Nalbandian, John. "Facilitating Community, Enabling Democracy: New Roles for Local Government Managers." *Public Administration Review* 59, no. 3 (1999): 187–197.

Nancy, Jean-Luc. *Being Singular Plural*. Edited by Werner Hamacher and David E. Wellbery. Translated by Robert D. Richardson and Annie E. O'Byrne. Stanford, CA: Stanford University Press, 2000.

Nancy, Jean-Luc. *The Birth to Presence*. Translated by Brian Holmes. Stanford, CA: Stanford University Press, 1993.

Nancy, Jean-Luc. "Church, State, Resistance." *Journal of Law and Society* 34, no. 1 (2007): 3–13.

Nancy, Jean-Luc. "The Compearance: From the Existence of Communism to the Community of 'Existence.'" *Political Theory* 20, no. 3 (1992): 371–398.

Nancy, Jean-Luc. "The Confronted Community." *Postcolonial Studies* 6, no. 1 (2003): 23–36.

Nancy, Jean-Luc. *Corpus*. Translated by Richard A. Rand. New York: Fordham University Press, 2008.

Nancy, Jean-Luc. *The Creation of the World, or Globalization*. Translated by François Raffoul and David Pettigrew. Albany: State University of New York Press, 2007.

Nancy, Jean-Luc. *Dis-enclosure: The Deconstruction of Christianity*. New York: Fordham University Press, 2008.

Nancy, Jean-Luc. *The Experience of Freedom*. Translated by Bridget McDonald. Stanford, CA: Stanford University Press, 1993.

Nancy, Jean-Luc. *A Finite Thinking*. Edited by Simon Sparks. Stanford, CA: Stanford University Press, 2003.

Nancy, Jean-Luc. *The Inoperative Community*. Edited by Peter Connor. Translated by Simona Sawhney. Minneapolis: University of Minnesota Press, 1991.

Nancy, Jean-Luc. *The Sense of the World*. Translated by Jeffrey S. Librett. Minneapolis: University of Minnesota Press, 1997.

Nancy, Jean-Luc. *The Truth of Democracy*. Translated by Pascale-Anne Brault and Michael Naas. New York: Fordham University Press, 2010.

Nancy, Jean-Luc. "The Unsacrificeable." Translated by Richard Livingston. *Yale French Studies* 79 (1991): 20–38.

Nancy, Jean-Luc, and Phillipe Lacoue-Labarthe. *Retreating the Political*. Edited by Simon Sparks. London: Routledge, 1997.

Nancy, Jean-Luc, and Phillipe Lacoue-Labarthe. *The Title of the Letter: A Reading of Lacan*. Translated by François Raffoul and David Pettigrew. Albany: State University of New York Press, 1992.

Negri, Antonio. *The Savage Anomaly: The Power of Spinoza's Metaphysics and Politics*. Translated by Michael Hardt. Minneapolis: University of Minnesota Press, 1991.

Negri, Antonio. *Insurgencies: Constituent Power and the Modern State*. Translated by Maurizia Boscagli. Minneapolis: University of Minnesota Press, 1999.

Negri, Antonio. "Letter to a Tunisian Friend." Translated by Nate Lavey. *Negri in English* (blog). February 14, 2011. http://antonionegriinenglish.wordpress.com/2011 /02/14/negri-letter-to-a-tunisian-friend/. Originally published as "Lettera ad un amico tunisino." *UniNomade 2.0*. January 28, 2011. http://uninomade.org/lettera-ad-un-amico-tunisino/.

Negri, Antonio. *Time for Revolution*. Translated by Matteo Mandarini. London: Continuum Press, 2003.

Neilson, Brett. "Potenza Nuda? Sovereignty, Biopolitics, Capitalism." *Contretemps* 5 (2004): 63–78.

New Oxford American Dictionary. 2nd ed. Oxford: Oxford University Press, 2005.

New Oxford American Dictionary. 3rd ed. Oxford: Oxford University Press, 2010.

Newhouse, Victoria, *Towards a New Museum*. New York: Monacelli Press, 1998.

Newman, Caroline, "Cemeteries of Tradition: The Critique of Collection in Heine, Nietzsche, and Benjamin." *Pacific Coast Philology* 19, no. 1–2 (1984): 12–21.

Nicholson, Zara. "Plan for District Six Angers Claimants." *Cape Times*, September 9, 2011. http://www.iol.co.za/capetimes/plan-for-district-six-angers-claimants-1.1134461.

Nietzsche, Friedrich. *On the Advantage and Disadvantage of History for Life*. Translated by Peter Preuss. Indianapolis, IN: Hackett Publishing, 1980.

Norbrook, David. "The Emperor's New Body? Richard II, Ernst Kantorowicz, and the Politics of Shakespeare Criticism." *Textual Practice* 10, no. 2 (1996): 329–357.

Norris, Andrew. "Jean-Luc Nancy on the Political after Heidegger and Schmitt." *Philosophy and Social Criticism* 37, no. 8 (2011): 899–913.

Norval, Aletta. *Deconstructing Apartheid Discourse*. London: Verso, 1996.

Norval, Aletta. "Memory, Identity and the (Im)possibility of Reconciliation: The Work of the Truth and Reconciliation Commission in South Africa." *Constellations* 5, no. 2 (1998): 250–265.

Nuttal, Sarah. "Subjectivities of Whiteness." *African Studies Review* 44, no. 2 (2001): 115–140.

Ochoa Espejo, Paulina. *The Time of Popular Sovereignty*. UniversityPark: Penn State University Press, 2011.

Olmi, Giuseppe. "Science-Honour-Metaphor: Italian Cabinets of the Sixteenth and Seventeenth Centuries." In *Grasping the World: The Idea of the Museum*, edited by Donald Preziosi and Claire Farago, 129–143. Aldershot: Ashgate, 2004.

Oklopcic, Zoran. "Constitutional (Re)Vision: Sovereign Peoples, New Constituent Powers, and the Formation of Constitutional Orders in the Balkans." *Constellations* 19, no. 1 (2012): 81–101.

Osborne, Peter. "Small-Scale Victories, Large-Scale Defeats: Walter Benjamin's Politics of Time." In *Walter Benjamin's Philosophy: Destruction and Experience*, edited by Andrew Benjamin and Peter Osborne, 59–109. New York: Routledge, 1994.

Pache, Claudine. "Content Curators: The DJs of the Web." *Journal of Digital Research and Publishing* (2011): 19–25.

Pan Africanist Congress of Azania. "Election Manifesto." http://www.pac.org.za/2009-Election-Manifesto.pdf, Accessed September 1, 2012.

Paris, Scott G. "How Can Museums Attract Visitors in the Twenty-First Century?" In *Museum Philosophy for the Twenty-First Century*, edited by Hugh H. Genoways, 255–266. Lanham, MD: Altamira Press, 2006.

Pascal, Blaise. *Pensées*. Translated by A. J. Krailsheimer. London: Penguin, 1966.

Pavlich, George. "On the Subject of Sovereigns." In *After Sovereignty: On the Question of Political Beginnings*, edited by Charles Barbour and George Pavlich, 22–36. London: Routledge, 2010.

Pavlich, George, and Charles Barbour. "Introduction." In *After Sovereignty: On the Question of Political Beginnings*, edited by Charles Barbour and George Pavlich, 1–11. London: Routledge, 2010.

Pollock, Griselda, and Joyce Zemans. *Museums after Modernism: Strategies of Engagement*. Oxford: Blackwell, 2007.

Pomian, Krzysztof. *Collectors and Curiosities: Paris and Venice, 1500–1800*. Translated by Elizabeth Wiles-Porter. Cambridge: Polity Press, 1990.

Poovey, Mary. *A History of the Modern Fact: Problems of Knowledge in the Sciences of Wealth and Society*. Chicago: University of Chicago Press, 1998.

Posel, Deborah. "Race as Common Sense: Racial Classification in Twentieth-Century South Africa." *African Studies Review* 44, no. 2 (2001): 87–113.

Posel, Deborah. "What's In a Name: Racial Categorisations Under Apartheid and Their Afterlife." *Transformation* 47 (2001): 50–74.

Pranger, M. B. "Politics and Finitude: The Temporal Status of Augustine's *Civitas Permixta*." In *Political Theologies: Public Religions in a Post-Secular World*, edited by Hent de Vries and Lawrence E. Sullivan, 113–121. New York: Fordham University Press, 2006.

Pratt, Mary Louise. *Imperial Eyes: Travel Writing and Transculturation*. London: Routledge, 1992.

Preziosi, Donald. "Art History and Museology: Rendering the Visible Legible." In *A Companion to Museum Studies*, edited by Sharon MacDonald, 50–63. Oxford: Blackwell, 2006.

Preziosi, Donald. *Brain of the Earth's Body: Art, Museums, and the Phantasms of Modernity*. Minneapolis: University of Minnesota Press, 2003.

Preziosi, Donald. "Philosophy and the Ends of the Museum." In *Museum Philosophy for the Twenty-First Century*, edited by Hugh H. Genoways, 69–78. Lanham, MD: Altamira Press, 2006.

Preziosi, Donald. *Rethinking Art History: Meditations on a Coy Science*. New Haven, CT: Yale University Press, 1989.

Preziosi, Donald, and Claire Farago. "What Are Museums For?" In *Grasping the World: The Idea of the Museum*, edited by Donald Preziosi and Claire Farago, 1–21. Aldershot: Ashgate, 2004.

Raffoul, François, and David Pettigrew. "Translators' introduction." In Jean-Luc Nancy, *The Creation of the World, or Globalization*, trans. François Raffoul and David Pettigrew, 1–26. Albany: State University of New York Press, 2007.

Raffoul, François and David Pettigrew. "Translators' Preface." In Jean-Luc Nancy and Phillipe Lacoue-Labarthe, *The Title of the Letter: A Reading of Lacan*, translated by François Raffoul and David Pettigrew, vii–xxiv. Albany: State University of New York Press, 1992.

Ramose, Mogobe B. "An African Perspective on Justice and Race." *Polylog: Forum for Intercultural Philosophy* 3 (2001): 14.

Ramose, Mogobe B. *African Philosophy Through Ubuntu*. Harare: Mond Books, 1999.

Ramose, Mogobe B. "In Memoriam: Sovereignty and the New South Africa," *Griffith Law Review* 16, no. 2 (2007): 310–329.

Ramose, Mogobe B. "Learning Inspired Education." *Caribbean Journal of Philosophy* 2, no. 1 (2010): 1–15.

Rancière, Jacques. *Dissensus: On Politics and Aesthetics*. Translated by Steven Corcoran. London: Continuum, 2010.

Rancière, Jacques. "Overlegitimation." Translated by Kristin Ross. *Social Text* no. 31–32 (1992): 252–257.

Rantete, J. M. *The African National Congress and the Negotiated Settlement in South Africa* (Pretoria: J. L. van Schaik, 1998).

Rasch, William. "Locating the Political: Schmitt, Mouffe, Luhmann, and the Possibility of Pluralism." *International Review of Sociology* 7, no. 1 (1997): 103–115.

Rasch, William. *Sovereignty and its Discontents: On the Primacy of Conflict and the Structure of the Political*. London: Routledge, 2004.

Rawls, John. *Political Liberalism*. New York: Columbia University Press, 1996.

Razack, Sherene, ed. *Race, Space, and the Law: Unmapping a White Settler Society*. Toronto: Between the Lines, 2002.

Ricoeur, Paul. "The Political Paradox." In *History and Truth*. 2nd ed., 247–270. Evanston, IL: Northwestern University Press, 1998.

Rifkin, Mark. *The Erotics of Sovereignty: Queer Native Writing in the Era of Self-Determination*. Minneapolis: University of Minnesota Press, 2012.

Robins, Claire. "Engaging with Curating." *International Journal of Art & Design Education* 24, no. 2 (2005): 149–158.

Rose, Nikolas, and Peter Miller. "Political Power Beyond the State: Problematics of Government." *The British Journal of Sociology* 43, no. 2 (1992): 173–205.

Ross, Alison. *The Aesthetic Paths of Philosophy: Presentation in Kant, Heidegger, Lacoue-Labarthe, and Nancy*. Stanford, CA: Stanford University Press, 2007.

Runnymede Trust. "About Us." http://www.runnymedetrust .org/about.html, accessed May 12, 2012.

Runnymede Trust. "The Year of Cohesion." *Bulletin 332.* http://www.runnymedetrust.org/uploads/projects/communityCohesion/theYearOfCohesion. pdf, accessed April 1, 2012.

Russell, Terry. "The Enquiring Visitor: Useable Learning Theory for Museum Contexts." *Journal of Education in Museums* 15 (1994): 19–21.

Rust, Jennifer. "Political Theology: Sacred Flesh and Social Form." *Journal for Cultural and Religious Theory* 12, no. 1 (2012): 5–10.

Sachs, Albie. "South Africa's Unconstitutional Constitution: Transition from Power to Lawful Power." *St. Louis University Law Journal* 41 (1997): 1249–1258.

Said, Edward. *Orientalism.* London: Vintage, 1979.

Sanger, Mandy. "Education Work in the District Six Museum: Layering in New Voices and Interpretations." In *City-Site-Museum: Reviewing Memory Practices at the District Six Museum,* edited by Bonita Bennett, Chrischené Julius, and Crain Soudien, 96–109. Cape Town: District Six Museum, 2008.

Sartre, Jean-Paul. Preface to Frantz Fanon, *The Wretched of the Earth,* xliii–lxii. New York: Grove Press, 1961.

Sayer, Derek. "Incognito Ergo Sum: Language, Memory and the Subject." *Theory, Culture, and Society* 21, no. 6 (2004): 67–89.

Schaap, Andrew. "Enacting the Right to Have Rights: Jacques Rancière's Critique of Hannah Arendt." *European Journal of Political Theory* 10, no. 1 (2011): 22–45.

Schaap, Andrew. "Introduction." In *Law and Agonistic Politics,* edited by Andrew Schaap, 1–14. Aldershot: Ashgate, 2008.

Scheuerman, William E. "Revolutions and Constitutions: Hannah Arendt's Challenge to Carl Schmitt." In *Law as Politics: Carl Schmitt's Critique of Liberalism,* edited by David Dyzenhaus, 252–280. Durham, NC: Duke University Press, 1998.

Schmitt, Carl. *The Concept of the Political.* Translated by George Schwab. Chicago: University of Chicago Press, 1996.

Schmitt, Carl. *Constitutional Theory.* Edited by Jeffrey Seitzer. Translated by Jeffrey Seitzer. Durham, NC: Duke University Press, 2008.

Schmitt, Carl. *Crisis of Parliamentary Democracy.* Translated by Ellen Kennedy. Cambridge, MA: MIT Press, 1988.

Schmitt, Carl. *Political Theology: Four Chapters on the Concept of Sovereignty.* Translated by George Schwab. Chicago: University of Chicago Press, 2005.

Schmitt, Carl. *Theory of the Partisan.* Translated by G. L. Ulmen. New York: Telos Press, 2007.

Schwab, George. "Introduction." In Carl Schmitt, *The Concept of the Political,* translated by George Schwab, 3–16. Chicago: University of Chicago Press, 1996.

Schwab, George. "Introduction." In Carl Schmitt, *Political Theology: Four Chapters on the Concept of Sovereignty,* translated by by George Schwab, xxxvii–lii. Chicago: University of Chicago Press, 2005.

Scott, David. *Conscripts of Modernity*. Durham, NC: Duke University Press, 2004.

Segal, Lauren, Karen Martin, and Sharon Cort. *Number Four: The Making of Constitution Hill*. Edited by Lauren Segal. Johannesburg: Penguin, 2006.

Ševčenko, Liz, and Maggie Russell-Ciardi. "Sites of Conscience: Opening Historic Sites for Civic Dialogue." *The Public Historian* 30, no. 1 (2008): 9–15.

Shepard, Benjamin, and Ronald Hayduk, eds. *From ACT UP to the WTO: Urban Protest and Community Building in the Era of Globalization*. New York: Verso, 2003.

Siegel, Jonah. *The Emergence of the Modern Museum: An Anthology of Nineteenth-Century Sources*. Oxford: Oxford University Press, 2008.

Sigmund, Paul E. "Law and Politics." In *The Cambridge Companion to Aquinas*, edited by Norman Kretzmann and Eleonore Stump, 217–213. Cambridge: Cambridge University Press, 1993.

Simon, Nina. *The Participatory Museum*. Santa Cruz, CA: Museum 2.0., 2010.

Simon, Roger. "The Terrible Gift: Museums and the Possibility of Hope Without Consolation." *Museum Management and Curatorship* 21, no. 3 (2006): 187–204.

Simpson, Audra. *Mohawk Interruptus: Political Life Across the Borders of Settler States*. Durham, NC: Duke University Press, 2014.

Simpson, Moira G. *Making Representations: Museums in the Post-Colonial Era*. London: Routledge, 2001.

Sinnerbrink, Robert. "Violence, Deconstruction, and Sovereignty: Derrida and Agamben on Benjamin's 'Critique of Violence.'" In *Walter Benjamin and the Architecture of Modernity*, edited by Andrew Benjamin and Charles Rice, 77–91. Melbourne: re.press, 2009.

Skinner, Quentin. *The Foundations of Modern Political Thought Volume 1: The Renaissance*. Cambridge: Cambridge University Press, 1978.

Skinner, Quentin. "The State." In *Political Innovation and Conceptual Change*, edited by Terence Ball, James Farr, and L. Hanson, 90–131. Cambridge: Cambridge University Press, 1989.

Sleeper-Smith, Susan. *Contesting Knowledge: Museums and Indigenous Perspectives*. Lincoln: University of Nebraska Press, 2009.

Smith, Andrea. "Queer Theory and Native Studies: The Heteronormativity of Settler Colonialism." *GLQ: A Journal of Lesbian and Gay Studies* 16, no. 1–2 (2010): 41–68.

Smith, Jason E. "Nancy, Justice and Communist Politics." In *Jean-Luc Nancy: Justice, Legality and World*, edited by B. C. Hutchens, 186–203. New York: Continuum, 2012.

Snyman, Johannes. "Interpretation and the Politics of Memory." *Acta Juridica* (1998): 312–337.

Sorel, George. *Reflections on Violence*. Translated by T. E. Hulma and J. Roth. London: Allen and Unwin, 1950.

Soudien, Crain. "Memory and Critical Education: Approaches in the District Six Museum." In *City-Site-Museum: Reviewing Memory Practices at the District Six Museum*, edited by Bonita Bennett, Chrischené Julius, and Crain Soudien, 110–119. Cape Town: District Six Museum, 2008.

Soudien, Crain. "Memory in the Re-making of Cape Town." In *City-Site-Museum: Reviewing Memory Practices at the District Six Museum*, edited by Bonita Bennett, Chrischené Julius, and Crain Soudien, 18–31. Cape Town: District Six Museum, 2008.

Sparks, Simon. Editor's Introduction Politica Ficta to Jean-Luc Nancy and Phillipe Lacoue-Labarthe, *Retreating the Political*, edited by Simon Sparks, xiv–xxvii. London: Routledge, 1997.

Spaulding, Norman W. "Constitution as Countermonument: Federalism, Reconstruction, and the Problem of Collective Memory." *Columbia Law Review* 103, no. 8 (2003): 1992–2051.

Spivak, Gayatri. "Subaltern Studies: Deconstructing Historiography." In *Other Worlds: Essays in Cultural Politics*. London: Methuen, 1987.

Stanziola, Javier, and Diego Méndez-Carbajo. "Economic Growth, Government Expenditure and Income: The Case of Museums and Libraries in England." *Cultural Trends* 20, no. 3–4 (2011): 243–256.

Steiner, George. "Introduction." In *The Origin of German Tragic Drama*, translated by John Osborne, 7–24. New York: Verso, 1998.

Strong, Tracy. "Foreword." In Carl Schmitt, *Political Theology: Four Chapters on the Concept of Sovereignty*, translated by George Schwab, vii–xxxv. Chicago: University of Chicago Press, 2005.

Sussman, Henry. "Booking Benjamin: The Fate of a Medium." In *Walter Benjamin and the Architecture of Modernity*, edited by Andrew Benjamin and Charles Rice, 9–38. Melbourne: re.press, 2009.

Thobani, Sunera. *Exalted Subjects: Studies in the Making of Race and Nation in Canada*. Toronto: University of Toronto Press, 2007.

Thurschwell, Adam. "Radical Feminist Liberalism." In *Imagining Law: On Drucilla Cornell*, edited by Renée Heberle and Benjamin Pryor, 31–58. Albany: State University of New York Press, 2008.

Tierney, Stephen. "'We the Peoples': Constituent Power and Constitutionalism in Plurinational States." In *The Paradox of Constitutionalism: Constituent Power and Constitutional Form*, edited by Martin Loughlin and Neil Walker, 229–246. Oxford: Oxford University Press, 2007.

Tomba, Massimiliano. "Another Kind of *Gewalt*: Beyond Law, Re-reading Walter Benjamin." *Historical Materialism* 17 (2009): 126–144.

Tomkins, Adam. *Our Republican Constitution*. Oxford: Hart Publishing, 2005.

Toscano, Alberto. "Always Already Only Now: Negri and the Biopolitical." In *The Philosophy of Antonio Negri: Volume Two*, edited by Timothy S. Murphy and Abdul-Karim Mustapha, 109–128. London: Pluto Press, 2007.

Tribe, Keith. "Introduction." In Reinhart Koselleck, *Futures Past: On the Semantics of Historical Time*, translated by Keith Tribe, vii–xx. New York: Columbia University Press, 2004.

Tully, James. *Strange Multiplicity: Constitutionalism in an Age of Diversity*. Cambridge: Cambridge University Press, 1995.

Tully, James. "Struggles Over Recognition and Distribution." *Constellations* 7, no. 4 (2000): 469–482.

Tully, James. "The Unfreedom of the Moderns in Comparison to Their Ideals of Constitutional Democracy." *The Modern Law Review* 65, no. 2 (2002): 204–228.

Tyson, Amy M. "Crafting Emotional Comfort: Interpreting the Painful Past at Living History Museums in the New Economy." *Museum and Society* 6, no. 3 (2008): 246–262.

Ullman, Walter. "The Carolingian Renaissance and the Idea of Kingship." *The Birkbeck Lectures 1968–69*. London: Methuen, 1969.

van der Walt, André J. "Dancing With Codes: Protecting, Developing and Deconstructing Property Rights in a Constitutional State." *South African Law Journal* 118, no. 2 (2001): 258–311.

van der Walt, Johan. "Hospitality and the Ghost. A Response to Emilios Christodoulidis's Article 'The Paradoxes of Sovereignty.'" *Tydskrif vir die Suid-Afrikaanse reg (TSAR)/Journal for South African Law* 2 (2002): 362–369.

van der Walt, Johan. *Law and Sacrifice: Towards a Post-Apartheid Theory of Law*. London: Birkbeck Law Press, 2005.

van der Walt, Johan. "The Murmur of Being and the Chatter of Law." *Social and Legal Studies* 20, no. 3 (2011): 389–400.

van der Walt, Johan. "Piracy, Property and Plurality: Re-Reading the Foundations of Modern Law." *Tydskrif vir die Suid-Afrikaanse reg (TSAR)/Journal for South African Law* 3 (2001): 524–547.

van der Walt, Johan. "Rawls and Derrida on the Historicity of Constitutional Democracy and International Justice." *Constellations* 16, no. 1 (2009): 23–43.

van der Walt, Johan, and Henk Botha. "Democracy and Rights in South Africa: Beyond a Constitutional Culture of Justification." *Constellations* 7, no. 3 (2000): 341–362.

van Marle, Karin. "Constitution as Archive." In *Law and the Politics of Reconciliation*, edited by Scott Veitch, 215–228. Aldershot: Ashgate, 2007.

van Marle, Karin. "Law's Time, Particularity and Slowness." In *Law, Memory, and the Legacy of Apartheid: Ten Years After AZAPO v. President of South Africa*, edited by Wessel le Roux and Karin van Marle, 11–32. Pretoria: Pretoria University Law Press, 2007.

van Marle, Karin. "The Spectacle of Post-Apartheid Constitutionalism." *Griffith Law Review* 16, no. 2 (2007): 411–429.

van Roermund, Bert. "Questioning the Law: On Heteronomy in Public Autonomy." In *Law and Agonistic Politics*, edited by Andrew Schaap, 119–132. Aldershot: Ashgate, 2009.

von Bertalanffy, Ludwig. "An Outline of General System Theory." *British Journal for the Philosophy of Science* 1, no. 2 (1950): 134–165.Vatter, Miguel. "The Idea of Public Reason and the Reason of State: Schmitt and Rawls on the Political." *Political Theory* 36, no. 2 (2008): 239–271.

Vatter, Miguel. "Legality and Resistance: Arendt and Negri on Constituent Power." In *The Philosophy of Antonio Negri: Volume Two*, edited by Timothy S. Murphy and Abdul-Karim Mustapha, 52–83. London: Pluto Press, 2007.

Vergo, Peter, ed. *The New Museology*. London: Reaktion, 1989.

Villa, Dana R. "Beyond Good and Evil: Arendt, Nietzsche, and the Aestheticization of Political Action." *Political Theory* 20, no. 2 (1992): 274–308.

Wagner, Andreas. "Jean-Luc Nancy: A Negative Politics?" *Philosophy & Social Criticism* 32, no. 1 (2006): 89–109.

Waldmeir, Patti. *Anatomy of a Miracle: The End of Apartheid and the Birth of the New South Africa*. New York: W. W. Norton & Company, 1997.

Wall, Illan. *Human Rights and Constituent Power: Without Model or Warranty*. New York: Routledge, 2012.

Walker, Neil. "Constitutionalism and the Incompleteness of Democracy: An Iterative Relationship." *Rechtsfilosofie & Rechtstheorie* 39, no. 3 (2010): 206–233.

Walker, Neil. "Constitutionalism and the Incompleteness of Democracy: A Reply to Four Critics." *Rechtsfilosofie & Rechtstheorie* 39, no. 3 (2010): 276–288.

Walker, Neil. "The Idea of Constitutional Pluralism." *The Modern Law Review* 65, no. 3 (2002): 317–359.

Walker, Neil. "On the Necessarily Public Character of Law." In *The Public in Law*, edited by Claudio Michelon, Gregor Clunie, Christopher McCorkingdale, and Haris Psarras, 9–34. Aldershot: Ashgate, 2012.

Walker, Neil. "Taking Constitutionalism Beyond the State." *Political Studies* 56, no. 3 (2008): 519–543.

Ward, Ian. "Beyond Constitutionalism: The Search for a European Political Imagination." *European Law Journal* 7, no. 1 (2001): 24–40.

Weber, Samuel. "Taking Exception to Decision: Walter Benjamin and Carl Schmitt." *Diacritics* 22, no. 3–4 (1992): 5–18.

Weeder, Michael. "Topographies of the Forgotten: Prestwich and Cape Town's Nineteenth Century Cemeteries." In *City-Site-Museum: Reviewing Memory Practices at the District Six Museum*, edited by Bonita Bennett, Chrischené Julius, and Crain Soudien, 32–49. Cape Town: District Six Museum, 2008.

Wellman, Peter. "Sustainability of South Africa's Water Miracle Questioned." *African Eye New Service*, May 9, 1999. www.thewaterpage.com/SAWS Problems. html.

Whyte, Jessica. "'I Would Prefer Not To': Giorgio Agamben, Bartleby and the Potentiality of the Law." *Law and Critique* 20, no. 3 (2009): 309–324.

Wilder, Gary. *The French Imperial Nation-State: Negritude and Colonial Humanism Between the Wars*. Chicago: University of Chicago Press, 2005.

Wilson, David. *The British Museum: Purpose and Politics*. London: British Museum Publications, 1989.

Wiredu, Kwasi. *Cultural Universals and Particulars: An African Perspective*. Bloomington: Indiana University Press, 1996.

Wiredu, Kwasi. "Democracy and Consensus in African Traditional Politics." *Polylog: Forum for Intercultural Philosophy* 2 (2000): 1–31.

Wiredu, Kwasi. "An Oral Philosophy of Personhood." *Research in African Literatures* 40, no. 1 (2009): 8–18.

Wright, Steve. *Storming Heaven: Class Composition and Struggle in Italian Autonomist Marxism*. London: Pluto Press, 2002.

Wolin, Richard. *Heidegger's Children: Hannah Arendt, Karl Lowith, Hans Jonas, and Herbert Marcuse.* Princeton, NJ: Princeton University Press, 2001.
Wolin, Richard. "Carl Schmitt, Political Existentialism and the Total State." *Theory and Society* 19, no. 4 (1990): 389–416.
Xali, Mthetho. "They Are Killing Us Alive": A Case Study of the Impact of Cost Recovery on Service Provision in Makhaza Section, Khayelitsha." In *Cost Recovery and the Crisis of Service Delivery in South Africa,* edited by David A. McDonald and John Pape, 101–122. London: Zed Books, 2002.
Young, James. "The Counter-Monument: Memory against Itself in Germany Today." *Critical Inquiry* 18, no. 2 (1992): 267–296.
Yuval-Davis, Nira, and Davia Stasiulis. *Unsettling Settler Societies: Articulations of Gender, Race, Ethnicity and Class.* London: Sage, 1995.
Zartaloudis, Thanos. "Without Negative Origins and Absolute Ends: A Jurisprudence of the Singular," *Law and Critique* 13 (2002): 197–230.
Zerubavel, Eviatar. "The French Republican Calendar: A Case Study in the Sociology of Time." *American Sociological Review* 42, no. 6 (1997): 868–877.

Cases

South Africa

MEC for Education: Kwazulu-Natal and Others v. Pillay, CCT 51/06 21 (2007).
Soobramoney v. Minister of Health (KwaZulu-Natal), CCT32/97 17 (1997).
State v. Makwanyane and Another, CCT3/94 (1995).

United Kingdom

Attorney-General v. Trustees of the British Museum, EWHC 1089 (2005).

United States of America

Payne v. Tennessee, 501 U.S. 808, 828 (1991).
Planned Parenthood v. Casey, 505 U.S. 833, 854 (1992).

Legislation

South Africa

Republic of South Africa Constitution Act 110, 1983.
Constitution of the Republic of South Africa, 1996.

United Kingdom

The British Museum Act, 1753 (26 Geo. II XXII).
The British Museum Act, 1963.
The Education Act, 1902 (2 Edw. VII).
Museum and Galleries Act, 1992.

Index

Printed and bound by CPI Group (UK) Ltd, Croydon, CR0 4YY

13/04/2025

14656536-0001